Living Philosophy

Living Philosophy

Reflections on Life, Meaning and Morality

Christopher Hamilton

Edinburgh University Press

For Mimi

© Christopher Hamilton, 2001

Edinburgh University Press Ltd
22 George Square, Edinburgh

Typeset in New Baskerville
by Hewer Text Ltd, Edinburgh, and
printed and bound in Great Britain by
MPG Books Ltd, Bodmin

A CIP record for this book is
available from the British Library.

ISBN 0 7486 1418 4 (paperback)

Contents

Acknowledgements

T O MY PARENTS-IN-LAW MARGARET and John Davis I owe especial thanks for material and moral support for much of the time during which this book was written. Their generosity and faith in me helped keep me going, and I thank them for all they have done for me.

I am grateful to John Anderson, Amy Eames, Bob Farquhar and Sue Ruben, all of whom read parts of this book at some point during its composition. Audri Day also read much of the book and responded most helpfully to what I had written. She has also been generous to me in many other ways, and I should like to record here my thanks for her support and encouragement. I also thank Jackie Jones at Edinburgh University Press who has been generous of her time, supportive and encouraging throughout. Bob Eaglestone gave me some timely advice, and I thank him.

I should like to thank my teachers of philosophy, especially Sebastian Gardner, Christopher Janaway, Roger Scruton and Michael Tanner, all of whom allowed me to explore my thinking without imposing on me any kind of academic straitjacket. To Sebastian Gardner in particular I am deeply grateful for years of support and encouragement.

Amongst contemporary philosophers I am indebted in particular to the writings of Raimond Gaita, R. F. Holland and Peter Winch. Amongst philosophers of the tradition my deepest debt is to Nietzsche: his influence is to be found everywhere in this book.

I thank my friends Harry Chapman and Michael Newton who both read parts of the book and discussed my ideas with me. I should also like to thank my friends John Armstrong and Arnim Wiek with whom

Acknowledgements

I have discussed many of the topics of this book and from whose philosophical insight I have benefited enormously.

My deepest debt of all, however, is to my wife Mimi. She has read and discussed with me everything I have written in this book and has helped me on numerous occasions to get clear on what it was I was trying to do and to express myself better. Throughout the time we have been together she has been a constant source of support, encouragement and consolation and my sense of life and philosophy has been touched at the deepest level by her. Her greatest gift to me has been, however, that she is a woman of tremendous depth, integrity and honesty, reassuring me that it is, after all, possible to get through life and wrest something uniquely valuable from it without selling one's soul.

I have throughout this book followed traditional practice and, where appropriate, used the masculine pronoun to refer indifferently to both men and women. I have done so for reasons of style, and no sexist implication is intended.

Chapters 1 and 2 are reworked versions of two earlier publications of mine:
'Virtue and Human Flourishing', *Cogito* 12:1, 1998, ed. Carolyn Wilde, © The Cogito Society.
'On Birth and Death', *Cogito* 13:1, 1999, ed. Carolyn Wilde, © The Cogito Society.
Other parts of the book rework small amounts of material from the following of my previous publications:
'Kierkegaard on Truth as Subjectivity: Christianity, Ethics and Asceticism', *Religious Studies* 34:1, 1998, ed. Peter Byrne, © Cambridge University Press.
'Ethics and the Spirit', *Philosophical Investigations* 21:4, 1998, ed. D. Z. Phillips, © Blackwell Publishers.
'The Great Critic and an Aesthetic Education', *Journal of Aesthetic Education* 33:2, 1999, ed. Ralph A. Smith, © Board of Trustees of the University of Illinois.
'The Nature of Evil: A Reply to Garrard', *Philosophical Explorations* 2:2, 1999, ed. Jan Bransen, © Van Gorcum & Comp.
'Nietzsche on Nobility and the Affirmation of Life', *Ethical Theory and Moral Practice* 3:2, 2000, ed. Robert F. Heeger and Albert W. Musschenga, © Kluwer Academic Publishers.
I am grateful to all the publishers concerned for permission to reuse material.

Acknowledgements

My thanks to the following publishers for permission to reprint copyright material.

Harcourt, Inc. for excerpts from 'East Coker' in *Four Quartets*, © 1940 by T. S. Eliot and renewed 1968 by Esme Valerie Eliot, reprinted by permission of the publisher.

Farrar, Straus and Giroux, LLC for excerpts from 'Afternoons', 'Aubade', and 'Continuing to Live' from *Collected Poems* by Philip Larkin. © 1988, 1989 by the Estate of Philip Larkin. Reprinted by permission of the publisher.

Faber & Faber Ltd for an excerpt from 'East Coker' from *Four Quartets, Collected Poems 1909–1962* by T. S. Eliot and excerpts from 'Aubade' and 'Continuing to Live' from *Collected Poems* by Philip Larkin. Reprinted by permission of the publisher.

The Marvell Press, England and Australia for 'Poetry of Departures' by Philip Larkin from *The Less Deceived*. Reprinted by permission of the publisher.

Laurence Pollinger Limited and the Estate of Frieda Lawrence Ravagli for extracts from 'Death' and 'Ship of Death' from *The Complete Poems of D. H. Lawrence* by D. H. Lawrence. Reprinted by permission of the publisher.

The publishers gratefully acknowledge permission to reproduce material previously published elsewhere. Every effort has been made to trace the copyright holders, but if any have been inadvertently overlooked, the publisher will be pleased to make the necessary arrangements at the first opportunity.

If we had a keen vision and feeling of all ordinary human life, it would be like hearing the grass grow and the squirrel's heart beat, and we should die of the roar which lies on the other side of silence. As it is, the quickest of us walk about well wadded with stupidity.

George Eliot

All our learned schoolmasters and educators are agreed that children do not know what they want. Yet no one is willing to believe that adults too, like children, stumble around on this earth and do not know where they come from and where they are going, seldom act for genuine motives and are just as governed as children are by biscuits, cake and the rod: yet it seems palpably clear to me.

Goethe

The gulf between how one should live and how one does live is so wide that a man who neglects what is actually done for what should be done moves towards self-destruction rather than self-preservation.

Machiavelli

One of the greatest reasons why so few people understand themselves, is, that most writers are always teaching men what they should be, and hardly ever trouble their heads with telling them what they really are.

Bernard Mandeville

Style is the ultimate morality of mind.

A. N. Whitehead

Introduction:

A Personal View of Philosophy

T HIS IS A BOOK of philosophical essays that may be read independently of each other but which together explore the nature of those values that fall roughly in the area we label with the term 'morality' or 'ethics'. Yet they differ in certain important ways from the kind of philosophy which constitutes the mainstream of the subject as this is studied and written in academic institutions in the English-speaking world and in other places. In this Introduction I try to explain some of those differences. But I must make it clear that what I say here about the nature of philosophy applies only to philosophy that concerns itself with values – with moral values, and also, by extension, with aesthetic, political and related values. I leave it open whether what I say applies also to other areas of philosophy. Further, although I speak in what follows of the way philosophers go about their business, I do not mean to say that all philosophers all the time operate in the way I describe. However, precisely because academic philosophy is a discipline studied at universities there is, as is only to be expected, a methodology which characterises the mainstream of the subject. It is this methodology and possible alternatives to it which interest me here.

The most natural assumption to make about philosophy is that it is an attempt to arrive at, and articulate, a deepened understanding of human life. 'Philosophy', after all, means 'love of wisdom', and it seems natural to suppose that wisdom will only accrue to someone if he understands life in a way less superficial than most do. However, few books in academic philosophy seem to concern themselves with

1

this task of providing such a deepened understanding. Reading philosophy books, one usually gets the very strong impression that philosophers do not try to describe and understand life in all its rich confusion, in all its absurdities, frustrations, joys, pains, highs and lows. On the contrary, the impression one gets is that the philosopher has a picture of life into which he then tries to make all the confusing phenomena fit. This involves his ignoring or distorting those bits of reality which do not fit into the picture of life he already has. Certainly anyone who has written the kind of philosophy which is expected by, and is considered acceptable for, an academic audience, will know first-hand that doing philosophy often seems to involve – even if one does not wish this – a kind of distortion of life as it is. This point has been well made by one very highly respected American philosopher, Robert Nozick:

> One form of philosophical activity feels like pushing and shoving things to fit into some fixed perimeter or specified shape. All those things lying out there, and they must be fit in. You push and shove the material into the rigid area getting it into the boundary on one side, and it bulges out on another. You run around and press in the protruding bulge, produc-ing yet another in another place. So you push and shove and clip off corners from the things so they'll fit and you press in until finally almost everything sits unstably more or less in there; what doesn't gets heaved *far* away so that it won't be noticed . . . *Quickly*, you find an angle from which it looks like an exact fit and take a snapshot; at a fast shutter speed before something else bulges out too noticeably. Then, back to the darkroom to touch up rents, rips, and tears in the fabric of the perimeter. All that remains is to publish the photograph as a representation of exactly how things are . . .
> [. . .] Why do they [philosophers] strive to force everything into one fixed perimeter? Why not another perimeter, or, more radically, why not leave things where they are? What does having everything within a perimeter *do* for us? Why do we want it so? (What does it shield us from?)[1]

There are, perhaps, very many answers to Nozick's different ques-tions. Two, in particular, seem to me to stand out. First, the tempera-ment of the philosopher is characterised by a desire, not simply to understand life, but to understand it in such a way that life itself makes sense. This should not surprise us, for there is nothing more natural. There is certainly something frightening in the thought that one might devote one's life to trying to understand the nature of human existence only to arrive at the conclusion that one cannot make sense of things or, even worse, that life itself cannot be made sense of. The philosopher is, as I understand him, someone who happens to be afflicted by such a fear to a greater degree than most. In a famous letter, Keats spoke of '*Negative Capability*, that is when a man is capable of being in uncertainties, mysteries, doubts, without any irritable reaching after fact and reason'.[2] The philosopher, one might say, is someone who possesses to a more than usual degree a lack of Negative Capability.

The second principal reason, I think, why philosophers go about things the way Nozick describes can be found in a certain style of thinking and writing. For, in general, those who write academic philosophy seek to write in an impersonal manner as if they were not individuals with specific concerns. They seek to write in an impersonal voice of reason or pure intellect, that is, a voice which is no particular person's voice. Raimond Gaita has put this by suggesting that the mainstream philosopher thinks of himself as a *res cogitans*, a mere thinking thing, and for such a philosopher 'to think philosophically is determined by an idealisation of thinking as such, thinking abstracted from the form which life takes for any thinking thing'.[3] This approach is, indeed, recognised within the subject, and philosophers pride themselves on it: it is supposed that the glory and power of the subject lie in such an approach, since it is thought that it frees the writer from personal prejudice. There are many reasons why this is so, but the central one is that philosophers have noted – it is not something that one can easily avoid noting – that we are all of us usually trapped in our own subjectivity. We can very rarely ascend to a level of understanding which releases us from the worries, fears, hopes, wishes, aspirations, regrets and so on which make up by far the largest part of our inner life. Life is for most of us most of the time something we live at the level of anecdote: we are caught in a web of self-concern which blinds us to much but the story of our own lives, and even when we tell that story to ourselves and to others what we relate is very often self-serving and distorted. And having seen this, the philosopher typically thinks that the way to escape this is to leave the self behind. Truth, it is supposed, is revealed to an eye which is untainted by any personal concerns and is revealed in a voice which is no particular person's voice. It is revealed by rational reflection which is fair to all competing views of the world and thus arrives at the one true account. Hence, the correct view on the world is, as it were, God's view, a view which sees everything unchangingly, calm, steady, free from any concerns of the self. However, not actually having God's view on the world, but longing for such a view, the philosopher is naturally led – perhaps *malgré lui* –

into forcing life to fit into a predetermined mould or perimeter in the kind of way Nozick describes. For, as he struggles to formulate his view in the light of the requirements which he takes philosophy to impose on him, this forcing and chopping of the phenomena of life comes to seem to the philosopher the next best thing actually to having God's view on the world. His own personality and experiences of life which could interfere with such a view are thus excised as far as possible from the work he produces; and, when not excised, concealed.

Similar points about the style of philosophy have been made by Martha Nussbaum. 'Our Anglo-American philosophical tradition', she writes,

> has tended to assume that the ethical text should, in the process of enquiry, converse with the intellect alone; it should not make its appeal to the emotions, feelings, and sensory responses. Plato explicitly argues that ethical learning must proceed by separating the intellect from our other merely human parts; many other writers proceed on this assumption, with or without sharing Plato's intellectualistic ethical conception.[4]

As Nussbaum notes, the mainstream philosopher takes himself to be appealing to nothing but the intellect of the reader, to nothing but his reason. It is not the imagination, still less the needs and desires of the reader, which makes the reader agree with the philosopher, but rather his reason alone. The philosopher, taking himself to speak in the voice of reason, speaks in a voice which is also the reader's voice when this has been purged of its personal elements. The meeting of minds between philosopher and reader, a meeting which produces conviction in the reader, is a meeting precisely because it is the coming together of two minds which have no individuating characteristics and thus are not two minds, after all, but one – the impersonal mind of reason, conversing, as it were, with itself alone.

As I have already suggested, one consequence of the fact that the philosopher does not present his work as someone in the thick of existence with his own concerns and interests is that he delivers what he has to say as – simply – the truth. Nozick, in his discussion of the methodology of philosophy, has noted this point, remarking that 'the usual manner of presenting philosophical work puzzles me. Works of philosophy are written as though their authors believe them to be the absolutely final word on their subject'.[5] And one way to express this is to say that academic philosophy is written as if there is no more work for readers to do once they have understood and absorbed the argument the philosopher offers. Philosophy aspires to a kind of completeness which settles the issues of which it treats. Hence, as A. C. Grayling has written in trying to characterise the nature of philosophy, '[p]hilosophy . . . remains a pursuit which . . . tries to bring itself to an end'.[6] To give one example which could stand for many: one of the greatest of philosophers, Immanuel Kant, tried in his writings to prove that we are morally required to act in certain ways on pain of falling into self-contradiction. In particular, he thought, roughly speaking, that it could be shown that as rational beings we must be committed to acting towards others in a way we would like them to act towards us. Now, if Kant is right, what this means is that a certain kind of moral requirement is simply settled for us. That is, if he is right then he has *brought discussion to an end* about this basic requirement. Of course, there might still be ways in which this requirement could be explored. One could, for example, discuss its concrete application. Or it might be important to explore its relation to other principles. But none of this undermines the central point: Kant writes as if, once the argument is completed, there is no room to discuss further whether the basic moral requirement he explores applies to us or not.

In one way, all this may seem reasonable. After all, the moral principle in question is one to which many people are committed, either implicitly or explicitly. But if Kant were right then it would mean that *nothing* in your experience of life could, if you are thinking clearly, lead you to question that principle in such a way as to find it mistaken. But this would surely be extremely odd: it would mean that one single man, living and teaching in Königsberg in the eighteenth century, thinking about morality, had solved for once and for all for you and me and the rest of us one of the most fundamental problems of human life, namely, how we should treat each other. Could one man, sitting alone in his armchair, however hard he thought, and however clever, really illuminate in this way the moral meaning of all of human history, both that which had passed before his chance appearance on earth and that which was to come?

It is not just that I think it *unlikely* that anyone could do this. I do not think the idea even makes sense: morality is not the kind of thing which can be settled in that way. And, for a variety of reasons which are not of immediate importance here, there are, of course, plenty of philosophers who are sceptical about Kant's moral theory. Nonetheless, as I have been suggesting, a great deal of mainstream philosophy continues to work on the basis that it can reflect on the nature of morality using the resources of reason or the intellect alone. That is, it continues to operate with the same kind of philosophical methodology employed by Kant.

It would be surprising if no philosophers objected to this state of affairs. And, of course, some have. Martha Nussbaum, for example, has, as we have seen, raised a protest against it, and has argued forcefully for the importance of emotion and imagination in moral philosophy. And again, Alasdair MacIntyre has argued that moral philosophy must take much more account than it does at present of historical variations in moral ideas and experience: rational reflection alone cannot grasp the nature of moral experience.[7] I agree with both these points and I am indebted, as many philosophers are, to both these thinkers for opening up within philosophy a broader approach to moral questions. Nonetheless, it seems to me that such thinkers have still not completely shaken off the most fundamental aspect of the approach they criticise. For even though Nussbaum and MacIntyre believe that philosophers need to employ more than reason alone in their reflections, and that they must openly and honestly appeal to more in their readers, they continue to share with the mainstream the idea that philosophers could, in principle, arrive at the truth – the Truth – about whatever aspect of the moral life it is that they investigate.

To see the difficulties inherent in such a stance, consider the following remarks of Bertrand Russell's:

> Philosophy has been defined as 'an unusually obstinate attempt to think clearly'; I should define it rather as 'an unusually ingenious attempt to think fallaciously.' The philosopher's temperament is rare, because it has to combine two somewhat conflicting characteristics: on the one hand a strong desire to believe some general proposition about the universe or human life; on the other hand, inability to believe contentedly except on what *appear* to be intellectual grounds. The more profound the philosopher, the more intricate and subtle must his fallacies be in order to produce in him the desired state of intellectual acquiescence.[8]

Fundamentally the same point had been made – though somewhat less politely – towards the end of the nineteenth century by Nietzsche.

> The thing that provokes one to look at all philosophers half mistrustfully and half mockingly is not that one again and again detects how innocent they are – how often and how easily they get things wrong and go astray, in short their childishness and childlikeness – but that they do not go

about things in an honest enough manner, whilst making a mighty and virtuous noise as soon as the problem of truthfulness is even remotely touched on. They all behave as if they had discovered and reached their real opinions through the self-development of a cold, pure, divinely unperturbed dialectic . . . whereas, in fact, an assumption, a notion, an 'inspiration', usually a desire of the heart sifted and made abstract, is defended by them with reasons sought after the event. They are one and all advocates who do not want to be seen as such, and even, indeed, usually no better than cunning pleaders for their prejudices, which they baptise 'truths' – and are *very* far from having the courage of conscience which admits this to itself, very far from having the good taste of the courage which makes this clear . . .[9]

Certainly Nietzsche and Russell are arguing that much more than reason alone drives the reflections of the philosopher. But they are saying something much more than this. The philosopher, they are saying, believes what he believes for a whole variety of reasons – including, sometimes, perhaps often, because he *wants* to believe it – but would like to get himself to believe that he believes these things on the basis of reason alone, for purely intellectual reasons. Where, then, does what he believe really come from if not only from reason? From the philosopher's temperament; from his experience and lack of experience; from his deepest needs, fears and the like; from the social and cultural milieu in which he happens to have grown up; from what was inculcated – or not inculcated – in him as a child; and so on. What Nietzsche and Russell are certainly *not* saying is that this renders the philosopher's work worthless, for saying that the philosopher's beliefs come from his temperament and the like is not to say that those beliefs are the fruit of thoughtlessness or something similar. Rather, they are trying to shift our sense of what the philosopher is doing. Here is how I would understand that shift, though both Nietzsche and Russell would probably put things at this point slightly differently: instead of thinking of the philosopher as trying to arrive at some kind of final truth for all, we should think of him – and he should think of himself – *as trying to find out what he really thinks.* Or, as Wittgenstein put it: 'Working in philosophy . . . is really more a working on oneself. On one's own interpretation. On one's way of seeing things. (And what one expects of them.)'[10] It goes without saying that this process will involve the use of reason, and it may lead the philosopher to views he might otherwise not have had, views which he could, perhaps, find uncomfortable. Moreover, he may well wish to persuade us of his point of view and he may be successful in doing so. But this view will remain the view of this individual philosopher, rooted in a specific life, namely, his own, and will appeal to us, if it does, as individuals rooted in *our* specific life.

But what, we might ask, is what any given philosopher thinks about life to us? Otherwise put: does this view on philosophy not simply evacuate it of any authority, turning it into mere personal revelation? I do not think it does.

We already have plenty of forms of writing and reflection where it is helpful to understand at least many of the writers and thinkers in question as exploring what they really think about whatever it is they are discussing: literature, poetry, plays and so on. We might say that such writers, far from seeking to speak in some impersonal voice, seek to find a personal voice, a voice in which they can have something substantial to say. Indeed, such writers say this of themselves. But this does not mean that their work lacks authority. On the contrary, it is crucial to, say, a novelist's having authority in what he says that he possess and evince his own personal voice in his writing. This is why we can criticise a novelist's work by discussing what sense of life, in the largest meaning of the term, he has. Hence we can say that a work is naïve or shallow or lacking in a sufficiently complex response to life; insightful or sensitive or richly responsive to life; and so on. We may even say that what he says is true, but what we are getting at in saying something like this is not, I think, that the novelist has solved anything, any problem of life, either for himself or for us, but that he deepens his and our sense of what the problems and nature of life are. This is why we sometimes speak in this context of the deep truth of things. None of this means that a novelist never seeks to persuade us of a particular point of view. But when he does seek to persuade us he does so, not by offering explicit arguments for his view, but by *showing* certain ideas in various contexts, perhaps then commenting on them. This not only allows the reader's mind space in which to move and think, but positively invites his mind into that space. This is why reading literature is so often an extremely refreshing experience. We could, perhaps, put this point by saying that novelists seek primarily to enter into conversation with their readers.

If there are forms of writing that have these features, then there is, perhaps, no reason in principle why the work of a given philosopher should not also possess such or similar features. So if we say that philosophers are trying to find out what they really think, this need not evacuate their work of authority. In any case, what the Nietzschean–Russellian view suggests is that finding out what they think is what philosophers have always been doing. It is just that they thought they were doing something else, namely, seeking to uncover the final truth about things, a truth which would settle matters in the area of which they treat.

I myself think the Nietzschean–Russellian picture is basically correct. I think that what philosophers most fundamentally doing is finding out what they really think, exploring their view on things. This is even the case in modern, highly professionalised philosophy where, as Martha Nussbaum has noted, everyone seeks to write like everyone else 'in order to be respectable and to be published in the usual journals' and where to suggest that all might not be well with this state of affairs and to try to do things otherwise involves 'training oneself in professionally irrelevant ways and risking ridicule'.[11] For even the most pared-down, dry academic writing style shows the mind of a particular individual at work, if only in the choice of subject-matter. As Stuart Hampshire has written:

> There are a thousand or more themes that might be pursued under the heading of moral philosophy . . . But in this part of philosophy strictly philosophical interests can be expected to fall short in determining the issues to be pursued and the difficulties to be emphasised. The experience and the interests of the author unavoidably play a part, and for two reasons. First, he will feel at ease in writing about those aspects of common experience which he knows at first hand. Second, his experience will normally have left him with particular doubts and uncertainties, and these, when pressed and probed far enough, will turn into philosophical doubts and philosophical uncertainties. His experience will usually have left him with some particular philosophical bias. He will pick out those themes that recall points of stress and of conflict in his own past and in his own thought.[12]

Further, I think that when we speak of a philosopher's revealing the truth, we do not mean that he has solved anything for us, but that he has helped us deepen our sense of what the problem really is. These ideas are certainly not capable of proof. But they derive at least some plausibility from our ability to look back over the history of philosophy and see how wildly mistaken most philosophers' thought has been: it is usually only the philosopher himself who is even remotely satisfied by his work, or perhaps an age which is particularly receptive to his work. But none of this renders philosophers' work worthless. On the contrary, there is wisdom there if we know how to look. Such points have been made eloquently and with humour by Richard Taylor.

St Thomas 'proved' that God exists, and numberless things besides. He 'answered' just about every question a thinking man might ask, setting out his philosophy as a seemingly endless series of questions *and answers*, and with a note of finality that seemed to leave no doubt. Very few today would concede that he really proved any of these things . . . Descartes and Spinoza similarly 'proved' that God exists, and a great deal more. Indeed, they both thought that we can achieve not only knowledge, but even certainty, concerning the soul, human motivation, free will, and virtually everything under the sun . . . We know now that the profession of knowledge of all these things was delusion, that they possessed knowledge of none of the things they set forth with such imposing proof . . .

If one reads Descartes he is rewarded mainly by the instructiveness of his errors. Such works stand as a lasting reminder that an intellect so great can nevertheless get everything so terribly wrong, so utterly out of accordance with what actually exists, so fantastically unbelievable, in spite of the most elaborate precautions against error. . . that it is possible for one to erect. The same type of distortion runs through Spinoza, whose imposing demonstrations have not the strength of a feather. Yet between Spinoza's proofs – in the corollaries, notes and asides – there resides a priceless philosophical wisdom for anyone who can disregard the intellectual window dressing.[13]

The window dressing, I would say, is the attempt – or the pretence – to speak for all, the impression created, or longed for, that one has arrived at some final truth.

As I see it, accepting the view of philosophy I am urging leads one to think that philosophy in some sense impossible. For if a philosopher is to remain true to his own experience and sense of things then surely he must find himself reflecting as Larkin did:

> And once you have walked the length of your mind, what
> You command is clear as a lading-list.
> Anything else must not, for you, be thought
> > To exist.
>
> And what's the profit? Only that, in time,
> We half-identify the blind impress
> All our behavings bear, may trace it home.
> > But to confess,
>
> On that green evening when our death begins,
> Just what it was, is hardly satisfying,
> Since it applied only to one man once,
> > And that one dying.[14]

But if this is so, then what is one to make of that requirement, internal to philosophy, to deal in argument, to seek to persuade the reader?

For does this not mean that the philosopher must represent himself to the reader as one in possession of the truth concerning the matter of which he treats? After all, even if one can read other philosophers and say of them that what they say is true, meaning that they deepen one's sense of the problems they discuss; and even if that is consistent with thinking that they make some claims which are false, as, say, certain religious beliefs might deepen our understanding of life and yet be false; how can one think this way of oneself as a philosopher? For even if one aims to deepen the sense of the questions one discusses, one cannot, it seems to me, be indifferent to the truth of what one says. There are, after all, as I have suggested, ways one could deepen one's understanding of a problem which would involve beliefs one thinks false. The task of philosophy thus becomes a task to seek to write in a way which respects the sense, as T. S. Eliot put it, that 'one has only learnt to get the better of words / For the thing one no longer has to say, or the way in which / One is no longer disposed to say it'.[15] But, with nothing more at one's disposal than 'shabby equipment always deteriorating', one knows one will fail in that task.

I have said that the chapters in this book deal with questions that fall in the area of experience we label 'morality'. When philosophers discuss morality they tend to focus on a very limited range of moral notions. They talk a great deal about rights, duties and rules, and about virtues and vices, but there is precious little, if any, discussion in the mainstream of the subject of a person's spirit and sensibility, of fate, of the nature of wholly conflicting moral world-views, of the mystery of birth and death, of the vanity of life, of a form of wisdom which is not mere practical astuteness, of the meaning of life, and of a whole host of other concepts, ideas and notions. What this means is that moral philosophy rarely has a proper sense, either implicit or explicit, of the way in which our inner life is made up of those innumerable cross-currents and undertows that give us a sense of leading a pointful or decent life, and which contribute to our relations to one another. We are at every waking moment living in complex and subtle interaction with others, responding to their gestures and tones of voice, to the look in their eyes, to their manner and manners, to their way of dressing, to their facial expressions, to their style and so on. We live also in the same kind of interaction with the natural and built environment, responding to the weather, to smells, to the light cast at different times of the day, to the change of the seasons, to cultivated and uncultivated land, to the look of buildings, roads and towns, and so on. Our inner life is in a state of permanent flux, adjustment, readjustment, enquiry, attraction, repulsion, curiosity, concern, solicitude, defiance, acceptance, and so on to all that we find about us. Most of these are left unaddressed by any talk of character – of virtues and vices – or of the following of rules and principles, or of belief in certain rights and duties.

A helpful way in which such points have been expressed is to be found in some comments of Hannah Arendt's concerning the nature of human individuality. She writes:

> The manifestation of who the speaker and doer unexchangeably is, though it is plainly visible, retains a curious intangibility that confounds all effort toward unequivocal verbal expression. The moment we want to say *who* somebody is our very vocabulary leads us astray into saying *what* he is; we get entangled in a description of qualities he necessarily shares with others like him; we begin to describe a type or a 'character' . . . with the result that his specific uniqueness escapes us.[16]

In these terms, I could put my point about the limitations of the concepts which are usually discussed in moral philosophy by saying that such concepts only ever give us the 'what' of a person, never the 'who'. But this does not quite capture the point. For part of what Arendt is saying is that *no* description can properly capture the 'who' of a person. Yet it does not follow from this that some descriptions are not better than others. For there are some descriptions which, even if they fail to tell us of the 'who', at least do a better job than, in my view, the standard philosophical vocabulary does. Such ways are usually to be found in poetry and literature, for these disciplines are able to capture something of those cross-currents and undertows of life to which I have referred.

I do not mean, in registering my sense of the limitations of the concepts usually taken to be central to moral philosophy, to suggest that we should abandon them or that we could get by without them. We cannot. Nor am I saying that philosophers should not discuss such concepts. Indeed, I do so in some of the chapters in this book, and I try to show some of the ways in which, as I see it, the philosophical mainstream has an understanding of them which is poor at getting at the *who* of those for whom they matter. Rather, what I am trying to get at is a scepticism about the nature of morality itself, of what we should think of as being the central moral concepts. For any account of what morality is can only be thought good to the extent that we know what it is an account *of.* So if we think a particular account of morality good, then we must already suppose ourselves to be possessed of a fairly strong sense of what morality is. Yet it seems to me to be the job of the philosopher to guard against that very supposition. There are many different conceptions of what morality is, some of which are themselves in conflict with one another, and I take it to be part of the aim of this book to try and hold these open as much as I can. This point could be expressed by saying that life seems to me a great deal more complicated, and much more resistant to complete, or completely satisfying, comprehension, than one would usually suppose from reading works of academic moral philosophy. And this signals the leading theme of the chapters in this book: the attempt to write a philosophy which takes seriously, as the best literature in all its forms takes seriously, the confusing, mysterious and exasperating nature of life itself. For a consideration of life from such a perspective brings us, I believe, closer than moral philosophy usually does to an understanding, in Arendt's sense, of the 'who' of who we each of us are.

One of the fundamental issues here is the mismatch between the perception of philosophy from outside academia and what the academic subject actually is. Many of those who want to read philosophy at university suppose that it is one of the most fundamental forms of reflection on the human condition. They often discover that it has precious little contact with, and therefore proper understanding of, life as it is actually lived. I have, indeed, taught or come across many students who were profoundly disappointed by the subject and whose sense of it was that it 'dwells in a bleak and arid desert; a very great distance separates it from green, fresh life, and it is highly questionable whether it will ever close the gap', as Georg Büchner put his response to the subject.[17] Further, there are many outside academic life who suppose that philosophical reflection must in some way be of relevance to their life and, finding out through the experience of trying to read some philosophy that it rarely is, have turned away from the subject in disappointment. Richard Taylor has put such points in terms of the concept of wisdom.

> Students of philosophy learn very early – usually the first day of their first course – that philosophy is the love of wisdom. This is often soon forgotten, however, and there are even some men who earn their livelihood at philosophy who have not simply forgotten it, but who seem positively to scorn the idea. A philosopher who, disclaiming any philosophical knowledge, dedicates himself to wisdom is likely to be thought of as one who has missed his calling, who belongs in a pulpit, perhaps, or in some barren retreat for sages, but hardly in the halls of academia . . . It

has been a matter of genuine concern to those 'outside' philosophy to realize, when wise men are sought, that not only do the philosophers not resemble very closely what they would suppose were men of great wisdom, but many do not even seem to profess a love for it.[18]

A central aim of this book is to seek to respect and respond to the sense that there should be some connection between the kind of reflection typical of academic philosophy and what those outside such philosophy usually take this discipline to be. I approach matters by trying to provide what Wittgenstein called, in another context, an *übersichtliche Darstellung* – a perspicuous representation. Others call this giving the 'grammar' of a concept. The idea is to attempt to trace for any given concept – say the notion of fate or destiny – the way in which it fits together with other ethical concepts. In this way, I seek to get clear on what it is that we are interested in, and what we wish to draw attention to, in speaking of the concept in question. The overall aim is thus partly descriptive, but it is also, and more importantly, an attempt to liberate our thinking to see sense or significance where before there was just an unclear, inchoate and unfocused awareness of a number of ethical concepts whose importance and relation to one another was dimly sensed but not seen for what it is. There is no question here of trying to suggest that anyone in particular *ought* to use the concept in question or, indeed, that if he does use it he must use it in the kind of way I suggest. Rather, the aim is to try to offer the best understanding I can in the hope that others will find this enlightening. Hence, I could say of this book what Virginia Woolf says of her thinking at the beginning of *A Room of One's Own*:

> [W]hen I began to consider the subject . . . I soon saw that it had one fatal drawback. I should never be able to come to a conclusion. I should never be able to . . . hand you . . . a nugget of pure truth to . . . keep on the mantelpiece forever. All I could do was to offer you an opinion . . . [W]hen a subject is controversial . . . one cannot hope to tell the truth . . . One can only give one's audience the chance of drawing their own conclusions as they observe the limitations, the prejudices, the idiosyncrasies of the speaker . . .[19]

Notes

1. Robert Nozick, *Anarchy, State, and Utopia* (Oxford: Basil Blackwell, 1984), p. xiii

2. John Keats, *The Letters of John Keats*, R. Gittings (ed.) (Oxford: Oxford

University Press, 1970), letter of 21 December 1817 to George and Tom Keats.

3. Raimond Gaita, *Good and Evil: An Absolute Conception* (London: Macmillan, 1991), p. 328.

4. Martha Nussbaum, *The Fragility of Goodness* (Cambridge: Cambridge University Press, 1986), p. 15.

5. Nozick, *Anarchy, State, and Utopia*, p. xii.

6. A. C. Grayling, 'Editor's Introduction', in A. C. Grayling (ed.), *Philosophy: A Guide through the Subject* (Oxford: Oxford University Press, 1995), p. 2.

7. He has done so in a number of books. The most important of these are: *After Virtue* (London: Duckworth, 1981); *Whose Justice? Which Rationality?* (London: Duckworth, 1988); and *Three Rival Versions of Moral Enquiry* (London: Duckworth, 1990).

8. Bertrand Russell, 'Philosophy's Ulterior Motive', in Russell, *Unpopular Essays* (London: George Allen, 1950), pp. 64–5, my italics.

9. Nietzsche, *Jenseits von Gut und Böse* in Giorgio Colli and Mazzino Montinari (eds), *Sämtliche Werke: Kritische Studienausgabe in 15 Einzelbänden* (Berlin: Walter de Gruyter, 1980), vol. 5, 'Von den Vorurteilen der Philosophen', §5, my translation.

10. Wittgenstein, *Culture and Value*, G. H. von Wright and Heikki Nyman (eds), tr. Peter Winch (Oxford: Basil Blackwell, 1980), p. 47^e.

11. Martha Nussbaum, *Love's Knowledge* (Oxford: Oxford University Press, 1992), p. 20.

12. Stuart Hampshire, *Innocence and Experience* (Harmondsworth: Penguin, 1989), p. 3.

13. Richard Taylor, *Reflective Wisdom*, J. Donnelly (ed.) (New York: Prometheus Books, 1989), pp. 28 and 35.

14. Philip Larkin, 'Continuing to Live', Larkin, in *Collected Poems*, Anthony Thwaite (ed.) (London: Marvel and Faber & Faber, 1988). I am grateful to Michael Newton for drawing my attention to the relevance of this poem for my thinking.

15. T. S. Eliot, 'East Coker', in Eliot, *Collected Poems 1909–1962* (London: Faber & Faber, 1986), pp. 202–3.

16. Hannah Arendt, *The Human Condition* (Chicago: University of Chicago Press, 1958), p. 181.

17. G. Büchner, 'Probevorlesung uber Schädelnerven', in Büchner, *Werke und Briefe*, K. Pörnbecher, G. Schaub, H.-J. Simm and E. Ziegler (eds) (Munich: Deutscher Taschenbuck Vorlag, 1988), p. 260.

18. Taylor, *Reflective Wisdom*, pp. 26–7.

19. Virginia Woolf, *A Room of One's Own/Three Guineas* (Harmondsworth: Penguin, 2000). I am grateful to John Armstrong for drawing my attention to this passage.

1

Birth and Death

At one point in *The House of the Dead*, his account of his time in Siberia doing hard labour, Dostoyevsky describes a spell he had in the prison hospital. Whilst he was in the infirmary, a fellow prisoner, Mikhailov – a man who had been sentenced for particularly unpleasant crimes – died of consumption. He died very slowly and painfully, and Dostoyevsky describes in detail the man's writhing in agony and his panting, fevered attempt to cling to life. After he had died, Dostoyevsky tells how the duty sergeant came in.

> [H]e was wearing his helmet and carrying a sabre . . . He approached the corpse, walking more and more slowly, and looking bewilderedly at the hushed convicts who were staring grimly at him from all sides. When he was about a yard away he stopped dead as though suddenly abashed. The sight of the completely naked, withered corpse, wearing nothing but its fetters, made a deep impression on him, and he suddenly unfastened his swordbelt, took off his helmet – something no regulation required him to do – and made the sign of the cross broadly over himself. This man was a hardbitten, grey-haired soldier who had put in many years of service. I remember that at the same moment Chekunov, another grey-haired man, was also standing close by. He was looking steadfastly, without saying a word, into the duty sergeant's face, observing his every movement with a strange attentiveness. But their eyes met, and for some reason Chekunov's lower lip suddenly started to tremble. He contorted it strangely, baring his teeth and, as if inadvertently drawing the duty sergeant's attention to the corpse, said quickly:
>
> 'He had a mother too!' and walked away.
>
> I remember that these words seemed to pierce me through . . . And why had he said them, what had put them into his head?[1]

It is natural to think that the duty sergeant and Chekunov shared fundamentally the same response to the sight of the dead man: they were suddenly gripped by a realisation of what it meant for this particular human being to die. But what does this mean? What, indeed, had put those words into Chekunov's head? Why did Chekunov's words have the effect on Dostoyevsky they did? What is their ethical and spiritual meaning?

Hundreds of thousands, perhaps millions, of people die every day. To the vast majority of those deaths we are utterly indifferent. Sometimes, however, someone dies who matters to us, someone whose death is a particular loss for us. For there are some people – a very few – who are irreplaceable to us. If we think about the nature of this irreplaceability we tend to describe the character of the dead man or woman. And, of course, differences of character are part of what we have in mind in speaking of someone's irreplaceability. But in the case Dostoyevsky describes he makes it clear that no one really knew Mikhailov well. When the duty sergeant, Chekunov and Dostoyevsky himself were moved as they were by Mikhailov's death this was not because they had suddenly been struck by the death of a man with such and such character traits, however interesting, noble or unusual they might have been. Chekunov's words on Mikhailov's death suggest that something else, something important in a different way from the nature of a person's character traits, was relevant to their response to the convict's death.

In the prison, the inmates had to endure all kinds of indignities, punishments, humiliations and torments. There was little or no sense in which, for the authorities, they existed as individuals. The same may be said of their relation to one another, for Dostoyevsky describes how the most common feature of the inmates was their profound need to impress one another: nearly all of them were ludicrously vain and proud, concerned about external appearances, boastful, and the like. This bespeaks, as Dostoyevsky suggests, a deep need to establish themselves as individuals in the eyes of their fellow inmates. In short, the prison environment was one in which the inmates were, and knew they were, without any individuality.

What Chekunov's words do is to indicate that he had been struck, as if for the first time, by the individuality of Mikhailov. For they bring him into relation to someone, his mother, for whom he was not, and could not have been, merely one amongst many. To his mother he was the irreplaceable individual he was. In speaking of him as he did,

Chekunov was recording his sudden realisation that there was a way of looking at Mikhailov in which he was understood to be a unique, irreplaceable individual. That way of looking at him is the way a mother looks at her infant. And what is most importantly relevant here is the love a mother feels for her child: a mother's love for her infant is itself an expression of her sense of the infant's unique individuality and irreplaceability.

This might seem an odd thing to say. After all, for all Chekunov knew, Mikhailov's mother might have resented her baby and have abandoned him. In that sense, Chekunov's words might be thought to be quite illegitimate, mere speculation on a relationship about which he knew nothing. But Chekunov was not speculating. He was not engaged in framing hypotheses about the relation of Mikhailov's mother to her child. Even if he had found out that Mikhailov's mother had resented him and had abandoned him as a baby, he would not have had to withdraw his comment. For Chekunov was articulating an ethical ideal of motherhood – precisely the ideal in whose light Mikhailov could be seen as an irreplaceable individual. If it turned out that Mikhailov had been an abandoned child, Chekunov would have judged the former's mother to have failed in the light of the ideal of motherhood which he was implicitly invoking.

But why, then, invoke the love of a mother here? After all, there might be many kinds of love which reveal the object of the love to be a unique and irreplaceable individual. What is special about the notion of motherhood? The answer lies in the fact that the love which a mother has for her baby is precisely not a love which depends upon any knowledge of the character traits – or, for that matter, any other detailed knowledge – of her infant. It could not, for, in any but a vanishing sense, a baby has no character. For sure, parents sometimes say, when a child is a little older, that all of its character was present from the first. But this is less helpfully thought of as a justification for the love that a mother has for her baby than an expression of it. And this is not to deny that one can see patterns of character emerge as a baby grows. But it is to say that the cherishing of, the delight in, witnessing that emergence is precisely what needs to be understood.

We can put the point this way. Philosophers sometimes ask whether we can justify our special concern for babies on the basis of their properties. For it is thought that what justifies our response to, and treatment of, an object – be it a human being, an animal or a stone – is its properties. And it is often thought that what justifies our special treatment of (adult) human beings are such facts as that they are rational or self-conscious or autonomous and the like. But babies possess none of these properties, and thus it turns out that we cannot justify our special regard for them.[2] Yet what this line of reasoning misses is how parents do in fact respond to their infants. For they clearly show in their behaviour that they think their infants' lack of rationality and so on is not what is significant in whatever it is that leads them to treat them as they do. Nor is it most importantly significant that their babies will become rational and the rest. A mother who is told that her new-born baby will only live a few months on account, say, of some congenital and terminal illness, does not for that reason think that care for her infant is misplaced. On the contrary. She may even think her baby all the more deserving of love and pity. The truth is, we are looking in the wrong place if we wish to 'justify' our responses to human infants by investigating their 'properties'.

A friend of mine who recently had a baby told me that, as she was bringing him home from the hospital in the car, she was suddenly struck, on driving through the polluted, grimy and noisy streets of London, by love and pity for him. Her response to her baby depended upon her sense of life as something tough and difficult, even as something hostile, at all events as something inextricably bound up with struggle, pain and confusion. It was also dependent upon her sense of the fragility of her infant, of his being a nascent soul in a body at once awkward and clumsy yet, in its own way, perfect.

But my friend's response also depended on something else. It depended on her sense of the *innocence* of her baby in the face of a world harsh and uncaring. Some philosophers are puzzled by this notion. They can see no sense in which a human infant is innocent in which creatures of others species are not also innocent. Thus Peter Singer claims that human infants are innocent in just the same way that laboratory rats are.[3] Implicit in this line of reasoning is the assumption that what makes any creature innocent is that it has not committed any morally reprehensible act, and since this is clearly true of both a human infant and a laboratory rat they must be innocent in the same sense. But what such reflections fail to notice is that the innocence of a human infant has little, if anything, to do with moral culpability. For the notion of innocence which was present in my friend's response to her baby is appropriate in the light of the idea that all human lives involve, in various ways, and to various degrees, compromise, loss and waste, and that her baby was destined to experience this but was as yet untouched by it.

We are in contact here with the very place where we get the notion of waste itself. Hannah Arendt has pointed out that everything in nature moves in a cyclical way. Accordingly, the concept of waste has, strictly speaking, no application in nature until we see nature in the light of human concerns. It is in a human life, unlike anything else in the world, that waste can be located: what we see as waste elsewhere is the image of the waste which afflicts every human life. This is because the path of a human life, from the moment of birth, is, as Arendt puts it, not cyclical but 'rectilinear', a path from birth to death.[4] We can tell the life story of any human being, the narrative of his journey through time. We cannot do the same with an animal's life. If we try to tell the story of an animal's life this is nothing more than relating the events in that life – what happened, and when. With a human life, things are quite different. For a human being can find his life meaningless; or feel that all has gone wrong in it; or come to curse the day he was born; or see that he has betrayed what he once was or might have been. The story of a man or woman's life is the story of such things. And a human infant who dies before maturity and who therefore cannot have this sense of his life can be pitied for having missed out on the extraordinary adventure, whereas this makes no sense for an animal, however intelligent or – like Washoe the clever ape – however many fragments of language it has been taught. A human life is always an attempt to make up for the fact that we live in a rectilinear fashion, at variance with our biological life which, like the life of all natural things, is cyclical. That attempt and its failure give us the sense of waste which, to a greater or lesser extent, haunts any and every human life and which can never apply to an animal's life. This, indeed, makes for us one of the fundamental differences between human life and animal life – in fact, defines our sense of what human and animal are. For this reason, those philosophers and others who wish to argue that animals have similar kinds of interests as humans have and that we should thus accord equal consideration to the preferences of animals and humans,[5] or grant animals some of the legal rights which humans have,[6] miss the point that a human life is something which is different in kind from an animal's life.[7]

A mother may often go on thinking her child innocent even when he or she is a grown man or woman. This need not mean that she mistakenly thinks that the child's life has not involved waste. Indeed, she may view him as innocent when she has a particularly keen sense of just that. For her sense of his innocence is an expression of her *pity* for this, just as her sense of the innocence of her infant involved pity for the fact that his life could not remain untouched by the unforgiving world. It is for this reason that a mother's sense of her son's innocence can be strongest when she knows, not merely that there has been waste, compromise and loss in his life, but when the form this has taken has been evil-doing or wickedness. If she insists on his innocence, she is not making a mistake about him and what he has done. Nor does she think that her sense of his innocence is anything that could be relevant in a court of law. It is rather, again, an expression of her pity for him: of her pity for him as an evil-doer – that *this* is what his life has come to.

The love and pity that a mother has for her infant, according to an ethical ideal we have of motherhood, is thus a form of recognition of the irreplaceable individuality of her child, and a sense of his innocence. But the former is not a conception of individuality dependent upon a knowledge of the character traits of her child, and the latter is not a conception of innocence dependent upon the thought that her child has done nothing wrong.

Chekunov's words about Mikhailov were not, as I have said, intended as some kind of hypothesis about the way his mother treated him. Rather, they call us back to the possibility that every human being can be seen in the light of the kind of love and pity of which we have an ethical ideal in the love of a mother, the nature of which I have tried to indicate. In its light one grasps the indifference of the world and the fragility of a human being in it. In this sense, Chekunov's words served to lift Mikhailov out of his anonymity and give him a dignity that he so singularly lacked as one among many hundreds of prisoners in the work-camp. But Chekunov's sudden sense of Mikhailov's dignity and individuality, as we have already noted, did not come from the fact that he or anyone else had suddenly seen what kind of person Mikhailov was, if we mean by that that he had come to some insight concerning his character. He did not suddenly come to see that Mikhailov was possessed of a fine or interesting character. Rather, the dignity and individuality in question came from seeing him in the way a mother sees her infant, that is, in the light of the kind of love and pity I have mentioned. And such a way does not wait upon a knowledge of character traits.

But there is another, connected, point. Chekunov knew, of course, that Mikhailov was an evil-doer: he would not have been in the prison otherwise. Yet when he said of him, 'He had a mother too!', he was articulating the possibility of seeing Mikhailov as innocent nonetheless. The sense of innocence in question was one which expresses pity for the fate of a human being, pity for the fact that such things come to pass in a man's life, that a man can end in this way.

Chekunov, I pointed out earlier, was struck by a sense of what it is for a given human being to *die*. What does it mean to be struck by this?

When someone dies who matters to us, a common reaction is one of disbelief. This disbelief is not that of failing to believe the truth of some such proposition as that 'X has died'. When someone says he cannot believe that his friend has died, he does not mean this at all. He is not *making a mistake*. Rather, his disbelief is an expression of perplexity in the face of the fact that there is now no more a world for his friend, that there is now no more that perspective on the world which was his friend's. The issue here has to do with the notion of the inner life of his friend. But this is not an inner life in the sense of what philosophers call the subject of experiences, that is, the having of beliefs, desires and the like. For that could be said of an animal. The inner life of which someone is thinking who says that he cannot believe it that his friend has died is rather an inner life which tells of his friend's struggles to make sense of his life. In this sense an animal has no inner life, which is why Heidegger said that an animal cannot die: it merely perishes (*verendet*).[8] And the extinguishing of a man or woman's inner life is received by the friend as a *mystery*. This is why the typical expression is one of disbelief. That sense of mystery is the sense of the individuality of his friend.

But to be struck by this mystery we do not need to know a lot about the character of the deceased. Even if we know nothing about it, we can still be struck by it. All that we need to recognise is that he had an inner life of the kind discussed, that is, one which is given by his struggles to find meaning in his life, whatever those struggles were.

The sense of mystery in question here is well captured by the reaction of those around him to Samuel Johnson's death.

> The same sense of incredulity was shared by everyone who had known him ... As Boswell said of himself ... 'My feeling was just one large expanse of Stupor ... I could not believe it. My imagination was not convinced.' William Gerard Hamilton put it best: 'He has made a chasm, which not only nothing can fill up, but which *nothing has a tendency to fill up.* – Johnson is dead. – Let us go to the next best: There is nobody; – *no man can be said to put you in mind of Johnson.*'[9]

When Chekunov spoke as he did of Mikhailov, he was intending to record his sudden sense of the mystery of the latter's death. And with this sense of mystery goes the realisation that Mikhailov had an inner life such that he could have thought his life wasted. There is here a sense of the appalling brevity of a human life, that everything in it can go wrong and that the man or woman whose life it is can see that this is so.

This idea of the inner life of a human being comes to the fore in the fact that we think of the dead human body as something which can be respected or desecrated. This is why Antigone is so keen to bury her brother, and why Achilles drags Hector's body around behind his chariot. But the idea of respecting or desecrating a human body cannot be the idea of doing good or harm to a subject of experience, for when someone is dead there is no such subject. Respecting or desecrating a human body has to do with the good or harm that can befall someone even when he is not such a subject. It has to do with the notion of the meaning or meaninglessness of a life.

A person's life can be meaningless even if he thinks it otherwise, and vice versa: the meaning of someone's life can be obscure to the one whose life it is.[10] And it is for this reason that our treatment of a dead human body is connected with the notion of the meaning of a person's life even where there is no conscious experience at all. When someone's body is desecrated, an attempt is being made to reduce that person's life to something *meaningless* or *pointless*. An attempt is being made to reduce his body to a mere piece of matter that might just as well not have existed. Similarly, when someone's body is treated with respect or reverence, this expresses a determination to see a point or purpose in his life. And in either case there is, of course, no thought that the person in question is aware of the (attempt to ensure the) meaninglessness of his life or otherwise, just as a living man or woman might be unaware of the meaning or meaninglessness of his or her life.

Chekunov's ability to look at Mikhailov as he did depended upon his being familiar with the love of a mother for her infant and his sudden ability to look at an adult human being in a way which bears witness to this kind of love. What is required for this familiarity is that a culture make this kind of love a possibility for its members. It might do this in a number of ways: through its writings, through particular persons it venerates or otherwise admires, through its music and so on. And indeed, the perspective on human infants we have been discussing seems very deeply entrenched in the way human beings view their babies. For we see the same kind of love for infants, the same sense of pity for them and of their innocence, throughout the literature of the world. However, the view on adult human beings which Chekunov expressed in the case of Mikhailov is not something which all cultures have shared and it is one which is well beyond the reach of most of us. There are no doubt very many reasons for this, but the central one is, for sure, that adult men and women do have a character and we may well, in one way or another, find this character inhibits the growth of the ethical perspective under consideration. We may just not like someone, or we may have been harmed by him, or we may despise him and so on.

For some, as for Dostoyevsky, this raises one of the most profound ethical tasks which they face: how can one nurture in oneself the love, pity and generosity towards human beings to which Chekunov's words bear witness when so much about what human beings are seems to make them unfit objects for such concern?

Notes

1. Dostoyevsky, *The House of the Dead*, tr. D. McDuff (Harmondsworth: Penguin, 1985 [1860]), p. 222.
2. See, for example, Michael Tooley, 'Abortion and Infanticide', in Peter Singer (ed.), *Applied Ethics* (Oxford: Oxford University Press, 1986), pp. 57–85.
3. Peter Singer, *Practical Ethics* (Cambridge: Cambridge University Press, 1979), pp. 123–4.
4. Hannah Arendt, *The Human Condition* (Chicago: University of Chicago Press, 1958), p. 19.
5. Peter Singer, *Animal Liberation* (Wellingborough: Thornsons, 1984), 2nd edn.
6. T. Regan, *The Case for Animal Rights* (Berkeley: University of California Press, 1983).
7. My argument here is indebted to: Cora Diamond, 'Eating Meat and Eating People', *Philosophy*, 53, 1978, pp. 465–79; and Raimond Gaita, *Good and Evil: An Absolute Conception* (London: Macmillan, 1991), ch. 8.
8. Heidegger, *Sein und Zeit* (Tübingen: Max Niemeyer Verlag, 1967 [1927]), §47ff.
9. Walter Jackson Bate, *Samuel Johnson* (London: Hogarth Press, 1978), p. 599.
10. Gaita, *Good and Evil*, pp. 135ff.

2

Virtue and Human Flourishing

Since the 1980s, moral philosophers have become increasingly interested in virtues and vices, that is, in such traits of character as kindness, generosity, cruelty and meanness. The reason for this growth of interest lies primarily in a dissatisfaction with two moral theories which had dominated the thinking of moral philosophers for a long time: utilitarianism, associated at its origins with the work of Jeremy Bentham and John Stuart Mill,[1] and Kantianism, deriving from the philosophy of Kant.[2] Both theories are very complicated, but, roughly speaking, the former claims that an action is right if it promotes welfare or happiness or pleasure, whilst the latter says that our actions must conform to certain principles or rules if they are to be morally praiseworthy. What is common to these two theories is that they locate moral value in the doing of one's *duty*.[3] On the utilitarian theory I have a duty to promote welfare or happiness or pleasure, whilst on the Kantian picture I have a duty to follow certain principles or rules. Many philosophers have come to feel that this is in various ways unhelpful, the most important consideration being that it seems to leave out of account the *character* of the agent or to make the value of the agent's character dependent on the value of his actions: the good agent is on this picture the one who does his duty. But surely, many philosophers now feel, the notion of character is more complicated than this: the moral worth of a person's character cannot derive wholly from his doing his duty.

Elizabeth Anscombe, in a paper which is very famous amongst philosophers,[4] argued that if philosophers wanted to get to a better understanding of the nature of the moral agent they should return to

25

a consideration of the work of ancient Greek philosophy, in particular that of Aristotle. For Aristotle has an extremely rich account of the virtues and vices, and Anscombe thought that philosophers could learn a lot from him. Many philosophers took up Anscombe's invitation,[5] with the result that virtue ethics has become very popular, and many philosophers now think of themselves as neo-Aristotelians. Others who do not use this appellation nevertheless follow Aristotle in many respects. In addition, many philosophers who were attracted by Kant's moral theory have gone back to look at Kant's texts in light of the rise of interest in the virtues and now argue that he was more interested in the virtues than was thought to be the case.[6]

When philosophers discuss the virtues, they are interested in a number of things. They discuss the nature of the education which is necessary to acquire the virtues; the relationship between individuals' virtues and the culture around them; whether there are any character traits which can plausibly be thought of as virtues for all individuals everywhere; the relation between reason, emotions and the virtues; and many other topics. But perhaps the central issue which philosophers discuss is that of the relationship between virtue and human flourishing or happiness. For many of those philosophers who work in virtue theory are interested in this area of philosophy because they believe that the life of virtue constitutes human flourishing or well-being or happiness.[7] Otherwise put, the idea is: if you are virtuous, you will flourish or be happy. And virtue theorists are not alone in thinking this. Indeed, it is a belief of many people both within and without academic life that somehow or other this idea is true. It is this idea that I intend to discuss here.

It is no doubt true that there are some people of whom it is true that they are happy through being morally good. Moreover, most of us get some happiness from being decent and tend to be miserable if – and because – we are nasty and mean. But I am sceptical about whether, in general, the claim is true that if you are virtuous you will flourish.

Consider Napoleon. He possessed particular ambitions for power, prestige and glory, all of which he fulfilled; he had a profound influence on the political map of France and the rest of Europe; he was fulfilled, at least for the most part, in his two marriages; he was well-read and had a roving, keen intellect; he associated with some of the most interesting and important men and women of the age; and he created for himself, as he longed to do, the Napoleonic legend. It is hardly any wonder that from his time to ours Napoleon has been seen and revered as someone who flourished in a uniquely human and enviable way.

In flourishing as he did, however, Napoleon was far from virtuous. He was in many ways cruel and grasping; vain and self-obsessed; treacherous and cunning. And these traits of character were actually necessary for his flourishing as he did. For example, at one point in his career he had the Duc d'Enghien, a nephew of Louis XVI, kidnapped and summarily executed on the vague suspicion that he might be part of a plot to restore the Bourbons. There is no doubt that this was an act of murder, but Napoleon was not in the least troubled by this. He saw it as necessary to retain his position and if he had been of more virtuous disposition than he was it is unlikely that he could have ordered the Duke's execution. Someone in his position with a more developed conscience would have been tormented or otherwise troubled by what he had done. As it was, Napoleon remained inwardly calm and self-assured. His inner life remained at this point, as it did throughout most of his life, harmonious and collected.

In being like this, Napoleon differed greatly from the virtuous, who always face the risk that they will be confronted by a moral dilemma. That is, they might have to face a situation in which there are two competing moral claims on them both of which they cannot fulfil and yet both of which they feel they are required to fulfil.

A good example is provided by Gerard Manley Hopkins. When Hopkins was at Oxford he took the decision to convert to Roman Catholicism. He felt that he had no choice about this, for he had become convinced that the Roman Church was the true Church and thus that it was no longer possible for him to remain with the Anglicans. For Hopkins, conversion was a matter of his moral and spiritual integrity. Nonetheless, he was acutely aware that, in converting, he caused great and deep pain to his parents, and he felt profound regret at this. He felt that there was no way in which he could do the uniquely right thing: whatever he did – converting or remaining within the Church of England – involved moral costs since these were competing and irreconcilable moral claims on him. The person with the most well-developed moral sensitivity is often the one who suffers most in life. Morality exacts its costs on us.

I am, of course, not claiming that Napoleon never found himself confronted by moral dilemmas, for it is not as if morality was nothing to him. However, he was far less prone to such experiences than those are who possess a greater degree of sensitivity to moral matters. And therefore we can say that he flourished in a way which is foreign to such sensitive individuals.

Could we say that Napoleon was not fitted for social life on account of his character, and that it is therefore wrong to say that he flourished, appearances notwithstanding? This is the kind of thing Martha Nussbaum has suggested: a proper conception of human flourishing, she argues, is one which could form the basis of human social existence.[8] Certainly it is true that not everyone could flourish in the kind of way Napoleon did, possessing his kind of character traits: the social world would collapse in a few days, if not a few hours. But this hardly seems to the point. For one thing, Napoleon was perfectly fitted for a certain kind of social life, one which involved – though was not consumed by – intrigue, cunning, the pursuit of power and the like, and which he could eventually come to form according to his own preferences. Even if we do not like that kind of social life, it was one in and for which Napoleon was eminently fit. For another, although it has to be granted that a social system in which no one was honest or disposed to refrain from injuring others, that is, in which no one had a minimum of virtue, would be, in Hobbes's words, nasty, brutish and short, this does not mean that everyone will flourish if he is virtuous. A nasty character, for example, might well be miserable were he to seek to be virtuous, but he will flourish all the more in a social system in which most others are virtuous, since he will be able to exploit and manipulate them all the more readily.

Aristotle, on whose work on the virtues many philosophers draw, as I have already mentioned, would have had an objection to saying that Napoleon flourished. He thought that the most fulfilled kind of human life was one in which all the best activities of which human beings are capable would be harmoniously combined – the life of the citizen, of the soldier, of the philosopher and so on. But Napoleon would have been hopeless as, say, a philosopher: he was a man of action through and through. So Aristotle would have had some doubt that Napoleon flourished: he would have thought him too special-ised, as it were. But what Aristotle missed in stressing the value of a life in which all good activities and social roles are balanced is that the kinds of virtues that someone has in a certain role in his life can be manifested as vices when he finds himself in a different role. Othello, for example, is a noble and grand general, without doubt a man who flourishes as a leader of men. One of his virtues which fits him for this is his sense of himself *as* grand and noble, *as* cutting a commanding and imposing figure. Without this, he would not be the general he is.

However, this same public virtue is, in his private life, a vice. It is, indeed, his downfall. For when Iago insinuates into his mind the thought that Desdemona is unfaithful, he immediately sees himself in the kind of grand role – this time, the grand role of a betrayed and tormented husband – that he is used to adopting on the battlefield. This prevents him from being able to see who and what Desdemona is as a person, even as she stands before him. His tragedy is the tragedy of a man whose public virtues are his private vices.[9]

There are many such examples. A conductor of an orchestra cannot afford to take note of his players' nerves, or tiredness, or of their different understanding of the work they are playing. He has simply to require from them that they play, and play to the best of their ability. The notoriously insistent demanding nature of such conductors is not a vice: it is the distinctive virtue of such a person. But often this public virtue is a private vice: in personal relationships it is often a form of childish wilfulness.

I am not suggesting that every great general or conductor is bound to be a failure in his private life. I am just pointing out that, as a matter of fact, it is very often the case that a great general or conductor is anything but great in his private life, and that there are important reasons – reasons, as I have suggested, to do with the relation between social roles and the virtues – why this is so. We are guilty of a kind of doublemindedness if we suppose that the great public figure could always retain his greatness if he acquired the virtues of private life. It is a doublemindedness which involves a refusal to see that the kinds of disposition we need in some areas of our lives can let us down in others. We may lament this, but it belongs to our condition as the limited creatures we are.

As I mentioned, Aristotle would have had his reasons to doubt that Napoleon flourished. Nonetheless, he would have seen in Napoleon a great deal that he admired, for he had an understanding of the virtues which is very far from that which most of us have. For him, the centre of the moral life was the idea of the noble. In particular, he thought that the truly praiseworthy person is the man who revels in worldly glory, especially in glory on the battlefield; who claims great honours and considers himself superior in body and soul to the mass, whom he disdains; who sees himself as the kind of person for whose sake society exists at all; who is free of all petty, small and quotidian concerns; and so on. Aristotle gives a memorable description of such a person – the 'great-souled man' – as follows.

[He]is concerned especially with honours and dishonours. And when he receives great honours from excellent people, he will be moderately pleased, thinking he is getting what is proper to him . . . But if he is honoured by just anyone, or for something small, he will entirely disdain it; for that is not what he is worthy of . . . The proud [great-souled] man wishes to be superior . . . When he meets people with good fortune or a reputation for worth, he displays his greatness, since superiority over them is difficult and impressive, and there is nothing ignoble in trying to be impressive with them. But when he meets with ordinary people he is moderate, since superiority over them is easy . . . He stays away from what is commonly honoured, and from areas where others lead; he is inactive and lethargic except for some great honour or achievement. Hence his actions are few, but great and renowned. Moreover, he is open in his hatreds and his friendships . . . He is concerned for the truth more than for people's opinion. He is open in his speech and actions, since his disdain makes him speak freely. He cannot let anyone else . . . determine his life. For that would be slavish . . . He is the sort of person whose possessions are fine and unproductive rather than productive and advantageous, since that is more proper to a self-sufficient person . . . He has slow movements, a deep voice and calm speech. For since he takes few things seriously, he is in no hurry, and since he counts nothing great, he is not strident . . .[10]

This could very well serve as a description of Napoleon. It is, of course, in almost every respect unlike the picture that most of us have of the virtuous person. The main reason for this is the influence of Christianity which came between us and Aristotle. For Christianity believes that the things of this world are unimportant: what is really important is what lies in the world to come. Hence the virtues of Christianity are profoundly unworldly, rejecting the goods and honours of this temporal existence as being so much straw. Thus Christianity emphasises love of one's enemies; the willingness to offer unconditional forgiveness for wrongs done us; poverty of spirit; humility; meekness; and so on. Most of us do not really believe in these things, though we often like to talk as if we did. And even our commitment to other virtues which are especially emphasised by Christianity, such as kindness, compassion and friendliness, is ambivalent. This is because to get on in the world we need many traits of character which cut against the grain of Christian thinking, for there are many walks of life in which too keen a sense of the kinds of virtues in question can only mean failure or misery. For example, politicians would get nowhere if they were meek and mild, always willing to forgive, always kind and generous, and business men would usually fail if they were generous and understanding towards their opponents in the marketplace. Moreover, in some social roles one has need of traits of character which can only be classed as vices according to Christianity and any catalogue of virtues that derives from Christianity. Thus, a journalist often needs to be stubborn, or prying, or dogmatic; a soldier often needs to be ruthless and cold; an artist must often be self-obsessed. And, in general, there are many ways in which emotions and motives such as envy, ambition, greed and the like spur us on to good and valuable things in many areas of life. The truth is, a perfectly virtuous person as many now understand such a notion – someone who is kind, generous, understanding and so on – would find little in this harsh world that he could do. Aristotle, whatever else we think of his account of the truly virtuous person, was right in seeing that those who wish for worldly success need worldly virtues, and he would have said that the virtues of Christianity can only lead to shame and failure in worldly terms. And about that he would have been right, too: the central figure of Christianity, Christ, was himself a complete failure in worldly terms, living in poverty without any material and social honours, and suffering a completely shameful death. Aristotle would have had nothing but contempt for such a figure and would probably have been amazed that he had such a power to capture the imagination of so many people. Those philosophers who have wanted to follow Aristotle in claiming that the life of virtue is the truly flourishing human life but have wanted to amend his catalogue of the virtues much more in a direction influenced by Christianity whilst rejecting the overall Christian view of things have been, I believe, less insightful than he was about what it takes to flourish in this world.

This raises an interesting question for the issue of education. For it is certainly true that most parents see it as one of their primary jobs to educate their children to have virtuous dispositions. And Roger Scruton is certainly right that, in the case of at least some virtues, it is in the child's interest that parents educate the infant to be virtuous. If, to take Scruton's example, I do not educate my child to have some disposition to courage, I am certainly doing him a disservice, for courage is needed in many areas of life.[11] But if I instil in my child too keen a sense of virtue, I may well be setting him up for harm in later life, as I have already suggested. Yet, even if I see clearly that envy and the like can help one flourish, it seems absurd to suppose I could seek to educate my child to be envious. On the contrary, I shall be inclined to do everything I can to get rid of this ugly emotion in him. Perhaps the answer is that, given that human nature is in so many ways unpleasant, I know that, whatever I do by way of educating him, my child is likely to possess his fair share of dispositions to envy, greed and so on. In this case, I should do all I can to ensure that these wither in him, even as I can be glad that they will not do so entirely. This is one of those areas of life where we may say we want virtue to prevail, but be rather glad when it does not.

It is, however, not just in fitting someone for certain social roles that what these days are thought of as vices can be seen as part of, or an expression of, a person's flourishing. We can see this in the life of Samuel Johnson.

Johnson was once party to a conversation where a friend stated that his wife's sister was really happy. The lady was called upon to confirm this, which she did. Johnson exploded.

> 'If your sister-in-law is really the contented being she professes herself . . . her life gives the lie to every research of humanity; for she is happy without health, without beauty, without money, and without understanding.' [When Mrs Thrale later] expressed something of the horrour I felt, 'The same stupidity (said he) which prompted her to extol a felicity she never felt, hindered her from feeling what shocks you . . . I tell you, the woman is ugly, sickly, and foolish, and poor; and would it not make a man *hang* himself to hear such a creature say, it was happy.'[12]

The thing that may seem odd about this outburst of Johnson's is that everyone who knew him testified to his extraordinary charity.[13] His house was, for example, full of waifs and strays for whom he cared, and many were shocked that he was happy to lodge with such persons. Moreover, he often gave to beggars so that they might, as he put it, at least beg *on* – and when it was remarked that the money he gave went straight on drink, he commented that we all need sweeteners for our existence. How are we to reconcile Johnson's outburst with this charity?

The answer is easier to find than might seem apparent. For there is, in fact, no need for reconciliation at all. What he thought the lady in question had manifested was a thoughtlessness about the world. He felt that she had shown no imaginative sympathy at all, but a smug self-satisfaction in the face of the sorrows of the world. His reprimand was itself an expression of his compassion for suffering humanity. Of course, Johnson's comment was in some ways shocking. Through it he had shown a certain vice – say the vice of critical intolerance. Yet the same sensibility underlay both Johnson's acts of charity and his unkind remark. That is, his sensibility of compassion found expression both in acts which were virtuous (charity) and in acts which were vicious (critical intolerance).

It might be objected that if Johnson were really possessed of a sensibility of compassion then it would always have found expression *as* that sensibility. Yet this is to hold to a philosophy of mind which is more prescriptive than descriptive. That is, it is to hold a view which does not tell us what we *are* but what we *ought to be*. There is, of course, a place for such thinking in moral life: that of ideals of human conduct and emotional response. And some people set for themselves the task of acquiring a kind of compassionate sensibility which only finds expression *as* compassion. But this should not blind us to the possibility that a genuine sensibility of compassion can find expression in words and gestures which are themselves harsh or otherwise unkind.

What are we referring to in speaking of someone's sensibility? Here is a suggestion. A person is not merely a collection of virtues and vices – or, for that matter, a collection of character traits of whatever nature. Rather, he possesses a lived and living presence or individuality. And when we speak of someone's sensibility we are trying to get at this individuality. We could put the point this way: people matter to us in ways that cannot be exhausted by a description of their character traits – however complete – and talk of someone's sensibility is a way of gesturing towards the fact that people matter to us as they do, that is, as individuals, with the kind of presence individuals have. An example will help make this clear. A friend recently wrote to me telling, amongst other things, of the death of an acquaintance. My friend remarked that the sudden absence of this woman seemed utterly *mysterious*. What she was referring to was the fact of being struck by the individuality of her acquaintance, of her presence, and that this had been forever extinguished. For it would not have captured her sense of mystery simply to say that someone with such and such character traits had died, not even if the account of such character traits were as detailed as possible.

What these reflections show is that supposing – as some philosophers do[14] – that virtues and vices are the fundamental concepts for appraising someone's ethical life and nature is misleading if those virtues and vices are not understood in the light of a proper sense of a person's individuality. And this individuality, I have suggested, is revealed by a person's sensibility. This means that the kind of sensibility which a person possesses is as important in understanding whether he is flourishing as is an account of his virtues and vices. And it is thus mistaken to think that someone's possessing certain vices need as such impugn the thought that he is flourishing. For we might be able to see (some of) his vices as at root expressing the same sensibility as (some of) his virtues. And if we admire his sensibility as showing him to be flourishing as a human being then the vices of his in question cannot be thought to be undermining of that flourishing. They can, indeed, be thought to be part of it. Such is, in fact, what many generations of readers have thought about Johnson. His sensibility of compassion is a central reason for recognising that he flourished, and many have drawn, and do draw, a great deal of spiritual nourishment and consolation from him on account of this. For they have felt, and do feel, that they, too, might flourish better by being brought into contact with him through his writings and through writings about him, even where his compassion has been expressed in the kinds of comment of his which we have considered.

If it is the case that, as I have argued, human flourishing does not coincide with the life of virtue, why is it that many moral philosophers suppose otherwise? A central reason lies in something I mentioned earlier. That is, the idea that the life of virtue is a flourishing human life constitutes an *ideal.* It is a description, not of how human beings are, but of how someone might like them to be.

Of course, a given philosopher may set for himself the ideal of living a life of complete or perfect virtue. And if he does this then it is highly likely that he will feel that it is only if he is truly virtuous that he is happy. He will be made miserable by his moral failures. But even if a philosopher sets himself such a goal, this does not mean that he has any business doing so for others or claiming that if they do set themselves such a goal they will be on the way to finding happiness.

Notes

1. Discussions of utilitarianism can be found in Mary Warnock (ed.), *John Stuart Mill: Utilitarianism, On Liberty, Essay on Bentham, Together with Selected Writings of Jeremy Bentham and John Austin* (London: Fontana, 1962).
2. Kant's moral theory is adumbrated in Kant, *The Groundwork of the Metaphysics of Morals*, tr. H. J. Paton as *The Moral Law* (London: Hutchinson, 1953 [1785]) and Kant, *The Metaphysics of Morals*, tr. Mary Gregor (Cambridge: Cambridge University Press, 1993 [1797]).
3. Cf. Daniel Statman, 'Introduction', in Daniel Statman (ed.), *Virtue Ethics: A Critical Reader* (Edinburgh: Edinburgh University Press, 1997), p. 3. This book as a whole gives a very good introduction to virtue ethics.
4. Elizabeth Anscombe, 'Modern Moral Philosophy', *Philosophy*, 33, 1958, pp. 1–19.

5. Prominent amongst these are: Alasdair MacIntyre, *After Virtue* (London: Duckworth, 1981) and Martha Nussbaum, *The Fragility of Goodness* (Cambridge: Cambridge University Press, 1986).
6. See, for example, Robert B. Louden, 'Kant's Virtue Ethics', in Daniel Statman (ed.), *Virtue Ethics: a Critical Reader* (Edinburgh: Edinburgh University Press, 1997), pp. 286–99.
7. See, for example, John Casey, *Pagan Virtue* (Oxford: Oxford University Press, 1990).
8. Martha Nussbaum, 'Aristotle on Human Nature and the Foundations of Ethics', in J. E. J. Altham and R. Harrison (eds), *World, Mind, and Ethics: Essays on the Ethical Philosophy of Bernard Williams* (Cambridge: Cambridge University Press, 1995), pp. 86–131.
9. Cf. F. R. Leavis, 'Diabolic Intellect and the Noble Hero', in Leavis, *The Common Pursuit* (Harmondsworth: Penguin, 1962), pp. 136–59.
10. Aristotle, *Nicomachean Ethics*, tr. T. Irwin (Indianapolis: Hackett, 1985), 1124a5–1125a15.
11. Roger Scruton, *Sexual Desire: A Philosophical Investigation* (London: Weidenfeld & Nicolson, 1986), ch. 11.
12. Quoted in Walter Jackson Bate, *The Achievement of Samuel Johnson* (Oxford: Oxford University Press, 1955), pp. 43–4.
13. See, for example, Walter Jackson Bate, *Samuel Johnson* (London: Hogarth Press, 1978), esp. pp. 314ff.
14. For example, Gary Watson, 'On the Primacy of Character', in Statman (ed.), *Virtue Ethics: A Critical Reader*, pp. 56–81.

3

Morality and Style

A T ONE POINT IN *Middlemarch,* George Eliot describes a scene
which takes place between Dorothea, her uncle, Mr Brooke,
and her suitor, Mr Casaubon. Dorothea very much wants Mr Casaubon to think well of her but during the conversation Mr Brooke
delivers the opinion that young ladies are flighty – just the kind of
characteristic which Mr Casaubon would despise. George Eliot writes:

> Dorothea felt hurt. Mr Casaubon would think that her uncle had some
> special reason for delivering this opinion, whereas the remark lay in his
> mind as lightly as the broken wing of an insect among all the other
> fragments there, and a chance current had sent it alighting on *her.*[1]

Reflecting upon this passage in the context of the novel as a whole, it
becomes clear that George Eliot is saying something quite general. She
is saying that most of our ideas about most things lie in our mind like the
broken wing of an insect. And they do so primarily because we are like
the souls or characters of Strindberg's plays, about which he said that
they are 'agglomerations of past and present cultures, scraps from
books and newspapers, fragments of humanity, torn shreds of once-
fine clothing that has become rags, in just the way the human soul is
patched together'.[2] Most of us, that is, are not much more than
receptacles or bearers of second-hand ideas. Our thoughts and emotions are in the main cobbled-together bits and pieces we pick up from
the circulating library of ideas which does the tour through newspapers
and magazines, television and radio, novels and self-help books.

Kierkegaard made this point by saying that we get most of our ideas
from the bargain-basement. One reason he put things this way was to

draw our attention to the fact that we are often especially attached to bargains we get in the sales: they seem such good value. And the same is often true of the ideas we get from the culture at large: they seem very good value because they cost us nothing by way of action in the world. We can enjoy having them because we do not have to pay much for them – even as we suppose that we do. The point is well brought out in an exchange between Boswell and Johnson.

> BOSWELL. 'I wish much to be in Parliament, Sir.' JOHNSON. 'Why, Sir, unless you come resolved to support any administration, you would be the worse for being in Parliament, because you would be obliged to live more expensively.' BOSWELL. 'Perhaps, Sir, I should be the less happy for being in Parliament. I never would sell my vote, and I should be vexed if things went wrong.' JOHNSON. 'That's cant, Sir. It would not vex you more in the House than in the gallery: publick affairs vex no man.' BOSWELL. 'Have not they vexed yourself a little, Sir? Have you not been vexed by all the turbulence of this reign, and by that absurd vote of the House of Commons, "That the influence of the Crown has increased, is increasing, and ought to be diminished"?' JOHNSON. 'Sir, I have never slept an hour less, nor eat an ounce less meat. I would have knocked the factious dogs on the head, to be sure; but I was not *vexed*.' BOSWELL. 'I declare, Sir, upon my honour, I did imagine I was vexed, and took pride in it; but it was, perhaps, cant; for I own I neither ate less, nor slept less.'[3]

In truth, when we are vexed in the way Boswell took himself to be, we are enjoying the play of our emotions. For the inner life is not at all well regulated by the outer world: it rather subsists in a kind of limbo, with emotions, hopes, fantasies and much else welling up and washing around inside us, waiting to attach themselves to some object outside.[4] And public affairs readily present themselves as such objects, not least because they distract us from the task of confronting the important and painful aspects of our own lives. This point is well made by Max Frisch in his *Biedermann und die Brandstifter* (*The Fire-raisers*), a profound and often amusing exploration of the attractions and destructive powers of human complacency.

> He who, in order to know what danger threatens,
> Reads the papers,
> Each day at breakfast outraged
> About some distant event,
> Each day supplied with explanations
> Which spare him the need to think himself,
> Each day finding out what happened the day before–
> He finds it hard to perceive what is happening now
> Under his own roof . . .[5]

Just as our inner life is, to use T. S. Eliot's words, a 'general mess of imprecision of feeling, / Undisciplined squads of emotion',[6] it is also often nothing more than a vacuum in which we try to conjure up emotions we do not have. Indeed, these two perspectives – emotions running riot and inner emptiness – are nothing more than different ways of speaking of the same thing. 'Lying', said Camus, 'is not only saying what is not the case. It is also, and especially, saying more than is the case and, as far as the human heart is concerned, saying more than one feels. This is what we all do, every day, in order to simplify life.'[7] And we do it particularly with respect to what we feel for others. In truth, we are often much more indifferent to the fate of our neighbours than we claim, but we fear admitting this, partly because we think that others will judge us to be morally reprehensible, and partly because we like to keep our inner life charged up in order to rid ourselves of the time of our life. A great deal of human activity, including the activity that goes on in our inner lives, resembles, as Samuel Johnson put it, 'getting on a horse in a ship'. 'The man who is *emotionally* educated', remarked D. H. Lawrence, 'is as rare as a phœnix.'[8]

These reflections about the hollowness and lightness of our thoughts and emotions are not new. On the contrary, they have haunted Western philosophy almost since its birth. It is, perhaps, with Socrates that we see these concerns for the first time in their full form. For he was deeply troubled by the practice of rhetoricians in ancient Greece. These were people who, like the spin-doctors of the modern political party or the PR advisers of big business, taught the unscrupulous and ambitious how to adopt a certain style of speech which allowed them to speak utterly convincingly and persuade the crowd, even as the content of what was said was empty and fatuous. Socrates was scared of the fact that *style* could be so powerful.

Socrates' worries are shared by many people, especially in an age where so many people go far with so little to say that is of substance. Or at least, they are shared in connection with morality. Style is all right if it is a matter of 'personal relationships', but it is nothing but an interloper, a distraction, when we get down to the serious business of morality. Morality has to do with rights and duties, with courage and honesty, not with something as exotic as style. For does not countenancing style in morality allow room for all the varied forms of humanity to find a place and flourish in an area of human life where we should all be alike? Is morality not about our all following the same rules rather than our developing and expressing our individuality?

Does style in morality not just open the door to anarchy, a free for all in which rights and rules go by the board?

Many have thought this and the history of moral philosophy is, in fact, in large part, the history of an attempt to extinguish the role of style in our interactions with one another and replace it with rules, obligations and duties which have nothing to do with style. The trouble with this is that a world in which such things prevailed would not have rid itself of style. There are two reasons for this. First, even if we all followed the same rules this would not make us all alike in this respect. Rules relate only to the outermost and most coarse aspect of human life. Think of all the different reasons there could be for someone to follow a certain moral rule: because it has never occurred to him not to; because he is scared not to; because he wishes to impress others around him with the force of his 'character'; because he sees doing so as a matter of integrity; because he is too tired to do anything else; because he wishes for revenge on his earlier self which was lax in just this regard; because he thinks he will get to heaven if he does; because he has no desire to do anything else; and so on. To the perceptive and patient eye someone's style will still show through even if he follows the same rules as everyone else.

The second reason why we will not get rid of style even if we all follow the same rules and acknowledge the same obligations and duties emerges from something Mary McCarthy says in her novel *Birds of America*. Peter, writing in Paris to his mother in the USA, is reflecting on Kant's moral philosophy:

> When Kant asks what would the world be like if everyone stole, that may be at bottom an aesthetic question. What would the world *look like?* . . .
>
> When I first studied the categorical imperative, I thought, like a lot of laymen, that it was the same as the Golden Rule. Don't steal from your neighbour because you wouldn't want him to steal from you. But the motive there is selfish. Sort of an imaginary deal or bargain; how would *I* feel if somebody stole *my* pocket-book? I'm projecting my petty self-interest outward. The categorical imperative is purer, like a theorem in geometry. Presented with the question of Should I steal or Why shouldn't I steal, Kant tells me to contemplate a world of thieves disinterestedly and accept it or reject it. If I reject it, that means that I don't care for the overall picture, regardless of where I might figure in it. But then, you might say, ethics boils down to a question of taste. Only, with Kant taste isn't relative. He assumes that everybody, the thief included, would reject the picture of a world in which everybody stole. Because the picture is self-contradictory. He was trying, in fact, to take the taste out of ethics, to base

ethics on a universal agreement that would spring from a common recognition of what is evident.[9]

Life is an extraordinarily confusing, entangled, snarled, deceiving and treacherous web of events, people and places, and from all of this each of us has to create some kind of sense or order to make things bearable – liveable – at all. But any way that we might have of bringing some order to life will itself involve various forms of compromise and waste, certain forms of self-betrayal and betrayal of others, particular costs and benefits: it is not possible to see life entire, still less – so to speak – live life entire. What someone like Kant possesses and offers to us is a vision of the world which claims to make the best possible sense of it, a vision which tells us which things are most important, and why, which things are less important and which not important at all. He offers us what he takes to be a vision of a kind of fulfilled life, a life as complete as we could hope for.

Yet Kant's view offers just *one* vision of life. It presents just *one* style of living – of how each of us might live and of how we might live together as a group. And there are many other visions of life that put things together in a way different from Kant's. McCarthy's Peter, I think, is right: if one accepts the Kantian view then one wants the world to look a certain way. For, even if we all came to accept Kant's view of things, following the same moral rules, acknowledging the same duties and obligations – and even waiving my first objection that under such conditions different individuals' style would show through – this would not mean that we had rid morality of style. It would just mean that we had got rid of all styles but one.

But this may seem to miss the fundamental point. For Peter says that for Kant ethics reduces to a question of taste. Nietzsche, thinking along the same lines, and from whom some of McCarthy's thoughts probably derived, made much the same point by claiming that everything is a matter of taste. And this is what we may balk at. For, we want to say, it surely cannot be right to think that it is just a matter of taste whether one believes that the moral attitudes prevailing in, say, the hierarchical and feudal world of medieval Europe are acceptable or not, or preferable to the moral world we in the West inhabit. Surely there is more here than a question of what one happens to like, which is what the invocation of the notion of taste seems to imply. And it will be no good trying to get round this problem by claiming that we have failed to see how important questions of aesthetics are in life. For, even though this is probably true, that proposal will in all likelihood amount to no more than smuggling in moral notions under the guise of the aesthetic. It would, for example, be useless to say that the greatest style would be found in a world where we were all Kantians, or that such a world evinces truly good taste. This subterfuge just forbids the word 'moral' and replaces it with 'taste', thus achieving nothing, since we should like to know what it is about the Kantian picture that makes it in such good taste, and then we are surely going to have to appeal to moral notions at some point.

After Peter has said that Kant was trying to take the taste out of ethics, he goes on:

> The way philosophers have always been trying to take the taste out of aesthetics.
>
> Pragmatically, nearly everybody, at least in the Western world, agrees that the Parthenon is beautiful. It isn't a question of taste, like Mannerism, for instance, which you can get to like, the way you do olives. Kant's ethics, as I see it, is a beautiful structure, based on a law of harmony and inner consistency, that in its way resembles the Parthenon, while yours, Mother, if you'll excuse me, is more like olives . . . Your ethics is based on *style*, which never has to give a consistent reason why it is the way it is.[10]

There is something to be said for the idea that Kantian ethics has prevailed and is now accepted in the West in the way that the belief that the Parthenon is beautiful is accepted. At any rate, almost everyone believes in a framework of rights and duties which is roughly Kantian in spirit and which it is supposed must govern our relations with one another, though there are, of course, plenty of disagreements about how exactly we should understand and apply them. As Alasdair MacIntyre has said: 'For many who have never heard of philosophy, let alone Kant, morality is roughly what Kant said it was.'[11] Suppose, in any case, that we all came to accept the Kantian ethics and that it is, indeed, harmonious and consistent as Peter says. It would not follow from this that we had a rational justification for it, for there could be any number of moral systems which are also internally harmonious and consistent, but which contradict the Kantian picture. Perhaps, then, what Peter means is that, because the Kantian picture is internally harmonious and consistent, once one accepts the picture – whatever reason one might have for doing so – any action one contemplates doing can be assessed for its rationality and consistency with other actions in terms delivered by that theory. This may be true, but then it is not clear why that should be thought to be an advantage. Emerson writes:

With consistency a great soul has simply nothing to do. He may as well concern himself with his shadow on the wall. Speak what you think now in hard words and to-morrow speak what to-morrow thinks in hard words . . . A character is like an acrostic or Alexandrian stanza; – read it forward, backward, or across, it still spells the same thing. In this pleasing contrite wood-life which God allows me, let me record day by day my honest thought without prospect or retrospect, and, I cannot doubt, it will be found symmetrical, though I mean it not and see it not . . . We pass for what we are. Character teaches above our wills . . . There will be agreement in whatever variety of actions, so they be each honest and natural in their hour.[12]

Emerson's point is that if one acts honestly from what one really is then one has a style of one's own. For sure, it must be agreed that from this point of view any action of any given person cannot give a reason why it is as it is on a specific occasion in the sense of being consistent with all others of this person's actions. But in a larger sense it can say why it is as it is: it expresses what one truly is.

One may not like that picture, and one may prefer Kantian consistency. Nonetheless, despite all the efforts of many philosophers to prove otherwise, we do not have a rational justification for the Kantian-inspired moral thinking of the modern West (or, indeed, for any other) which can claim anything remotely approaching universal assent at a theoretical or philosophical level. This does not mean that our moral thinking is simply empty or foolish or something similar. But it might mean that it is an expression of a particular taste. And this just returns us to the original problem.

Perhaps the central issue here is why it is that someone might wish to say that ethics is a question of taste. One possibility is that one has actually gone and lived in another culture which has a morality quite unlike that prevailing in one's own culture. And one may have found that one could accept it much more readily than one would have supposed. In this case, one would have a very good reason for saying that ethics is a matter of taste. For the point is not that this other morality could or should be instituted here, but that it is clear that there are many who, had they gone to this other culture, would have been morally appalled. That one accepted that morality with ease depends to a great extent on the fact that one *happens to be a particular kind of person* whilst others' rejection of it depends on the fact that they *happen to be a different kind of person*. But this is analogous to the case in art. If I like, say, Baroque music, whilst you do not, then at some level we shall just have to say that this is a matter of taste: I happen to be the kind of person who likes Baroque music, you are not. It is true that we shall have to say a lot to one another to explain why we have the taste we do, talking, perhaps, about our educational background, our upbringing, our deepest needs and fears and the like. But the point will remain that at some level we shall just have to say: you happen to be like this, I happen to be like that. As Wittgenstein said in another context: 'If I have exhausted all the justifications I have reached bedrock, and my spade is turned. Then I am inclined to say: "This is what I do." '[13] The fact that in talking of art – and in many other things – many people appeal to such a notion before any discussion gets under way and thus use it to stifle debate does not mean it is a useless notion. It just means we have to be careful about when we wish to appeal to it.

To give an example. Tobias Schneebaum wrote about his stay with the Asmat tribe in New Guinea, a tribe of warriors and cannibals.[14] He gives examples of some of their practices. They put the heads of their dead enemies in a fire to remove the skin, and when the skin is torn off, a hole is made in the skull and the brains poured out for the elders to drink. Their enemies' flesh, and sometimes that of their dead relatives, is mixed with sago, wrapped in leaves, cooked and eaten with relish. The young men of the Asmat are subjected to excruciatingly painful initiation rites: stalks of sugar cane are pushed up the nose until it bleeds freely; they are forced to swallow cane until they vomit (and they often defecate in fear); the tongue is pierced; and the penis head is scraped with rough leaves and cut until it bleeds profusely. And amongst the Asmat there is an elaborate system of ritualised homo-sexuality in which young boys take part as a matter of course: it is believed that unless they absorb the semen of older men when they are young they will not grow into strong warriors. Schneebaum felt com-pletely at home with this tribe, whilst many others would be morally appalled. And at some level we would have to say that he enjoyed life with the Asmat as he did because he happened to be a particular kind of person, and that the reason others would be disgusted and appalled is because they happen to be a different kind of person. This, as I have said, gives some sense to the idea that ethics is a matter of taste.

One thing one might take this to show is that if one is going to claim that morality is a question of taste then there must be a serious sense in which one could suppose oneself able, without self-decep-tion, to live in quite another moral climate. Otherwise, there will always be the suspicion that one's claim is a mere pose, just empty rhetoric. One must, in other words, earn the right to make this claim.

Perhaps not much short of going and living in a very different moral world is what is required here, but there are analogous situations. For example, Jean Genêt, who spent half of his life amongst criminal gangs and prostitutes, clearly could have lived in – indeed, flourished in – a variety of moral environments more brutal than most of us could stand. And another related case is, I think, that of those who have suffered long and hard. For, if their suffering has not destroyed them and has led them to a greater wisdom, then it will almost certainly have given them the capacity to cope with, even prosper in, extreme conditions of life. To that extent, they will in all likelihood have less need than most of the prevailing moral climate, whatever it might be, but especially the extremely cosy one by which we are now surrounded. There is a kind of flexibility of spirit which can be gained only through experience, and it is, perhaps, the possession of this flexibility which entitles one to speak of morality as a question of taste. Most of us, including those of us who think we are very liberal, are probably far too rigid of spirit to be entitled to speak in this way.

None of this should be taken to mean that the idea that morality is a question of taste implies that any moral outlook is to be as welcomed as any other. This would no more be the case than it is the case that any work of art or style of art is as good as any other. But we are strangely willing to adopt in the case of morality an equivalent to an 'I-know-what-I-like' attitude to art. Indeed, we are often praised for such an attitude to our moral opinions, for it is taken to show that we have principles or character. The reflection that morality is a question of taste may be helpful in loosening up our complacency or, at the very least, making us explore what we really mean in saying that we know what we like in morality.

Aside from such questions, however, we can safely assert that, one way or another, style is and always will be important to us. David Pole has well described its significance:

> [I]ts power over the mind and imagination remains undeniable and vast. Nor need this surprise us. In a thousand daily situations these are the things we must go by; in trivial or crucial decisions, it is a man's manner, the sound of his voice, that affect us, in which we find something that reassures or disquiets us ... [I]ntuitive people can amaze us by how much they rightly read from what seems like mere absence of evidence.[15]

It is someone's style which brings his virtues and vices alive; which shows him to be full of life or dead within; which excites our interest in him or makes us turn away from him in boredom. 'Le style, c'est l'homme même', said Buffon. Style is one of the most fundamental things about a person and reveals the deepest layers of his mind. The way a person converses, eats, drinks, gets angry, smokes a cigarette, gesticulates, makes love, walks, laughs, smiles, weeps, sits – all of these aspects of a person's style tell us *what kind of person he is*. Style can be manifested in the smallest of things. The song by George and Ira Gershwin 'They can't take that away from me', which sounds for all the world like pure entertainment, contains a profound truth. 'The way you wear your hat, / The way you drink your tea /. . . The way your smile just beams, / The way you sing off-key /. . . The way you hold your knife /. . . No, no, they can't take that away from me.' One action or kind of action can express for us the very essence of another person – the essence we love or hate, admire or despise, long to emulate or shy away from. It is not absurd to think that we can find in the style of the tiniest action the whole of the inner life of another person if only our perceptions are subtle and deep enough – a thought, indeed, which animates much of the writing of Henry James, especially in his later work.

The real problem is not with style, but with a particular employment of it. For there are kinds of style which reveal a deep and rich mind just as there are kinds which reveal a shallow and deceiving – or self-deceiving – mind. And it is primarily through someone's style that we see him as being in touch with reality or living a life of illusion. We can see this if we think for a moment about the fact that it is in a person's speech that we most clearly see his style. If someone can speak only in clichés then his style is not his own: it is merely the style of the masses, of the crowd, of a worn-out vocabulary. And the inability to speak in anything other than clichés is a profound moral disease. It means that one is empty within, that there is nothing there that is really one's own. Malcolm Pender, in a discussion of Frisch's *Biedermann und die Brandstifter*, has well described the moral disease of clichéd speech.

> There is a distorted relationship to language in the world of Biedermann. People are accustomed to saying what they do not mean. This ranges from the mechanical clichés of social intercourse . . . to the presentation of a [falsely] favorable picture of the world . . . In this way, language ceases to be a reliable mode of communication because there is always a different meaning below the surface. And the corollary of people not meaning what they say is that they cannot say what they mean, so ingrained in them has become the acceptance of language as a medium which dissimulates rather than reveals or communicates.[16]

But someone who speaks with real style finds new ways of speaking or new ways of giving a tired vocabulary fresh life. Such a person speaks with a kind of vitality and energy which mean that he is fully present in his words. He is able to stand behind his words, and this betokens a form of spiritual integration or integrity. Such speech reveals him to be possessed of a deepened understanding of the most important or significant aspects of his life. In this way we can see that he is bearing witness to what life has taught him. And there can be no question here of someone's repeating or reciting the views of another, not even if he is convinced by his words. For even if he is thus convinced he must be able to show that there is something in his own life which gives him the right to speak in this way, and that means that he must find his own words and his own style of speech in which to offer the thoughts in question. This is a way of making them his own.[17]

In 'A Prayer for Old Age', W. B. Yeats put the point this way:

> God guard me from those thoughts men think
> In the mind alone;
> He that sings a lasting song
> Thinks in the marrow bone . . .[18]

We might say that someone who speaks in this way speaks as a *whole* man (or woman). He does not appear in his words a mere abstract intellect or, alternatively, as possessed of passion which is uninformed by thought and the tough discipline of reflection (which is a form of sentimentality). D. H. Lawrence spoke in this connection of *real* beliefs, and he described a real belief as 'a profound emotion that has the mind's connivance'.[19]

Many of the greatest thinkers have been profoundly distressed by the fact that we live second-hand lives, that our only style is that of the mass. They have placed enormous demands on their own minds in order to remove themselves from such a condition. For them, the fact that so much in what we are is second-hand assumes the image of something like the fall of man. Nietzsche spoke in this connection of the possibility of creating oneself, and he was constantly amazed and appalled by the fact that the human soul can never fully escape the condition of soiled goods. And Martin Heidegger claimed that the fundamental condition of man is that of his 'thrownness': he simply finds himself in existence, trapped in a web of human lives which are not of his making, over which he has very little control and whose influence penetrates to the very core of his soul. He spoke with barely concealed disgust of the idle chatter which

46

characterises so much of human life and which, like some fluid – viscous and sticky – seems to stick to us and drag us down. Jean-Paul Sartre, developing Heidegger's thought, claimed that man has a primitive disgust of sticky substances. Yet disgust always contains an element of fascination and what these thinkers did not explore sufficiently is the relief that can come from giving oneself up to the idle chatter of the moment.

For we have created a world for ourselves in which idle chatter can be a way of getting through the day. Many of our contemporaries spend a great deal of their lives in occupations – their job and all that this brings with it – which gradually wear them down, turning their souls to dust. It is, in general, not the great moral catastrophes of life which destroy people but the grind of everyday experience: the unceasing requirement to go without sufficient sleep, the battle through the rush-hour, the lack of an environment which gives the eye anything refreshing to rest on, and the like. When in Kafka's story 'Die Verwandlung' ('The Metamorphosis') Gregor Samsa wakes up and finds that he has metamorphosed into a beetle, Kafka suggests that one reason for this is that Gregor's work has done this to him – destroyed his soul.

> My God . . . I really have chosen a strenuous career. Day in, day out travelling. The trials connected with the business are greater than the business itself in the office, and on top of that I have to cope with the torture of travelling, the worry about train connections, the irregular, bad food, relationships with others which are impermanent and unsettled and which never become intimate . . . And always having to get up early makes one completely crazy. A man needs his sleep.[20]

In such circumstances, idle chatter can, in the short if not the long term, provide a form of refreshment to the mind and spirit. Socrates said the unexamined life is not worth living. But the examined life may not, for some, be liveable.

In being so intolerant of idle chatter, Nietzsche, Heidegger and others were, as I mentioned above, partly motivated by the idea that, in such chatter, one loses all style of one's own. The only style available there is that of the majority. Nietzsche thus came to the conclusion that 'Eins ist not' – 'one thing is needful' – namely, to give style to one's character. In saying this he probably had in mind, amongst other things, the passage in the Bible (Luke 10: 38–42) where Jesus enters the house of the sisters Martha and Mary. Mary sat at Jesus' feet.

> But Martha was cumbered about much serving, and came to him, and
> said, Lord, dost thou not care that my sister hath left me to serve alone?
> bid her therefore that she help me. And Jesus answered and said unto
> her, Martha, Martha, thou art careful and troubled about many things:
> But one thing is needful: and Mary hath chosen that good part, which
> shall not be taken away from her.

Christ's style, whatever else we say about it, was one which disdained
the things of this world – goods, possessions, fame, success and the
like, that is, the things most of us, including most Christians, want. It
comes out here in a hostility – shown in the passage I have quoted – to
an anxious watching over the minutiae of daily life to make it run
smoothly. Christ, like Nietzsche, had little but contempt for that, and,
again like Nietzsche, he praised that style of living which (as Nietzsche
put it) squanders the energies of the spirit, which thrives on con-
tinuously drawing deeply on one's emotional reserves, forever ready
to expend oneself in both action and inaction. Such was the style of
both men. And again both of them despised the anxious following of
rules and prescriptions of life: for both of them, individual style was
everything – or almost everything.

Part of the urgency which the search for his own style assumed for a
thinker like Nietzsche came from the fact that he associated having
his own style with giving meaning to his life. He was afflicted by a
dreadful sense of having to make something of himself and his life, by
a horror of the destructive effects of time. Most of us are affected by
this at least occasionally. Some have counselled a relaxed attitude.
Thus Montaigne:

> What great fools we are! 'He has spent his life in idleness,' we say. 'I
> haven't done a thing today.' – 'Why! Have you not lived? That is not only
> the most basic of your employments, it is the most glorious.' – 'I would
> have shown them what I can do, if they had set me to manage some great
> affair.' – If you have been able to examine and manage your own life you
> have achieved the greatest task of all . . . Our duty is to bring order to our
> morals not to the materials for a book.[21]

But what if one is like the German film-maker Rainer Werner
Fassbinder who said that he never really felt he had experienced
something until he had made a film about it? And Montaigne was
pretty much afflicted by the same need: writing to convince himself of
the superfluity of writing. This kind of processing of experience – it
could be the making of a film, the writing of a book, the painting of a
painting, and much more besides – is an attempt to get it in one's
control, to stop it being something whose meaning one cannot fully

grasp. It is an attempt to create oneself, to stamp one's experiences with one's own nature, not letting them run out beyond one's control.

This attempt is the exertion of inner pressure on oneself: it is the struggle to live without waste. Consider how much of life just flows over us when we know we could get so much from it. Of course, one person's waste is another's pleasure. But someone like Nietzsche was caught in the appalling tangle of trying to strike some balance between a sense of waste which threatened to make his life seem pointless and a feeling that the waste of his life was only increasing because he was applying the inner thumb-screws ever tighter in the effort not to waste anything, in the effort to make something of all his experiences. For him, as for others in this predicament, it was in the experience of art that this compromise could best be struck. For art seems to offer a refreshment to the spirit whilst yet filling the self with a sense of time well spent, used to the full. But if someone has noticed that art offers the possibility of moments free from waste then before long he will get the idea that he could try to make of himself a work of art and to make life approach the condition of art. And Nietzsche, of course, saw the point.

> *One thing is needful.* – 'To give style' to one's character – a great and rare art! It is exercised by him who has an overview of all that his nature offers by way of strengths and weaknesses and who fits it into an artistic plan until everything appears as art and reason and even weakness delights the eye. Here a great mass of second nature has been added, there a piece of first nature carried away – both times with long practice and daily work at the task. Here the ugly, which could not be carried away, is hidden, there reinterpreted as something sublime. Much that is vague or resistant to being formed has been saved up and exploited for the view from a distance – it should signal to what lies off, into the immeasurable distance. At last, when the work is complete, it becomes clear that it was the constraint of one and the same taste which ruled and formed in big and small things alike: whether the taste was good or bad is of less consequence than one thinks – it is enough, that it is *one* taste![22]

The idea that nothing in what one is should be wasted is clear in this passage, as is the general idea – which is not to deny that there are plenty of problems here, such as knowing what counts as a strength or a weakness in one's character. But the thing that has most worried commentators on this passage of Nietzsche's is his idea that what is important is that a single taste prevail. For he is interested in this passage in the way bits of character fit together in a formal sense, rather than in the content of that character. Hence there surely are characters who might fit Nietzsche's description of having style and yet be far removed from being morally praiseworthy. This is not a thought that many philosophers have been happy to accept, for they would like to reconcile a liberal and humane, even gentle, moral perspective with Nietzsche's beguiling thought about giving style to one's character. Alexander Nehamas, for example, in what is a very fine book on Nietzsche, avoids facing the issue by writing:

> It is not clear to me whether a consistently and irredeemably vicious person does actually have a character . . . In some way there is something inherently praiseworthy in having character or style that prevents extremes of vice from being praised in Nietzsche's formal sense.[23]

In fact, it seems to me clear that Nietzsche *did* think that a person could have style and yet be far from being morally praiseworthy in any modern sense. He mentions, for example, Cesare Borgia, the violent criminal-soldier of the Italian Renaissance, and he is explicit about his agreement with Dostoyevsky in admiring the kinds of characters the latter describes in *The House of the Dead*. About one of them, Orlov, who had cut up old men and boys in cold blood, Dostoyevsky says:

> He was a man with a terrible strength of will and a proud awareness of his strength . . . [He] . . . was not really quite an ordinary mortal . . . I can say unequivocally that never in my life have I met a man of stronger, more adamantine character . . . This was truly a case of total victory over the flesh. It was evident that this man had a boundless self-mastery, that he had nothing but contempt for any kind of torture and punishment, and that he was not afraid of anything under the sun. All that could be seen in him was an infinite energy, a thirst for activity, for revenge, and for the attainment of the goal he had set himself . . . I do not think that there was any being in the world that could have influenced him by its authority alone . . . I tried to talk to him about his exploits. He would frown during these questionings, but his replies were always frank. But when he realised that I was trying to get at his conscience, to secure at least some kind of repentance from him, he looked at me contemptuously and haughtily; as though I had suddenly become a silly little boy to whom it was impossible to talk as one would to an adult. His features even expressed something approaching pity for me . . . [H]e could not help despising me and seeing me as a weak, pathetic, submissive creature, in every way his inferior . . .[24]

Surely this man had style: he is in many ways magnificent.[25] And, in a discussion of Dostoyevsky's book, Nietzsche suggests that the criminal type is simply the strong human being – like Orlov – under unfavourable conditions. Examples of criminals under favourable conditions might include Caesar and Napoleon, whom many people still admire enormously. So Nehamas seems to me wrong in what he says in interpreting Nietzsche. But the important point is not really one about the interpretation of Nietzsche's thinking. The real issue is this: we like people to have style, and we also want the world to be *safe*, yet these two usually pull in different directions. For most of us there is no solution to this problem: it is one of the deep tensions in modern moral thought, and we are not going to get everything we want here.

Such issues may seem in some way distant from everyday concerns. Yet the idea of making oneself into a work of art is not, perhaps, so foreign to such concerns as one might imagine. It may, after all, be a secret truth behind the reason there can be so much pleasure in listening to music through a walkman whilst going about the world that what this does for us is make us think we are works of art in a work of art. For the experience in question is something like that of watching a film whilst fantasising that one is a character in it. And film, in fact, exerts a powerful influence in other ways, for it is almost certainly true that many styles of speech and behaviour are adopted because we see them in films. There is, indeed, a theatricality to everyday life which is part of what makes it bearable.

Another way in which one can seek to make oneself into a work of art is to cultivate inwardness. This notion is not at all easy to understand, but central to it, I think, is a kind of willing acceptance of all that life can throw at one, an ability to accept all that might otherwise, or naturally, be thought to harm one. One will then have a self utterly secure and sufficient unto itself and life itself will seem a huge spectacle. Anyone who thinks this way will have to accept that such inwardness is a fragile possession: if he does not grant – and feel to the depths of his soul – that tomorrow his life could be reduced to ashes then his inwardness is not wholly authentic. This view is not inconsistent with trying to change things in the world, but what it excludes is resentment and hatred if one's best efforts to change things come to nought. This kind of attitude towards existence was a key aspect of Christ's life, and it is central to the thinking of some Eastern mystics. Nietzsche, too, was attracted by this way of looking at things, but could never reconcile it with his admiration for such a man as Napoleon, in many ways the very antithesis of the man of inwardness. It must be said, though, that Napoleon also looked at life as if it were a work of art, conceiving of himself as the central player

51

on the stage of European politics. Hence his constant references to his destiny or fate. For someone who thinks in terms of following his fate or destiny tends towards thinking of himself as a player in a piece: and a player has no control over his life, he is at the mercy of the playwright. But then, he is, after all, a work of art within a work of art. It is no accident that Nietzsche thought that the highest form of inwardness, which he thought of as an affirmation of life, involved *amor fati* – love of one's fate.

Kleist would have disagreed. For he had a horror of being what he called a plaything of fate. His attempted solution was to formulate a plan of life.

> [I]t is incomprehensible to me how a human being can live without a plan of life . . . [W]ithout a life-plan, without a fixed purpose, always wavering between uncertain desires, always at variance with my duties, a plaything of chance, a puppet on the string of destiny – this degrading state seems to me so contemptible, and would make me so unhappy, that death would be preferable to me by a long way.[26]

Kleist was, in fact, as good as his word, for when he came to the conclusion that the plan of life which he had set up for himself could not give him what he needed he blew his brains out. He saw that there is a basic problem with setting up a plan of life for oneself. This is that it is only by trying to limit the impact of life on one that the plan could bring what one hopes for. For if one remains open to life then part of this very openness must involve the possibility of the repudiation of one's plan of life. But these are both things which it is possible to feel that life demands of one. That is, it is possible to feel – it is, indeed, common to feel – that life demands of us both that we remain open to it in all its richness and confusion and that we seek to tame it and bring order to it by formulating a plan of life. Some philosophers, such as Kant, have tried to reconcile the two by arguing that by obeying the moral law we are also open to life and truly free. Perhaps he felt peace in his own life with this way of living. Others might find that Kafka's comment on Kant's moral philosophy will ring truer to life than that philosophy itself: in his short story 'Vor dem Gesetz' ('Before the Law') a man waits his entire life before the gates of the law – gates which exist for him and for him alone and through which he and he alone may pass – without gaining entrance. He is called to that which excludes him. He is doomed to failure. For Kafka, that was the fate to which all of us are condemned.

Notes

1. George Eliot, *Middlemarch* (Harmondsworth: Penguin, 1994 [1872]), pp. 21–2.
2. Michael Meyer, *Strindberg* (Oxford: Oxford University Press, 1988), p. 195.
3. Boswell, *Life of Johnson* (Harmondsworth: Penguin, 1980 [1791]), p. 1235.
4. Cf. Michael Tanner, 'Sentimentality', *Proceedings of the Aristotelian Society* LXXVII, 1977, pp. 127–47.
5. Max Frisch, *Biedermann und die Brandstifter* (Frankfurt: Suhrkamp, 1958), Scene 3 (chorus leader), my translation.
6. T. S. Eliot, 'East Coker', in Eliot, *Collected Poems 1909–1962* (London: Faber & Faber, 1986), p. 203.
7. Albert Camus, quoted by W. J. Strachan in his edition of *La Peste* (London: Methuen, 1965 [1947]), p. xxxiii, my translation.
8. D. H. Lawrence, 'John Galsworthy', in Lawrence *Phœnix I*, Edward D. McDonald (ed.) (London: Heinemann, 1961), p. 539.
9. Mary McCarthy, *Birds of America* (Harmondsworth: Penguin, 1974), pp. 129–30. The importance of this passage was first drawn to my attention by Michael Tanner in lectures at the University of Cambridge in the academic year 1991–2.
10. McCarthy, *Birds of America*, p. 130.
11. Alasdair MacIntyre, *A Short History of Ethics* (London: Routledge, 1987), p. 190.
12. Ralph Waldo Emerson, 'Self-Reliance', in Emerson, *Selected Essays*, Larzer Ziff (ed.) (Harmondsworth: Penguin, 1985), pp. 183–4.
13. Ludwig Wittgenstein, *Philosophical Investigations*, tr. E. Anscombe (Oxford: Blackwell, 1983 [1953]), Pt I, §217.
14. Tobias Schneebaum, *Where the Spirits Dwell* (London: Weidenfeld & Nicolson, 1988).
15. David Pole, *Aesthetics, Form and Emotion*, George Roberts (ed.) (London: Duckworth, 1983), p. 206.
16. Malcolm Pender, *Frisch: Biedermann und die Brandstifter* (Glasgow: University of Glasgow, 1998), pp. 24–5.
17. Cf. Raimond Gaita, 'Integrity', *Proceedings of the Aristotelian Society, Supplementary Volume* 1981, pp. 161–76; and *Good and Evil: An Absolute Conception* (London: Macmillan, 1991), pp. 272–3.
18. W. B. Yeats, 'A Prayer for Old Age', in Yeats, *The Poems*, Daniel Albright (ed.), (London: Dent, 1991), p. 332.
19. D. H. Lawrence, 'A Propos of "Lady Chatterley's Lover"', in Lawrence, *Phœnix II,* Warren Roberts and Harry T. Moore (eds) (New York: Viking Press, 1970), p. 493.
20. Franz Kafka, 'Die Verwandlung', in Kafka, *Das Urteil und andere Erzählungen* (Frankfurt: Fischer, 1989), p. 20, my translation.

21. Montaigne, 'On Experience', in Montaigne, *The Complete Essays*, tr. M. A. Screech (Harmondsworth: Penguin, 1991), p. 1258.
22. Nietzsche, *Die fröhliche Wissenschaft*, §290, in Nietzsche, *Sämtliche Werke: Kritische Studienausgabe in 15 Einzelbänden*, Giorgio Colli and Mazzino Montinari (eds) (Berlin: Walter de Gruyter, 1980), vol. 3, my translation.
23. Alexander Nehamas, *Nietzsche: Life as Literature* (Cambridge, MA: Harvard University Press, 1985), p. 193.
24. Dostoyevsky, *The House of the Dead*, tr. D. McDuff (Harmondsworth: Penguin, 1985), pp. 81–4.
25. Cf. K. Mochulsky, *Dostoyevsky: His Life and Work*, tr. M. A. Minihan (Princeton: Princeton University Press, 1967), p. 195.
26. Heinrich von Kleist, letter of May 1799 to Ulrike von Kleist in Kleist, *Sämtliche Werke und Briefe in zwei Bänden*, Helmut Sembdner (ed.) (Munich: Deutscher Taschenbuch Verlag, 1994), vol. 2, p. 490, my translation.

4

Truth and Reality

K AREL ČAPEK'S NOVEL *The Cheat* is the story of a man, Foltýn, who, from his earliest days, longs to be an artist. He is, in fact, self-absorbed, vain and pompous, and he lacks the discipline necessary to write anything great. Dimly aware of this, he constantly puffs himself up and consoles himself with empty words concerning the necessity of the artist to sacrifice all for his art, be impulsive, act beyond the ordinary moral requirements and the like. In fact, all these words provide him with is a justification for his indifference to the others around him. Living from the spiritual energy of others, he sucks them dry, ruining their lives by being unable to face what his own life is: an empty vanity. Čapek says this about him: '[I]nveterate lying killed him, poor chap; he stumbled into the world of lies and he never got out again. He was nothing but spurious phantasy and no truthful reality; he had suspended all moral connection with it, you know.'[1]

Čapek says of Foltýn that he had lost touch with reality, and he indicates this by appeal to the notions of lies and fantasy. These are only two of the numerous concepts we have at our disposal through which we might seek to indicate our understanding of someone's relation to moral reality. For as well as being able straightforwardly to say that someone is in touch with, or is out of touch with, reality, we can also say that he has his feet firmly on the ground. Or that he has his head screwed on. Or that he is clear-sighted and sober in his thinking. Or that there is no bullshit in what he says. Or that he is full of illusions. Or that he is self-deceived. Clearly the idea of moral reality plays an enormous and important role in the moral life. But what are we getting at in invoking the notion of reality in this way?

Some philosophers, who call themselves moral realists, think that 'moral opinions are beliefs which, like other beliefs, are determined true or false by the way things are in the world', as David McNaughton, himself a moral realist, puts it.[2] At one level, no one could disagree with this idea, since all it amounts to is the thought that my holding some moral opinion cannot, by itself, make that opinion correct: I can make mistakes in my moral judgements.[3] Moral realists, however, take themselves to be saying something more than this. They have suggested two analogies in order to articulate their understanding of the way in which moral beliefs are determined true or false by the way the world is.

The first analogy, to be found in the writings of John McDowell,[4] David McNaughton and others, is that the world contains moral properties in the way in which it contains what philosophers call 'secondary properties' like colours. For we can certainly say that objects really are blue or red or whatever. However, the blueness or redness of an object depends upon its being perceived by creatures with our kind of sensory and cognitive equipment: a rabbit or a Martian might see a flower's colour quite differently from the way we do. On this analogy, then, moral properties really are properties of objects, yet they would not be perceived but for the presence of human beings to see them. This picture suggests that the presence of moral properties in the world depends partly on us and partly on the way the world is, and that they are objective properties of objects.

The second analogy is between moral notions and arithmetic. Discussing the possibility of convergence in moral matters, that is, the possibility that we might come to agree in our moral judgements, David Wiggins writes:

> [T]here is at least one general way in which we might try to conceive of the prospects for moral judgments' commanding the sort of convergence that truth requires. This is by analogy with the way in which arithmetical judgments command it. There is an impressive consensus that 7+5=12; and, when we rise above the individual level and look for the explanation of the whole consensus, only one explanation will measure up to the task. There is nothing else *to* think that seven and five add up to . . . Since any other answer besides 'twelve' will induce a contradiction in arithmetic, no wonder we agree. We believe that 7+5=12 because 7+5 *is* 12. We have no choice.[5]

These analogies seek to explain the way in which moral values are out there in the world, *facts of the matter*. Mark Platts has put the point with exemplary clarity:

> [M]oral judgements are . . . *factually cognitive* . . . presenting claims about the world which can be assessed (like any other factual belief) as true or false, and whose truth or falsity are as much possible objects of human knowledge as any other factual claims about the world.[6]

No philosopher, not even a moral realist, thinks that the analogy between secondary and moral properties or that between arithmetic and morality is perfect. It is obvious, for example, that it is usually easy to perceive correctly the colours of objects, whereas this is very difficult in the case of putative moral properties. Further, we have a much clearer sense of what it is to receive a training in arithmetic than of what it is to receive a moral training. And variation in moral ideas as between different individuals and cultures seems to have no analogy in the case of secondary properties or arithmetic.

Such variation actually raises an interesting issue concerning why anyone should want to be a moral realist in the sense under discussion. For moral reality might turn out to be rather uncongenial: what guarantee do we have that it might not require us to carry out female circumcision, persecution of Christians, human sacrifice, torture and cannibalism? After all, many have thought such activities morally legitimate. There is nothing in the theory as such which could rule this out. Suppose that we took seriously the idea that we might be massively deceived concerning what we think moral reality demands of us. Then it is far from obvious that it would not be better to say that, whatever moral reality turned out to be like, we should ignore it. Whence the confidence that the truth will not be painful?

Still, waiving such worries, we might perhaps suggest, in line with the thinking of the moral realists, that what we mean when we say that someone is in touch with reality is that he has a large number of morally correct beliefs, that is, beliefs which are correctly responsive to the presence of certain moral properties in the world. Such a person is in touch with reality because he possesses a great many moral truths. And many moral realists seem to have such an idea in mind when they speak of moral reality and, by implication, of what it would be to be in touch with it.

A key difficulty with this suggestion is that the proposed relation between beliefs and reality seems to have most plausibility for what appear at any rate to be relatively simple moral claims such as 'It was mean to make that remark', or 'That was a very generous act'. If someone says, rather, that he finds all of life a vanity or that life is meaningless, then, at the very least, we shall have to resolve each such claim into many, possibly tens, hundreds or even thousands of other moral claims and assess each one individually. And then, how are we to judge whether the person who says this is in touch with reality or not? Should we say that he is in touch with reality if more than 50 per cent of his beliefs are true? Or some other figure?

This idea is, of course, absurd, and no philosopher or anyone else would be inclined to accept it: being in touch with, or out of touch with, reality is not a question of possessing a number of true beliefs about moral facts. But perhaps this is so because the very idea of moral truths, thought of as facts of the matter, is unhelpful.

Consider in this context the following comments of Walter Jackson Bate's in his biography of Samuel Johnson. Reflecting on the fact that Johnson can be a source of great consolation and help to us in the confusions of life, Bate writes:

> He [Johnson] could write as well as he did about grief or despair, about remorse and guilt, about boredom, satiety, and the hunger for novelty, about pride, aggressive competition, and the habit of arguing 'for victory,' because he himself was so susceptible to all of them yet was constantly putting them at arm's length in order to see them for what they were.[7]

And he goes on:

> There is a refreshing dauntlessness in the way he cuts through to the essentials of human psychology and need . . . We begin to feel as though a mine sweeper were moving in front of us, clearing the path of so much that we darkly feared. Or, if dangers remain, they now seem more reduced to size, because of that marvelous union of two forms of perspective that Johnson combines – the union of comic reduction (which would never succeed for us unless we were also aware that he was overlooking and dismissing nothing) and of sympathetic under-standing and compassion (which again would never convince, never prove contagious, unless we knew it had been hard-earned).[8]

And Bate ends by saying that '[t]hough what he writes is pervaded with his own experience and emotion, he is constantly able to keep them from imposing subjective distortions'.[9]

Johnson, in the tradition of the so-called 'wisdom writings' of the Old Testament, especially Ecclesiastes, thought that all of human life was vanity: nothing in this world can satisfy the incessantly craving, hungry, grasping human mind. And Bate's point is that when Johnson spoke of the vanity of human life – in one way or another it is a central theme of a great deal of his writings – he brought all of his experience of life to bear in such a way that his words have an authority which arrests our attention and speaks to us at a deep level.

We may not agree with everything Johnson says – we may even disagree with his general view on life – but we see through his words that what he has to say claims our attention and gives us cause to think in a deep and serious way about ourselves. And it is not just that Johnson brought his experience to bear in reflecting on moral matters. It is also that he did so in such a way as to avoid sentimentalising or indulging himself in that experience. This is what Bate means by saying that Johnson kept his experience and emotion from imposing subjective distortions on what he wrote.

But now compare this with the case of a 14-year-old boy who also says that all of human life is vanity. Both he and Johnson might utter the same words, namely, 'Human life is vain', but in the case of the boy there will be nothing about his life as a whole to make what he says carry any weight or authority. He has too little experience of life even to know what he is really saying in saying such a thing.

What this example shows is that there is no such thing as assessing the idea that all of human life is a vanity outside the context of the life of the person who offers this view of things. Further, what we make of someone who says this will depend not only on the kind of person he is, but also on the kind of person we are. We might ourselves have too little experience of life to know properly what someone might be saying in saying such a thing. On the other hand, we might have suffered deeply in a way which shows us that this person uttering this idea is, we judge, being little more than self-indulgent. And so on.

Of course, it is possible that we make mistakes in our judgement of another: someone's style can fool us and we can think something someone says or writes profound but realise later that it was shallow and commonplace. This is, indeed, a constant experience as we emerge from youth. And as adults we can always find ourselves fooled in this way. Perhaps it is even a central task of the moral life to be on our guard against this. Further, at some point we have to trust in our own capacities to distinguish the real from the bogus, and we can be sure that we get it wrong some – or even a lot – of the time, for we are always too ready to trust ourselves. But despite these complications the central point remains: it is in the context of someone's life as a whole – or a large part of it – that we can sensibly understand and assess what he means by saying that all of life is a vanity. There is no such thing as the truth of the claim: 'Human life is a vanity' independently of the man or woman who thinks this way.

The points I have made about the notion of the vanity of life can be generalised. That is, any given moral notion has no substantial meaning outside the context of the life of the given individual who is using it. Iris Murdoch has suggested why this should be so. She noted that our understanding of moral ideas changes over time, sometimes becoming deeper and sometimes shallower.[10] The understanding that one has of concepts such as loyalty or honesty or integrity or justice at forty differ markedly from the understanding one has of these at seventeen. At forty they bear, for better or worse, the imprint of the experience of the years one has lived and are invested with layer upon layer of accretions which intermingle and cross-fertilise one another. Hence, each of us has different understandings of the moral concepts we employ from the understanding others have of them – slightly different or radically so, as the case may be. Moreover, some of us make use of some such ideas which are a blank to others. Some, for example, have little or no use for notions such as redemption, sanctity or piety, whilst for others these are central to their life.

What these reflections show is that we cannot properly understand what someone means by making a moral judgement without understanding the details of his life with at least some measure of completeness. Moral notions have, for different individuals, a personal meaning which overlaps at best only partly with the meaning they have for others. Of course, it is quite true that we usually do not have the time or energy to be responsive to this in our dealings with one another. And it is also true that we do not always need to have such time and energy at our disposal in order to understand what someone means to be saying in using specific moral notions: there is sometimes enough overlap between different individuals' understanding of such ideas for us to get enough of a sense, however rough and ready, of what someone is talking about in making a moral judgement, offering a moral opinion and the like. Be that as it may, the concept of a moral truth, if this is to be understood on analogy to truths about the colours of objects or truths in arithmetic, misses the point that moral notions have a largely personal or private meaning for each individual. For one's understanding and use of such notions as colour or arithmetical concepts do not depend in the same way upon one's experience of life. Raimond Gaita has put the point in a helpful way: if there were moral facts as there are facts about the colours of objects or arithmetic then it would make sense to think that God could put into your head in a flash all truths about all moral facts, in the way he could put into your head all the truths about the colours of objects or arithmetic. But it makes no sense to think that one could have all moral facts at one's fingertips in this way, as if, once one had them, one could then go on living one's life in such a way to render redundant all further experience from the point of view of deepening one's sense of morality: for this deepening is part of what it *means* to lead a human life and part of what we *mean* by the very notion of morality.[11]

If what I have said is right, then any notion of morality which seeks to show that there are *moral facts of the matter* in any sense which goes beyond the thought that one might get things wrong in moral reflection gives us a misleading picture of moral concepts.

If, however, we reject the idea of moral truths in the sense of moral facts, this does not mean that there is no place for the concept of truth in moral matters. There is, first of all, as I have already noted, the notion of truth and falsity which we can use simply to mark our sense that someone is, in our opinion, mistaken in his moral views, or that we agree with him, though it is usually only philosophers who will tend to employ the terms 'true' and 'false' in an emphatic way: ordinarily, one might say that the other was, or his ideas were, silly or foolish or insightful or sensitive or gullible or whatever. (We also use vulgar expletives a great deal in this context: the role of swear-words and insults in our moral vocabulary has not at all been adequately explored by philosophers. There is a whole philosophy of abuse yet to be written.) Secondly, and much more importantly, even if the man or woman who is in touch with reality is not so in virtue of possessing many moral truths, this does not mean that truth has nothing to do with the matter. But the way it enters the discussion is – or should be – via the notion of *living in the truth* or *love of the truth*, a notion wholly unlike that of love of truths. Many, for example, have judged that Johnson lived in touch with reality, because he had a love of truth, even though they also think that he believed some, perhaps many, things that are false. For example, Johnson believed in the Christian God who would reward him if he were righteous and punish him if he were wicked. But if one has no such belief and thinks there is no such God, one should not feel that one must assert that Johnson was out of touch with reality after all.

How is this possible? Here is a suggestion. Scepticism about whether God exists is consistent with thinking that Johnson possessed a love of the truth because the notion of truth here is something like the idea of it we are invoking when we say that something *rings true*, or when we speak of a *true* friend. And in such cases there is room for scepticism of various sorts without this impugning or rendering inappropriate the notion of truth. Thus, if we say that something someone says rings true, then we are not saying that we simply accept it as we might accept some fact of the matter. We are saying, rather, that we find what he says enlightening, that it casts things in a helpful light, gets us to think more imaginatively about the issue and the like. Analogously, a true friend might well disappoint us or set himself against us in various ways without this at all undermining the thought that he is a true friend. Indeed, we might see such opposition as integral to his being so: otherwise, he would just be a slave. There are thus, as I have said, uses of the term 'true' which are consistent with various kinds of scepticism or difficulty concerning the object under discussion. Such is the case with the idea of living in the truth or having a love of the truth. So even if we reject Johnson's belief in God it is still possible to acknowledge that his faith in God was itself an aspect of his love of truth. It is so because there was a kind of purity in his faith which we can see was part of his attempt to rid himself of those tawdry and squalid emotions and attitudes which render us small of soul: vanity, affectation, complacency, envy, greed and the like. For example, he was hostile to prayers of petition for he thought them nothing more than an expression of such movements of the soul, a refusal to consent to difficulties and suffering in their various forms: prayer for him was part of what was necessary that he might avoid becoming bitter about the fact that the world is not all we want it to be. We see this in the note that he wrote when he woke on the morning of 17 June 1783. He had suffered a stroke and wrote to his neighbour thus:

> DEAR SIR, – It has pleased GOD, this morning, to deprive me of the powers of speech; and as I do not know but that it may be his further good pleasure to deprive me soon of my senses, I request you will on the receipt of this note, come to me, and act for me, as the exigencies of my case may require. I am, sincerely yours,
>
> SAM. JOHNSON[12]

Johnson was himself no doubt unaware of the humour of this note which accompanies its good humour. But it is part of the very sense we have in reading it that his religious belief, even if we think it false, does not detract from the idea that Johnson was possessed of a love of the truth. Quite the contrary: it expressed it.

It is, indeed, in a person's response to his suffering that we have a central insight into whether we want to say of him that he is in touch with reality. This is because it is when we suffer that we are most prone to the self-consoling fantasy which blinds us to reality. Johnson himself spoke in this context of what he called the 'treachery of the human heart', by which he meant to indicate the fact that we are all of us trapped to a greater or lesser – usually greater – extent in more or less self-generated webs of fears, anxieties, wishes, illusions and delusion and so on. He also spoke in this connection of the 'hunger of the imagination', that is, of our near-on permanent need to make up for the felt inadequacies of the present by seeking 'supplemental satisfactions' in reflections on the past or in anticipation of the future. Iris Murdoch has also spoken of such fantasies.

> The psyche is a historically determined individual relentlessly looking after itself. In some ways it resembles a machine; in order to operate it needs sources of energy, and it is predisposed to certain patterns of activity. The area of its vaunted freedom of choice is not usually very great. One of its main pastimes is daydreaming. It is reluctant to face unpleasant realities. Its consciousness is not normally a transparent glass through which it views the world, but a cloud of more or less fantastic reverie designed to protect the psyche from pain. It constantly seeks consolation, either through imagined inflation of self or through fictions of a theological nature.[13]

And again:

> Our minds are continually active, fabricating an anxious, usually self-preoccupied, often falsifying *veil* which partially conceals the world . . . [O]ur fantasies and reveries are not trivial and unimportant, they are profoundly connected with our energies and our ability to choose and act.[14]

Someone who exemplified in his own life a profound hostility to the kind of fantasy Murdoch has in mind and who, I would judge, manifested in doing so his love of the truth, is Dostoyevsky. For example, whilst in prison awaiting trial for his activities with the radical Petrashevsky Circle, Dostoyevsky wrote to his brother that he felt the need 'to compare my ideas with someone else's or remould my ideas in accordance with someone else's turn of mind'.[15] His capacity to be concerned about such things in such circumstances reveals an openness of mind, a willingness to change, of which few of us are capable even at the best of times. But this was at least in part because he used his very sufferings and misfortunes as material to explore what he called 'the mystery of the meaning of man'. About this exploration he said:

> To learn the meaning of man and life is something I am making progress in . . . Man is a mystery which must be solved, and even if you were to

spend your whole life in solving it, you could not say that you had wasted your time. This mystery interests me, for I want to become a man.[16]

When Dostoyevsky spoke of his desire and need to become a man, what he was expressing was his desire to live in the truth. He possessed what R. F. Holland has called the concern *not to falsify*,[17] a kind of ruthless honesty about oneself and one's place in the world. And although he spoke of the possibility of solving the mystery of man, he would not, in fact, have thought that it made sense to suppose that this mystery could be solved. For in speaking of the need to become a man, he was speaking of his sense of the task by which human beings are faced in this world, of what we are here to do. He would no more have thought it possible to complete this task than he would have thought it possible, as I argued earlier, that one could possess all moral facts. And he would have thought this for the same reason: it makes no sense to think that one might have solved the mystery of man, and then live on with that solution at one's disposal.

I have spoken of various possibilities: of living in the truth, of the love of truth and of living in touch with reality. These are all expressions of a certain quality of spirit which has the power to attract us as manifesting an attitude to life, and a way of living, which has some kind of ultimate meaning. These notions may seem far from everyday life, yet, in fact, they express something with which we are all readily familiar. The shelves of bookshops throughout the Western world are heaving under the weight of books – self-help books, popular psychology books, 'how to' books and the rest – whose express aim is to teach people how to live in the truth, though the idea goes by many different names. Indeed, the very notion of living in the truth seems all the more urgent in the modern world where old religious and cultural certainties have broken down. We all identify to a greater or lesser extent with the character of Emilie in Ingmar Bergman's film *Fanny and Alexander* who, after the death of her first husband, marries the bishop in the hope that this will allow her to live in the truth.

> The bishop spoke to me of another life. A life of demands, of purity, of joy in the performance of duty. I had never heard such words. There seemed to be a light around him. And I saw he was lonely, unhappy, haunted by fears and bad dreams. He assured me that I would save him. He said that together with the children we would live a life in God's nearness. In the truth. What he said about the truth, that was most important. I was so thirsty. It sounds dramatic and overstrung . . . but I thirsted for truth. I felt I had been living a lie.

Unfortunately, like Emilie, most of us discover that it is much harder than we supposed to live in the truth. 'Find your deepest impulse and follow that', recommends D. H. Lawrence. He thinks of that as living in the truth. But what if you do not have a deepest impulse? Where can living in the truth be then?

Part of the problem is that there is no *one* way of life which can be called 'living in the truth'. P. F. Strawson speaks of the ideals of

> self-obliterating devotion to duty or to the service of others; of personal honour and magnanimity; of asceticism, contemplation, retreat; of action, dominance and power; of the cultivation of 'an exquisite sense of the luxurious'; of simple human solidarity and cooperative endeavour; of a refined complexity of social existence; of a constantly maintained and renewed sense of affinity with natural things . . . [18]

and all of these can seem to us to be ways of living in the truth. This is so despite the fact that there is no way of combining all of these in one life. The different ways of life these ideals express and demand cannot all be lived by one and the same person: choices have to be made, compromises struck. Yet, as I have said, we can see that two people who wholly oppose one another in what they think life demands of them could both be living in the truth.

One reason why we may think that there are many different ways of living in the truth is that the notion of moral reality is itself contentious. Consider in this context what Stephen Spender says of T. S. Eliot's view on things.

> His poetry . . . is an instrument which has very strong and deep low notes and very beautiful and transcendental high ones, but which is weak in the middle register. He seems always to have had a vision of Hell, and he attained, perhaps, a vision of Heaven. By the middle register between Heaven and Hell, I mean ordinary living. Most people's lives are spent preoccupied with this, and for them it means reality. If they have an idea of Hell or Heaven they form their idea of them from their everyday experiences . . . Eliot does just the opposite. Life for him is measured by the experience of Heaven and Hell and ordinary living denies those conditions which are to him the real life, and without which so-called life is for him a kind of death. [19]

According to Spender, Eliot had a view of what reality was which differs profoundly from that which most have. And Eliot's is only one perspective. As Erich Auerbach has discussed in great detail, since at least Homer human beings have been trying to understand and articulate different conceptions of what moral reality is, for reality has been represented in profoundly different ways by different writers. [20]

At one level, what these writers disagree about is which objects the universe is made up of: religious believers believe in God, or the gods, whilst atheists do not, and that they think such exist (or do not) both depends upon, and supports, their general moral perspective on life. And I suppose that it at least makes sense in such cases to think that one might find out definitively which of these things exist and which do not, though even then one would not have disposed of the world-view in question: one may not believe in God, but it is possible nonetheless to have a keen sense of Heaven and Hell in a quasi-religious sense, as the writings of Kafka make clear. However, it is certainly not true that what most fundamentally distinguishes all different moral perspectives is their lists of the objects that the universe contains. It is quite possible that two individuals disagree deeply about the nature of moral reality whilst agreeing in their account of which objects there are in the world. The differences reside in how they see those things. This is why, for example, we say that different novelists create different worlds, and the same may be said of serious painters, film-makers and the like. And such worlds do not simply differ one from the other: they often contradict one another in many ways.

Some people think, of course, that there is only one way of living in the truth and thus that the nature of moral reality is not, after all, contentious. Religious systems, for example, are notoriously good at claiming that there is only one such way to live and they know what it is. However, even if one does think that there are many ways of living in the truth which cannot all be lived by one person, one might not give up hope that one could forge some attitude towards one's life which would allow one to think it had been pointful in some ultimate sense. This is, at any rate, one way of looking at Nietzsche's doctrine of the eternal return of the same. He thought that if you could find one experience in your life that was so glorious that you would be willing for its sake to live all the rest of your life as it was without change over and over again to eternity then this would mean that there had been, after all, nothing in your life that you could properly regret. Everything would lead into and out of that one experience which would stand at the centre of your life, redeeming all the dross in it. It is hard to make sense of Nietzsche's idea, but the spirit behind it is clear enough. The idea is that life itself is such that there is more to be borne in it than enjoyed, but that the pain of life – life itself – can be redeemed.

The notion of redeeming life or redemption – which seems so

deeply religious a notion – may seem alien to modern, secular thinking, but it plays a role in our lives since it is only another way of speaking of reality. We are constantly on the lookout for things in life that will allow us to make sense of all the confusions and pains by which we are faced, for things, that is, which put us in touch with reality and give us a sense of really being alive. Love, particularly romantic love, is the central hope for most. In this we betray our Christian heritage since for us in the West it is Christianity which has decisively structured our consciousness and this system of belief placed love right at the centre of its conception of things. And it is not just that we value romantic love on account of Christianity's high evaluation of it. It is also that Christianity told us that true love was completely selfless. In longing for love as we do we can thus tell ourselves that we are longing for something morally admirable in that we are longing to be good to the one – or the ones – we love. Unfortunately, many find that love is greedy, covetous and possessive. This is why most of those who long for it as promising the redemption of life find it, in the end, disappointing: it just leads us back again to our own lonely self, encumbered as it is with its miserable round of worry and struggle.

Perhaps it is, indeed, loneliness which is the final reality of our situation. But if that is so, then it is not the kind of loneliness which comes from having no one around us, no one to talk to – though that can be bad enough. It is rather the kind which Conrad's Marlow discovers when trying to help and understand Jim.

> It is when we try to grapple with another man's intimate need that we perceive how incomprehensible, wavering, and misty are the beings that share with us the sight of the stars and the warmth of the sun. It is as if loneliness were a hard and absolute condition of existence; the envelope of flesh and blood on which our eyes are fixed melts before the out-stretched hand, and there remains only the capricious, unconsolable, and elusive spirit that no eye can follow, no hand can grasp.[21]

And who could live fully in the light of this reality?

Notes

1. Karel Čapek, *The Cheat*, tr. M. and R. Weatherall (London: George Allen & Unwin, 1941), p. 132.
2. David McNaughton, *Moral Vision* (Oxford: Basil Blackwell, 1996), p. 39.
3. Cf. Paul Johnston, *Wittgenstein and Moral Philosophy* (London: Routledge, 1991), pp. 143–4.

4. John McDowell, 'Values and Secondary Qualities', in T. Honderich (ed.), *Morality and Objectivity* (London: Routledge, 1985), pp. 110–29.
5. David Wiggins, 'Truth as Predicated of Moral Judgments', in Wiggins, *Needs, Values, Truth* (Oxford: Basil Blackwell, 1987), p. 153.
6. Mark Platts, *Ways of Meaning* (London: Routledge, 1979), p. 243.
7. Walter Jackson Bate, *Samuel Johnson* (London: Hogarth Press, 1978), pp. 312–13.
8. Bate, *Samuel Johnson*, p. 313.
9. Ibid., pp. 313–14.
10. Iris Murdoch, *The Sovereignty of Good* (London: Ark, 1970), p. 29.
11. Raimond Gaita, *Good and Evil: An Absolute Conception* (London: Macmillan, 1991), p. 271.
12. James Boswell, *Life of Johnson* (Harmondsworth: Penguin, 1980 [1791]), p. 1240.
13. Murdoch, *The Sovereignty of Good*, pp. 78–9.
14. Ibid., p. 84.
15. Quoted in David Magarshack, *Dostoyevsky* (London: Secker & Warburg, 1962), p. 161.
16. Quoted in Magarshack, *Dostoyevsky*, p. 74.
17. R. F. Holland, 'Is Goodness a Mystery?', in Holland, *Against Empiricism* (Oxford: Basil Blackwell, 1980), p. 107.
18. P. F. Strawson, 'Social Morality and Individual Ideal', in Strawson, *Freedom and Resentment and Other Essays* (London: Methuen, 1974), p. 26.
19. Stephen Spender, *Eliot* (Glasgow: Fontana, 1975), p. 213.
20. Erich Auerbach, *Mimesis: The Representation of Reality in Western Literature*, tr. Willard R. Trask (Princeton: Princeton University Press, 1953).
21. Joseph Conrad, *Lord Jim* (Oxford: Oxford University Press, 1983 [1900]), pp. 179–80.

5

Wisdom

I T IS ONE OF the peculiarities of modern life that a great deal of our experience of morality is mediated for us by confrontation with large and impersonal bureaucratic organisations. Greenpeace, Amnesty International, the UN, Animal Aid, Oxfam and other pressure groups and government agencies certainly do valuable work, but the contact that most of us have with them and with the moral issues with which they concern themselves is limited to such things as filling in a banker's covenant or putting money in a tin waved under our nose. We have, indeed, turned over a great deal of our moral experience to such organisations, letting them get involved in the big issues for us, whilst we struggle on with the banality of quotidian existence. Their very presence creates a vacuum in our moral life. And then, thanks to television, radio and the newspapers, we attempt to fill up the void by following assiduously the diverse activities of these very organisations. We have become consumers of morality as we are consumers of washing machines, cars and holidays abroad.[1]

One odd feature of the fact that there is for many a vacuum at the heart of their moral experience is that that experience has become deeply and disturbingly moralised. Indeed, the modern age is more moralised than any other epoch has ever been, even as it has – probably because it has – less genuine moral substance than previous ages. For more and more of the details of our lives are governed by rules, regulations, systems and theories which tell us how to live and what to think. We are now living in what Adorno called 'the administered society'.

However, between the gaps in this moralisation and bureaucratisation of existence we sense the presence of richer moral concepts, concepts which we acknowledge to be indispensable for any proper understanding of life. One of these is wisdom.

Amongst philosophers, it is perhaps Aristotle in *Nicomachean Ethics* who has most emphasised this notion. He was, in fact, torn between two competing conceptions of wisdom. On the one hand, he was attracted by the idea that true wisdom was to be found in a life of philosophic contemplation, and when he spoke of this he spoke of *sophia*, which is the term usually translated into English as 'wisdom'. For Aristotle, such wisdom had nothing to do with action. On the other hand, he also felt the pull of a different image of wisdom, one which refers to activity in the world and which equates wisdom with success. When he had this notion of wisdom in mind and wished to speak about the capacity to order one's affairs in such a way as to achieve happiness he talked of *phronesis*. This is often translated as 'intelligence', but it is clearly pretty much the thing that we often have in mind when we talk about wisdom. For we too want to be successful in our actions in the world, and we often praise people for their wisdom where we mean to praise their prudence in arranging things in such a way as to provide the maximum scope for achieving such success. 'Received wisdom' is the name by which this sometimes goes, and someone who shares in this wisdom can reasonably expect to reap some of the good things life has to offer.

One of the reasons why Aristotle was attracted to the notion of wisdom as philosophical contemplation was that he, like many of his fellow Greeks, was troubled by the fact that each human life is deeply dependent upon good fortune for its success, and he was interested in limiting the impact that bad luck or ill-fortune could have on human existence. For the Greek mind was haunted by the stories of those whose lives had been destroyed by reversals of fortune: Priam, successful and powerful as the King of Troy, who then had to supplicate to Achilles that the latter might return him Hector, whom Achilles had slain in the Trojan war;[2] Croesus, King of Lydia, who was so successful that he was filled with anger at Solon's refusal to pronounce him one of the happiest men he knew, and whose son was subsequently killed in error by Adrastus, to whom Croesus had given shelter;[3] Polycrates, Tyrant of Samos, who had tried, whilst at the height of his powers, to forestall a disastrous fate by throwing away a precious ring which was then returned to him;[4] and others. Aristotle thus made an ideal of self-sufficiency, in particular, the self-sufficiency of philosophic contemplation – something, it is true, not to be obtained in a human life but a condition to which we might approximate.

For most, the image of the self-sufficient thinker, withdrawn from the world, is one of the stock or clichéd conceptions of the man or woman of wisdom. But whilst many feel or see the attraction of such an image of wisdom, few of us feel completely comfortable with it. We may even find it embarrassing because we are unclear as to how it could find a place in our lives so taken up with everyday survival and 'getting on'.

But our uneasiness with the notion of wisdom has other sides to it. One of these resides in the fact that the relationship between knowledge and wisdom is too profoundly complicated for us properly to understand it. For the person of wisdom may not know anything more than others yet be in a kind of actively engaged interaction with what he knows. Boswell put it well in thinking about Johnson.

> [H]is superiority over other learned men consisted chiefly in what may be called the art of thinking, the art of using his mind; a certain continual power of seizing the useful substance of all that he knew, and exhibiting it in a clear and forcible manner; so that knowledge, which we often see to be no better than lumber in men of dull understanding, was, in him, true, evident, and actual wisdom.[5]

The difference Boswell indicates here is crucial. It is the difference between possessing inert knowledge, on the one hand, and, on the other, living inside that knowledge so that it becomes part of a whole which informs the diverse aspects of one's life. It is the difference between a person's ideas remaining what F. R. Leavis called 'amassed externalities',[6] mere adornments of the self, or their really being fully *alive* in him, possessing a certain generative quality which leads their possessor to an active grasping and assimilation of the various forms and aspects of life around him. And the deadness of a person's ideas is, Leavis suggests, like the kind of deadness which ideas in an examination often have: it is not of the least consequence whether the thoughts a candidate offers in an examination have any vital connection with his life as a whole.

There are many examples of knowledge which we all have, but which for most of us remain dead. One is our knowledge of our own mortality. Like Tolstoy's Ivan Ilyich we can all see the validity of the syllogism: 'Caius is a man, men are mortal, therefore Caius is mortal.' We can all apply this reasoning to ourselves. But, as Ivan discovered, knowing these things is utterly different from understanding without

71

clichéd consolations the meaning of one's own death, and living a life in the light of this understanding. Our knowledge of our own mortality is for most of us, as Heidegger emphasised, mere inert knowledge, containing no wisdom which could make our life less wasteful or frivolous.

A second, less obvious example is provided by our knowledge that the human condition is extraordinarily frail. This normally sits lifeless in us, doing nothing serious to inform our sense of ourselves and the men and women around us. With Johnson things were otherwise. As A. R. Humphreys has written:

> His sense of moral truth is one which operates on life to help mankind in its basic soundness and its daily struggle: he does not seek to make life seem easier than it is, yet he discountenances those who exact too much of human nature. His sense of human fallibility (his own, in particular) leads him to sympathy, not condemnation; he checks conventional judgements by his own experience and is prepared to defend, for instance, those who rise in the world and forget their friends, those who think better of themselves than circumstances warrant, those who are generous through vanity, and those who write better than they live.[7]

Knowledge which is lumber in the mind and knowledge which is wisdom: the difference makes us uncomfortable because it makes us see how hard it is to come to a deepened understanding of human life. And it does this partly because it makes clear to us that morality is not most helpfully thought of as something about which one can have knowledge at all.

This fact sits very uneasily with a moral idea to which many in modernity subscribe, namely, egalitarianism. For the egalitarianism of the age claims that everyone – or, at any rate, everyone who is of age – has something worth saying on morality. Naturally we know deep down that some people have got more to say than others on such matters. But we are reluctant to think of this in terms of their possessing wisdom. We like to think that the reason they have more to say is, not that they have made more of their experience, or that they have a deeper understanding of themselves and their fellow men and women, but that they have mastered some kind of discipline. We think, that is, in terms of the acquisition of techniques. This is why we have in modernity ceded the role of the sage to that of the expert. Hence it is that we have courses in so-called 'practical ethics' – a growth area in philosophy – which are supposed to communicate competence in making moral judgements through teaching students how to construct and criticise arguments for and against particular moral positions, such as, for example, the permissibility of abortion. It goes without saying that thinking intelligently about moral problems can be useful and is important. But as soon as we ask ourselves what kind of form such arguments should take, we see difficulties with the approach. For example, is personal experience relevant to such arguments and should it be included in them? If so, whose experience? And what should we count as personal experience in this context? Is it enough to have read about case histories or must one also have worked in the area? And if we say that such experience is irrelevant to the kinds of arguments we wish to construct what should go into them? Answering these questions is itself, it seems to me, a moral task, and thus any argument which one might construct for or against abortion, for example, already involves, I believe, a substantial moral input which cannot itself be properly represented within the argument itself. As I have already said, none of this means that thinking about practical moral problems is a waste of time. The point is rather that construing such thought as a matter of expertise in wielding arguments already raises more questions than it answers.

The point that having deeper moral insight is not a matter of possessing knowledge is one which Plato makes through the mouth of Socrates in his dialogue *Meno*. In that dialogue, Socrates argues that virtue is not knowledge and hence cannot be taught. In fact, this idea is part of a larger claim which Socrates makes, namely, that nothing can actually be taught at all. He thinks that what we call teaching and learning is really reminding and remembering, for he believes that the soul of a human being is immortal and previously existed in another realm, whence it has knowledge of all things. And, once born, this knowledge lies dormant in the soul until the possessor is reminded of it. The speculative metaphysics notwithstanding, Plato is making here an extremely interesting and insightful point. For there really is a mystery about how a student learns anything. At some point in all teaching there comes a time when the teacher can do nothing but *hope* that the student cottons on to what is being communicated. Of course, it may be that the teacher is not very good and a better teacher could explain things in such a way that the student grasps the point. And there are usually many ways of trying to get the point across. But eventually even the best teacher who has exhausted all the possible ways there might be to explain things will still have to hope that the student understands. In this sense Socrates is right: it is impossible to teach or learn anything. Rather, one must wait for something *to happen* in the mind and soul of the student: there is an irreducible element of *passivity* in learning which leaves it beyond the reach of human supervision.

Still, if there is a mystery about all learning, the situation is even more disconcerting in the case of the acquisition of wisdom. For even as we can agree that we do not properly understand the process of learning and teaching, we nevertheless have some idea how to go about it. This is so, at any rate, unless we are wholly mistaken about the possibility of training some people to be teachers, though there are, of course, plenty of disagreements about how best to do that. But we have no real idea how it is that wisdom is acquired. Wisdom opens up the sense of the mystery of the self. And this is not a mystery which could be solved by, say, increased psychological knowledge. It is a mystery whose roots lie in the fact that we always live outside ourselves. As Emerson has it:

> If any of us knew what we were doing, or where we are going, then when we think we best know! We do not know to-day whether we are busy or idle. In times when we thought ourselves indolent, we have afterwards discovered that much was accomplished and much was begun in us. All our days are so unprofitable while they pass, that 't is wonderful where or when we ever got anything of this which we call wisdom, poetry, virtue. We never got it on any dated calendar day. Some heavenly days must have been intercalated somewhere . . .[8]

Emerson's point is not simply that wasted and pointless days can bring us wisdom. His point is rather that, given that so much can flow from what seems like pointless, aimless, undirected time, we do not really know what it is for time to be wasted. But if we do not know that then we can begin to feel that we do not know anything much at all. For then we are in a position where our sense of, and pride in, purposive and pointful human activity is unseated. This is why many of those who have thought hard about the human condition have been attracted by the idea that human activity is fundamentally nothing but an elaborate attempt to free ourselves of boredom.

Once one has become affected by this thought the chances are that it will never leave one, and life will assume the figure of a ceaseless attempt to find something that can sustain one spiritually together with the recognition that there is nothing in this world which can do so. This is one of the spiritual points of entry into Christianity which says that we have, indeed, got it all wrong and there is no human activity which is ultimately pointful: happiness and meaning lie in a world beyond this. This is why Christian thought has a strong tendency to upset our understanding of wisdom and foolishness in the image of the folly of the cross. Christ's failure in worldly terms was deeply bound up with what he wanted to achieve. For it is of the essence of his work that he spurned the world and worldly success and if Christ had not been a failure in worldly terms then he simply would not have had the powerful attraction over the moral and spiritual imagination that he has had and continues to have for so many. The whole of his ministry was directed to saying that those who are failures in worldly terms would live forever, and his own ignominious death makes this point as clearly as could be desired. In Christ wisdom and foolishness come together.

But what if one cannot accept Christian belief? What if one has a sense of the evanescence of meaning in human life but cannot turn to Christian belief for consolation? No one has faced this more honestly than Nietzsche. His attempted solution was to seek to rise from the depths of such a sense and live on the surface as if he had never been down there. He called this being 'superficial out of profundity': the cultivation in oneself of a lightness of spirit and cheerfulness when one knows that everything in life gives one every reason not to possess them. This is why he thought that the great mind was one that loved the *mask*, that wanted to be *mis*understood by his fellow men and women.

> One of the most refined forms of disguise is Epicureanism and a certain ostentatious bravery of taste . . . There are 'cheerful people' who employ cheerfulness in order to be misunderstood. They *want* to be misunderstood . . . There are free insolent spirits who would like to conceal and deny that they are broken, proud, incurable hearts . . . and from time to time foolishness itself is the mask for a cursed, all too certain knowledge. – From which it follows that it is part of a more refined humanity to have reverence 'for the mask' . . .[9]

Wisdom presenting itself as foolishness: the idea appealed strongly to Nietzsche, and yet he never could quite convince himself that this was not itself yet one more vanity, since he suspected his own suffering of being itself just a pose – or, at any rate, as something ultimately not to be taken too seriously. '[T]he worst is not / So long as we can say "This is the worst." ', says Edgar in *King Lear*.[10] And for a long time Nietzsche could say 'this is the worst'. Hence he did not reach that condition until a combination of mental and physical strain threw him into total mental paralysis which lasted eleven years until his death. This was, indeed, the worst for him, and he could not say it, for he could say nothing.

Wittgenstein urged his pupils to go 'the bloody hard way'. He did not just mean that it was important to do this if their philosophical thinking was to be of any worth. He meant – and this was even more important to him – that they should do this in their life. He thought that only going the bloody hard way gave one any hope of acquiring some wisdom. In a letter he commented on how hard it is to do philosophy. He then goes on:

> But it is, if possible, still more difficult to think, or *try* to think, really honestly about your life and other people's lives. And the trouble is that thinking about these things is *not thrilling*, but often downright nasty. And when it's nasty it's *most* important.[11]

It is appropriate that these comments come directly after Wittgenstein has remarked on the nature of philosophy. For he in fact thought – at least, he often thought – that intellectual work not only did not help in thinking honestly about one's life but actually made it more difficult. This is because thinkers and writers are exposed to a very strong temptation to wish to impress others, show how clever they are, and so on, all of which Wittgenstein viewed with a profound repugnance. Those who think honestly about their lives need not be, and perhaps usually are not, thinkers in the sense of being intellectuals or academics.

Kierkegaard, like Wittgenstein, was sceptical about whether thinking in the sense of being an intellectual could be at all helpful in the task of reflecting honestly on one's life. He would have said that the only hope of combining the two is to remain what he called a 'negative thinker'. Kierkegaard contrasted such a person with the positive thinker, the person who thinks, as Kierkegaard puts it, that he has got a result, that he has arrived at the answer to the deepest problems of human life. But the negative thinker himself is prone to becoming a positive thinker. Thus Kierkegaard:

> [A]mong the so-called negative thinkers, however, there are a few who, after gaining an inkling of the negative, succumb to the positive and go roaring out into the world to recommend, urge, and offer their beatifying negative wisdom for sale. These . . . hawkers are not existing thinkers. Perhaps they were so once, until they found a result; from that moment they no longer exist as thinkers, but as hawkers and auctioneers.[12]

We are back once again with the problem of teaching. For Kierkegaard saw that it is more or less impossible to remain a negative thinker. And therefore the issue is: how can one avoid being a teacher? Kierkegaard suggested that one should try and write entirely in the subjunctive rather than the indicative mood. How one does that is a question of developing a certain style of writing and it may well be that such a style is only to be found after many failed attempts to do so. And the greatest virtue of such a style is probably tact: the tact to leave others alone with their thoughts and see what they make of what one might have to say. Kierkegaard found such negative thinking in Socrates. He did so for two reasons. First, Socrates never wrote anything. He simply talked with the people he came across and asked them to tell him what they thought and why they thought it. Secondly, he himself claimed no wisdom, except the wisdom that he had no wisdom, unlike all those around him who professed great insight. One can find such negative thinking in other places, and the scepticism of the work of Montaigne is one key place.

The roots of Montaigne's scepticism are various. One is that each of us is, inevitably, so limited and has so narrow a view on the world that it is absurd to claim more than temporary allegiance to any particular point of view. Life is so rich and confusing that an increase of experience of howsoever small a measure can, in a sensitive mind, have a massive impact on, and work great changes in, one's view on things. A second is that human thought is itself so fragile, halting and awkward that it would be foolish to think that one could arrive at anything definitive by way of a conclusion about life as a whole. Thirdly, it is clear that there are so many thinkers so much greater than one is oneself who have arrived at conclusions different from, sometimes opposed to, one's own, that it would be foolhardy to suppose that one had alighted on the truth. And fourthly, it just always is possible to find arguments for opposing views on those questions which are of deep and lasting concern to human beings.

Montaigne, in cultivating a healthy scepticism towards his own ideas and encouraging others to do likewise, did not intend that one should believe in nothing at all, but that one should seek for an equanimity and equilibrium of mind in the face of the fact that most are unlikely to agree with one on much of what one thinks. The image here is something of that of the sage, fully engaged in the world, as Montaigne was, but calm and accepting. Most of us are, I think, attracted by such an image, but there are reasons to find it inadequate as it stands. To see this, consider the following comments of Dostoyevsky's in response to a woman who had written to him complaining of what she called a 'dualism' in her nature.

> Why talk of a dualism? It is the most ordinary trait of people's character . . . It is something that is peculiar to human nature in general,

but it is not by any means as pronounced in every one's character as yours. That is why I feel such a strong affinity to you; for this dualism of yours is exactly like mine, and I have had it all my life. It is a great torment, but at the same time also a great delight . . . If you were not so mature spiritually, if your mental development had been limited, you would not have suffered from this dualism . . . But this dualism is nevertheless a great torment.[13]

It would be silly to think that Dostoyevsky would have been a deeper and wiser man had he possessed greater equanimity of mind than he did. The very wisdom of his reflections on good and evil, on suffering, humiliation, anger, joy, defiance and so on depended upon his possessing what he called an 'insufferable' character. His epilepsy was only the most catastrophic form of all kinds of cravings, disorders, compulsions and vices to which he was prey, though he liked to think of it as in some way emblematic of the whole of his inner life. Indeed, he had a tendency to think of this disease, as did ancient thought, as being sacred. For he thought, again in line with a long tradition of reflection on the human situation, that states of suffering ecstasy – states, that is, in which one loses oneself in intoxication, frenzy, raving and the like – were states which afforded one deeper insight into the human condition. In other words, such states are ones of wisdom. Such a view of wisdom was explicitly rejected by Montaigne in favour of calm scepticism.[14]

Nonetheless, Dostoyevsky and Montaigne shared something important in their sense of where wisdom lies. For they both searched throughout their lives for an understanding of what they most fundamentally were as men beneath the manifold and changing surface of their personality. They both searched for what Montaigne called a person's 'master-form', and they identified understanding this as possessing wisdom. In this they were following the most famous of the commandments of the Delphic Oracle: Know Thyself.

Achieving such insight into our nature is profoundly difficult, for what we really feel is something which depends upon a vast network of hopes, fears, needs, fantasies, desires, memories and so on which are laid down on top of one another, next to one another, impacted in and distorted by one another, now in tension with, now nurturing of, one another and so on. The mind of each of us has grown in peculiar, idiosyncratic and distorted ways as a result of our experience or lack thereof: we are each of us starved in some respects and suffering from a surfeit in others. We are all of us, one might say, a mixture of health and disease. And even if we come to know what we really feel there are many forces which combine to render us incapable of admitting this. The dead weight of convention plays a role here, but there is also the fact that we fear that if we are honest about the reasons we have for what matters to us in our life others may find – or claim they find – what we have to say weird or vague or absurd. Our attachment to works of art, to people, places, historical epochs, landscapes and much more besides often depends largely upon profoundly personal reasons which cannot readily find a voice in the domain of public reason-giving.

However, the greatest impediment to our coming to know ourselves is without doubt the censure of morality, exercised either by others over us, or by us over ourselves, or both. In fact, the pressure here may be so intense that even someone who seemed to have so clear an insight into himself as Montaigne did, and was prepared to speak about what he saw, may have been concealing a great deal – from others, but perhaps also from himself. Certainly Rousseau thought so:

> I have always been amused at Montaigne's false ingenuousness and at his pretence of confessing his faults while taking good care to admit only likeable ones; whereas I, who believe, and have always believed, that I am on the whole the best of men, felt that there is no human breast, however pure, that does not conceal some odious vice.[15]

About this kind of thing Stefan Zweig writes:

> When you are reading an autobiography, and come to a passage where the narrator appears amazingly frank, attacking himself ruthlessly, it behoves you to walk warily, for the probability is that these reckless avowals, these beatings of the penitent's breast, are intended to conceal some secret which is even more dreadful. One of the arts of confession is to cover up what we wish to keep to ourselves, by boldly disclosing something far more tremendous . . .
>
> Jean-Jacques Rousseau . . . trumpets his sexual irregularities. In the contrite vein, he deplores that he, author of *Emile*, the famous treatise on education, should have rid himself of his offspring by depositing them in the revolving box at the foundling hospital. Such frankness is suspect. The pseudo-heroic admission was, perhaps, a mask of inhumanity to hide something he found it impossible to acknowledge. The probability is that he never had any children at all, being incompetent to procreate them. Tolstoy, in his *Confessions*, shrilly proclaimed himself whoremonger, murderer, thief, and adulterer; but he would not write a line acknowledging the meanness which made him treat his great rival Dostoyevsky so ungenerously.[16]

As Johnson said, we only speak of those sufferings of which we are at least a little proud.

If it is true that wisdom consists in knowing oneself but that morality can often stand in the way of such knowledge then this is most fundamentally because wisdom and moral goodness only partially overlap with one another. This was implicit in the example of Dostoyevsky offered a little earlier. For not only can wisdom co-exist with a great many vices, it can actually depend for its growth in some people on their possessing certain vices. It may be the very recognition of this aspect of the human soul which is a principal reason why in our moralised age we often ignore the concept of wisdom.

Notes

1. Cf. Keith Tester, *Moral Culture* (London: Sage, 1997), pp. 11ff.
2. Homer, *The Iliad*, tr. Robert Fagles (Penguin: Harmondsworth, 1990), bk. 24.
3. Herodotus, *The Histories*, tr. Aubrey de Sélincourt, rev. John Marincola (Harmondsworth: Penguin, 1996), bk. I, 30ff.
4. Herodotus, *The Histories*, bk. III, 40ff.
5. J. Boswell, *Life of Johnson* (Harmondsworth: Penguin, 1980 [1791]), p. 1401.
6. F. R. Leavis, 'Introduction' in Leavis (ed.), *Mill on Bentham & Coleridge* (London: Chatto and Windus, 1971), p. 4.
7. A. R. Humphreys, 'Johnson', in B. Ford (ed.), *The Pelican Guide to English Literature 4: From Dryden to Johnson* (Harmondsworth: Penguin, 1966), p. 410.
8. Ralph Waldo Emerson, 'Experience', in Emerson, *Selected Essays*, Larzer Ziff (ed.) (Harmondsworth: Penguin, 1985 [1844]), p. 286.
9. Nietzsche, *Jenseits von Gut und Böse* in Nietzsche, *Sämtliche Werke: Kritische Studienausgabe in 15 Einzelbänden*, Giorgio Colli and Mazzino Montinari (eds) (Berlin: Walter de Gruyter, 1980), vol. 5, §270, my translation.
10. William Shakespeare, *King Lear*, Kenneth Muir (ed.) (London: Arden, 1991 [1608]), IV, i, 28–9.
11. Letter of 16 November 1944 to Norman Malcolm. Quoted from Norman Malcolm, *Ludwig Wittgenstein: A Memoir* (Oxford: Oxford University Press, 1989), p. 94.
12. Kierkegaard, *Concluding Unscientific Postscript*, tr. David F. Swenson and Walter Lowrie (Princeton: Princeton University Press, 1974 [1846]), pp. 84–5.
13. Quoted in David Magarshack, *Dostoyevsky* (London: Secker and Warburg, 1962), pp. 1–2.

14. Cf. Michael Screech, *Montaigne and Melancholy* (Harmondsworth: Penguin, 1991).
15. Quoted from Lionel Trilling, *Sincerity and Authenticity* (London: Oxford University Press, 1972), p. 59.
16. Stefan Zweig, *Casanova: A Study in Self-Portraiture*, tr. Eden and Cedar Paul (London: Pushkin Press, 1998 [1928]), p. 151.

6

Relativism

P HILOSOPHERS USUALLY DISCUSS THE issue of relativism in terms
of the juxtaposition of one system of belief, prevalent amongst
one group of people, with a different system of belief, prevalent
amongst another group. Thus worries about moral relativism might
arise, for example, when we see that our moral beliefs are not shared
by those of another group. The other group might, for example,
believe that women should have no choice but to stay at home and
tend the hearth whilst men go out and earn the daily bread. We, on
the other hand, consider such an arrangement to be a violation of
women's rights. The issue is then what we should say – or do – about
this. Do we say that the other group has simply got things wrong? Or
do we say that in our group it is wrong for women to have no choice
about whether to work outside the home whereas in the other group
such a moral belief is in order? Is the truth of moral claims thus
relative to a given group or culture? Or, to take another example,
within the Muslim world a man is allowed up to four wives, whereas
within Judaism a man may have only one wife. Should we say that
there is no absolute moral truth about how many wives a man may
have and that all moral truth on this matter will be relative to the
social or religious or cultural group to which he belongs? In general:
are moral truths never true *simpliciter*, that is, 'true for all', but 'true
for us', 'true for them' and so on, that is, true relative to a given group
as relativism would have it?

Let us put things this way. The dominant aspect of the liberalism of
modernity is the belief in the equality of all persons. For, although not
everyone in the modern West believes in this, and although not all

who do so share the same understanding of it, enough believe it – that is, there is enough of a shared understanding of it – to make it a central feature of the modern moral consciousness. Our question, then, given the context of this discussion, must be: should we think that, in believing in the fundamental equality of all persons, we have arrived at some moral notion which has a truth beyond all cultural boundaries? Were the Greeks and Romans, for example, mistaken in not believing in equality? Or were they right in their own terms?

In Mary McCarthy's *Birds of America*, Peter Levi, an American student in Paris, writes back home to his mother. In the course of his letter, he writes:

> My theory is that equality is a sort of poison; once it got into the human bloodstream, nobody could eliminate it. It just stayed there, corroding us. I mean, it might have been better if nobody had ever thought of it in the first place. But they did, and once they did, it should have been thought *through*. Which never happened.
>
> When you consider that mankind lived for centuries without this idea's ever seriously entering anybody's mind! It never occurred to Socrates or Plato or any of the old philosophers. The idea of *everybody*'s being equal, not just Athenians or free men . . . Yet you couldn't say that Socrates . . . was stupid . . .[1]

And Peter goes on to say that the reason why the idea of equality is like a poison is that no society has been able to embody it fully in its moral and political life, yet the very idea that it should be has made most people feel guilty about their position in society. In the past, both rich and poor accepted their status in society as part of a natural order. Now the rich need to *justify* their having wealth.

> [N]obody today really feels comfortable inside his own skin. The poor feel guilty for being poor, and the rich feel guilty for being rich. The poor are afraid that it's not an accident that they are poor but that there is something ghastly wrong with them, while the rich are afraid that it *is* an accident that they are rich.[2]

If the notion of equality is like a poison in the way Peter suggests, this may lie in the fact that human beings are driven by too many forces that run counter to the desire – however genuine – to embody egalitarianism in institutions and practices. Yet Peter is clearly pointing to something deeper than this, and deeper than any issue about the distribution of wealth. When he says that the notion of equality has not been thought through, what he means to be suggesting, I think, is that there is, in one sense, no way in which it can be thought through. For all attempts to ground or justify a conception of the equality of all on empirical features of human beings are doomed to failure. In terms of their intelligence, creativity, physical beauty and strength, moral and aesthetic sensitivities, quick-wittedness and so on no two human beings are equal. Attempts have therefore been made to justify the belief in question in terms of something more abstract, say, the capacity to suffer, or the very fact of having interests or desires at all, or being rational in some minimal sense, or possessing, *qua* human being, inalienable rights. None of these proposals has met with anything more than qualified acceptance on the part of the majority of philosophers. What this suggests is that belief in the equality of human beings is probably grounded on nothing: it rather expresses a moral perspective from which it is determined to treat individuals in a given way, a form of life, as Wittgenstein would say.

Even if this is right, it should not be thought to render the notion empty. For the concept of equality is probably no worse off in this respect than many another – perhaps every other – moral notion. The search for foundations to the moral life which justify that life continues unabated in the mainstream of moral philosophy as it has done for centuries, but no one has come up with any perspective on the issue which could settle matters. About the best that anyone has, in the end, been able to do is to point out that *any* society of people will have to have *some* constraints concerning the requirement to tell the truth, not to steal, to kill, to injure and so on, which constraints must be followed by *most* people *most* of the time if that society is not to collapse (and even these stresses may be over-optimistic). But this hardly gets us to anything like a justification of a particular morality, still less of such a morality for everyone.[3]

There can be little doubt that the material conditions of our life form a significant element in leading us to accept certain moral notions. For example, it is certainly true that the extraordinarily vast and rapid change in beliefs about the moral respectability of certain kinds of sexual behaviour between the end of the Second World War and, say, 1975 was brought about partly on account of the invention of the pill as a convenient, cheap and extremely reliable form of contraception. It would not be right to think that people came to some moral insight as to the moral acceptability of pre- and extra-marital sex and that this then led to the invention of the pill. Things are more complicated than that. And we might also note in this context that the rapidity with which many people changed their views on sexual morality in the period concerned shows that our moral attitudes are far more flexible than we often suppose. Similarly, we can afford to believe in equality because to do so involves us in little cost so far as keeping going the material comforts of our life is concerned – that is, belief in equality does not threaten our material well-being. We simply do not know which moral claims we could come to believe tomorrow or the day after if such comforts were seriously threatened. I am not, however, being cynical, or offering some reductive Marxist line to the effect that material conditions are the only things that change moral thinking. It is rather a question of reminding ourselves that history shows us that people can believe just about any moral ideas given specific circumstances. We should seek not to lose sight of the fact that we are the children of our time, contingently formed as we are by political, historical, social and other factors.

If we consider these points whilst bearing in mind the fact that, as Mary McCarthy's Peter says, it can hardly be right to accuse someone like Socrates, to whom the idea of equality did not seriously occur, of stupidity, then it seems that we should feel the strain of insisting that we have alighted upon some timeless moral truth in accepting the notion of equality.

One might conclude from this that relativism concerning equality is true, but that this should do nothing to undermine one's commitment to this value. This kind of conclusion was favoured by Isaiah Berlin.[4] Yet I am inclined to think that the situation is more complicated than Berlin suggests. The point is not, as Richard Rorty has suggested, that we should look at this value with some kind of *irony* in the sense of being attached to it whilst recognising it to be the product of certain historical contingencies – or, at any rate, it is not simply that.[5] It is rather that it raises for us an unclarity concerning whether we really know what it is to believe in the concept of equality. The point has been brought out extremely well by George Orwell.

> Here am I, a typical member of the middle class. It is easy for me to say that I want to get rid of class-distinctions, but nearly everything I do is a result of class distinctions. All my notions – notions of good and evil, of pleasant and unpleasant, of funny and serious, of ugly and beautiful – are essentially *middle-class* notions; my taste in books and food and clothes, my sense of honour, my table manners, my turns of speech, my accent, even the characteristic movements of my body, are the products of a special kind of upbringing and a special niche about half-way up the social hierarchy. When I grasp this I grasp that it is no use clapping a proletarian on the back and telling him that he is as good a man as I am; if I want real

contact with him, I have got to make an effort for which very likely I am unprepared. For to get outside the class-racket I have got to suppress not merely my private snobbishness, but most of my other tastes and prejudices as well. I have got to alter myself so completely that at the end I should hardly be recognizable as the same person.[6]

It would be false to say, flatly, that Orwell was not committed to equality, but just as false to say, flatly, he was so committed. That is his point. The truth lies in an uncomfortable area in-between, where it is unclear just what we mean in saying – or Orwell meant in saying – that Orwell was attached to a belief in the equality of all persons. One might say: Orwell believed in equality, all right, but he did not believe it in his heart – his did not *really* believe it.

One way to put this would be to say that the moral attitudes of groups and cultures seemingly alien to Orwell were, in fact, closer to Orwell's sensibility and thinking on the issue of equality than we might have supposed at first blush. For he expresses a sense of class distinctions no different in principle from the feeling that there is a rank order amongst people which was the normal view of things prior to the rise of egalitarian moral and social thinking. Orwell's moral understanding is, he sees, after all not wholly dissimilar to that of a pre-modern culture.

Orwell is surely not alone. William Ian Miller has even argued that contempt between social groupings is not only one moral reaction we often find in modern democracies but one that is actually essential for the maintenance of democracy.[7] Many of us who believe in equality can, if we are honest, also recognise that we too have the same kind of fractured relation to this value as Orwell did.

There is a general point in all this. This is that there is an idealisation in speaking, as we usually do – and as I already have – of the different moral identities of different groups.[8] This point has been interestingly discussed by Peter Winch who notes that it is possible to feel alienated from the members of one's own group whilst finding oneself in great sympathy with the members of another culture.

It is . . . misleading to distinguish in a wholesale way between 'our own' and 'alien' cultures; parts of 'our' culture may be quite alien to one of 'us'; indeed some parts of it may be *more* alien than cultural manifestations which are geographically or historically remote. I see no reason why a contemporary historical scholar might not feel himself more at home in the world of medieval alchemy than in that of twentieth century professional football.[9]

Winch's point suggests the following. In our culture there is agreement across certain areas on what behaviour is required from a moral
point of view and this agreement itself expresses and helps nurture a
similarity in the moral sensibilities in those who accept this way of
behaving. Thus, no one now in Western culture practises cannibalism
or religious sacrifice, and that we share a moral sensibility is part of
this agreement in practice. However, it does not follow from this that
we share such a sensibility all the way down. In fact, we do not. For just
as Winch's scholar might find himself in some way spiritually at home
in the world of medieval alchemy, some other scholar or historian
could find himself in some ways spiritually at home in, say, the
practices of Aztec ritual sacrifice. There might be all sorts of reasons
for this: because those practices express a religious sensibility which is
sadly lacking in modern life; because they are part of a noble view of
the natural world which is lost to us; because they evince an honesty
about the brutal and cruel impulses of the human soul which modern
life seeks to cover up; and so on. In other words, the historian's
imagination could be captured by the Aztecs' practices of ritual
sacrifice. Others might be left quite cold by such things.

   The point has a general import: when we explore in any detail the
moral sensibility of different individuals of our culture, we shall surely
find that, even as we agree in a certain measure, there are profound
differences between us. For we all of us stand at various distances to
both our own practices and those of other, putatively alien cultural
groupings: affirming, accepting, identifying with, being repelled by,
being at one with, disliking but finding inescapable, being excited by,
longing for, being puzzled by, shying away from, fantasising about,
and so on. As soon as we look below the surface of what we do and
why we do it, we shall find that it becomes increasingly difficult, and
often impossible, to identify what it is that 'we' believe. To that extent
relativism, which relies upon our being able to identify what *we*
believe and distinguish this from what *they* believe, is an unhelpful
way of understanding the moral life.

Even if what I have said so far is accepted, it might be argued that this
does not alter the fact that there are certain practices which, whether
or not we can find our imagination captured by them, are abhorrent
and morally forbidden wherever they are done and whoever does
them. *Qua* things to do they simply are wrong or evil or whatever,
quite independently of any particular culture's thinking so.

   One example one might offer of such a case is slavery. For we might say that slavery simply is evil and that those who practised it were practising evil, regardless of the fact that they no doubt thought it was not evil. It is, we might say, a universal moral truth that slavery is evil. However, I think that there are two reasons to be worried about this way of putting things.

First, we might ask ourselves what it does for us if we suppose we have got hold of some universal moral truth such as that slavery is evil. Perhaps what we suppose we have got in believing such a thing is a sense that we have a certain power over the world. But this does much less for us than we usually suppose. It certainly provides us with no guarantee whatsoever that we would have the courage and strength to do anything about slavery, or resist it, were we to be confronted by it. We can be quite sure, for example, that many ordinary, decent individuals in the Weimar republic and in the early years of Hitler's supremacy in Germany would sincerely have assented to the idea that slavery is evil. But only a few years later they were living in a country where slave labour was regularly practised, and they kept quiet to save their own skins and the skins of those they cared about. If we are honest, we know that very few of us would behave any differently. Our moral opinions are often little more than reflections of our complacency in our good fortune to be alive at a certain place and at a certain point in history.

The second reason to doubt that it is helpful to suppose that in believing slavery to be evil we have got hold of a final, culture-independent moral truth is that what we actually have to go on in making and offering moral judgements are our best – that is, our most insightful, sensitive and honest – moral reflections. There is nothing else that anyone has ever had to go on nor, I think, anything else we could have to go on. This does not mean that we should suppose that all moral ideas and opinions are as good as any other. Nor does it mean that we should suppose that all of our moral ideas are equally open to question or (worse) possibly absurd. It is just to say that we achieve nothing by supposing that we have more than our best thoughts to go on. Is that not enough?

Some think that it is not, and they might say that here, after all, we uncover an argument for relativism. For, if all one has with respect to some practice of another group which one finds abhorrent is one's best and most honest thoughts and reasons about why one sees things this way, then could one not say that the others in that group who carry out such activities also have their best and most honest thoughts about what they are doing, in which case there is no final moral truth but truth relative to a given society?

In fact, I do not think the argument I have offered provides any kind of defence of relativism at all. Look at things this way: philosophers and others often talk of the 'threat of relativism'. But what is the threat supposed to be? Is it that in the face of the differing moral practices of other groups we have no justification for going about things the way we do? But that would be absurd: it is not as if there is *nothing at all* between, on the one hand, conclusive proof beyond one's best moral thinking of the truth of the moral value of one's own ways of going on and, on the other, a complete and total lack of justification for one's practices. Moreover, what *difference* would it make to suppose that one had anything more than one's best and most honest thought to go on in making one's moral judgements? None, I think, to those whom one judges. They would be hardly likely to listen to one giving one's reasons, however conclusive one takes them to be, and, even if they did, why is there any reason to think that they would accept what one has to say?[10] Looked at this way it is hard to resist Nietzsche's thought that what is called 'the threat of relativism' is little more than the expression of a fear, namely, of the fear of living with less than complete certainty about the positive worth of our moral practices. Whether Nietzsche was right to see in that a form of weakness is another matter.

The scepticism I have expressed about the possibility of conclusive arguments against a practice one abhors is thus not an argument for relativism, for it involves a scepticism about what the value and point of having such conclusive arguments would be anyway.

It might be suggested that what I have said so far has left a – perhaps the – crucial issue unaddressed. This is: what is one supposed to *do* if confronted with the practices of another group which one finds abhorrent?

Consider the case described in Kafka's short story 'In der Strafkolonie' ('In the Penal Colony') about a foreign visitor to such a colony where he is to witness the execution of a soldier by an officer for a minor offence. There has been no trial in which the prisoner has had the chance to defend himself, and the execution is to be carried out through the offices of a machine which, in an operation lasting four hours, inscribes with large pins the name of the offence committed on the back of the victim that he might, for the first time, learn exactly what it is that he has done before he dies. The traveller reflects:

It is always a serious matter intervening decisively in other people's affairs. He was neither a citizen of the penal colony nor a citizen of the country to which it belonged. Were he to attempt to pass judgement on, or worse, prevent this execution, they could have told him: be quiet, you're a foreigner. He would have had no rejoinder; he could only have added that in this instance he found his own behaviour puzzling, travelling as he did purely for the purpose of seeing things and not at all, for example, in order to alter the way in which other countries constituted their legal systems. Here, though, the circumstances were extremely tempting. The injustice of the procedure and the inhumanity of the execution were beyond doubt.[11]

Through the traveller's reflections Kafka is able to bring out the kinds of thoughts which are in reality relevant in thinking about what to do about practices of others which one finds abhorrent. The traveller has to ask himself what he is doing in the penal colony; what kind of relationship he has with the people there; what the people themselves think of the procedure which repels him; whether he is in a position of power to influence anyone; and so on. The most important point in all this for our purposes is that nothing is solved for the traveller about whether to intervene despite his belief that what the officer is doing is unjust and inhumane – not even if he believes this claim to be true in a way which goes beyond his own best thinking about the situation. And even when it becomes clear to him that he should intervene, this does not solve the problem of how to do so: by physical force; by seeking to get others from his own land to take action; by talking to those in authority? Or again, suppose the populace of the Penal Colony all supported the officer's procedure – as they recently did, according to the story, in the time of the Old Commandant – and that the traveller believed in moral relativism. This would also solve nothing for him about whether to intervene or not since he is standing there with his thoughts and feelings about the inhumanity and injustice of the procedure. It is not as if belief in relativism will simply cut such reactions out or neutralise them in him. And given that he has them he still faces the question: what, if anything, should I do?

This example, as I said, brings out the kind of complexity that characterises any serious thought about what to do about practices of other groups which one finds abhorrent. In truth, *neither* belief in relativism *nor* belief that one possesses some universal, culture-independent moral standard *nor* belief that one has nothing more, but nothing less, than one's best thoughts to go on in judging of the moral practices of other groups will settle that question. Of course, if one believes any one of these things such belief will be relevant to, and can be presumed to influence, one's decision. But the form that that influence takes is itself deeply influenced by the way one answers the prior question: *how* is what I believe relevant to the decision of what to do? To answer that question is itself to make a moral judgement. And making that judgement is itself a burden from which one cannot be released by holding to any particular one of the beliefs in question.

Notes

1. Mary McCarthy, *Birds of America* (Harmondsworth: Penguin, 1974), p. 134.
2. McCarthy, *Birds of America*, p. 136.
3. Cf. Bernard Williams, *Ethics and the Limits of Philosophy* (London: Fontana, 1985), p. 153.
4. Isaiah Berlin, 'Two Concepts of Liberty', in Berlin, *Four Essays on Liberty* (Oxford: Oxford University Press, 1989), p. 172.
5. Richard Rorty, *Contingency, Irony, Solidarity* (Cambridge: Cambridge University Press, 1992), *passim*.
6. George Orwell, *The Road to Wigan Pier* (Harmondsworth: Penguin, 1987 [1937]), p. 141.
7. William Ian Miller, *An Anatomy of Disgust* (Cambridge, MA: Harvard University Press, 1997), ch. 9.
8. Cf. Bernard Williams, 'The Truth in Relativism', in Williams, *Moral Luck* (Cambridge: Cambridge University Press, 1986), p. 132.
9. Peter Winch, 'Can We Understand Ourselves?', *Philosophical Investigations*, 20: 3, 1997, pp. 193–204, at p. 198.
10. Cf. Williams, *Ethics and the Limits of Philosophy*, pp. 22–3.
11. Franz Kafka, 'In the Penal Colony', in Kafka, *Stories 1904–1924*, tr. J. A. Underwood (London: Futura, 1983), p. 161.

7

Vanity and Destiny

I N JOHN BUNYAN'S *The Pilgrim's Progress* Faith and Christian are on their way to the celestial city. In order to get there they must pass through a town called Vanity. This town keeps a fair all year, known as Vanity-Fair. More or less everything under the sun is available to buy at the fair, but Faith and Christian are not interested in what is on offer: 'houses, lands, trades, places, honours, preferments, titles, countries, kingdoms, lusts, pleasures and delights of all sorts, as whores, bawds, wives, husbands, children, masters, servants, lives, blood, bodies, souls, silver, gold, pearls, precious stones, and what not'.[1] Faith and Christian's lack of interest causes offence amongst the stall-holders, who bring the two to examination. They are cast into a cage, and, when disputes break out amongst those at the fair over their fate, they are put on trial. Faithful is burnt at the stake, whilst Christian manages to escape and go on his way.

In Bunyan's allegory, Vanity is, of course, this world and, as his name for the place indicates, he wants to communicate to us his sense of the emptiness of worldly goods and the pointlessness of worldly human endeavour. In his presentation of the journey to the celestial city he is articulating a Christian variation on the theme that human life is a vanity. It is only in the celestial city, he says, that we can find truly pointful activity.

There are two central sources for the idea that human life is vain: first, that even when one's desires are satisfied one often remains unsatisfied oneself, at least in the middle- and long-term, and one can even be sickened by the satisfaction of one's desires; secondly, that even if one manages somehow to be happy in life, death will come and put an end to it all.

It is not just that death comes. It is that it comes so *fast.* We are all familiar with the terrifying sense that the years are passing with a rapidity which makes the journey through life resemble nothing so much as a free-fall across the sky in which we stretch out our hands for support and find nothing but air rushing through our fingers. One of Kafka's short stories runs:

> My grandfather used to say, 'Life is so astonishingly short. As I look back on it now it becomes so telescoped in my mind that, for example, I have difficulty in understanding how a young man can come to a decision to ride to the next village without being afraid that – leaving possible misfortune quite out of account – even the span of a normal, fortune-favoured existence will be wholly inadequate for the trip.'[2]

W. G. Sebald describes in *The Rings of Saturn* a visit to a desolate railway station in Suffolk, once the pivotal point for a whole way of life: the transport of goods, the meeting of people, the working-life of officials. 'It takes just one awful second, I often think, and an entire epoch passes.'[3] What was it all for? This sense of time, its destructive, all-consuming passage, hardly begun before it has laid waste to all in its path, provides perhaps the deepest sense of the vanity of human affairs.

Schopenhauer, the only great pessimist of Western philosophy since the onset of Christianity, expended a great deal of energy in trying to *prove* that life was utterly dreadful. He thought that one could marshal arguments to show that this was so and it is a consequence of his way of proceeding that, if one disagrees with him, he will convict one of intellectual error. His central idea is that pleasure is always experienced as a negative, that is, as the mere absence of pain, whilst pain itself is experienced as a positive. He has two key arguments for this claim.[4] Neither is very good. The first is that it is impossible properly to be aware of pleasure except as a contrast to pain. But the converse may equally be said of pain, in which case we could conclude that pain is only ever negative and pleasure positive. The second is that when we experience pleasure we 'lose ourselves' whereas when we experience pain we are acutely aware of our own existence. This proves 'that our existence is happiest when we perceive it least; from this it follows that it would be better not to have it'.[5] But what Schopenhauer claims follows from his observation does not in fact follow, for he fails to note the obvious and banal difference that exists between loss of ourselves in an activity and loss of ourselves through death: in the one case we are conscious and in the other not. We may be happiest when, absorbed in an activity, we perceive our own existence the least, but this is because we are conscious, not of nothing, but of the very object of the activity.

Aside from the weakness of his arguments, Schopenhauer's way of going about things here is based on a profound misunderstanding. For he presents the issue of the vanity of life as if it were a matter of intellectual conviction. But it is not that at all: it is not something of which one can become convinced through argument. It has rather to do with one's spiritual condition. And nothing but experience of life and reflection on that experience can make one think that life is, as Schopenhauer would have it, a debt to be paid off with one's death.

When Bunyan alighted upon the figure of the fair as an image of the vanity of life, he was clearly expressing a sense of something he found quite repellent. The very variety of things on offer at the fair, the multitude of distractions, the evanescent quality of its pleasures, the whirl of sights, smells and sounds, the masks and jesters – all of that seemed to him inappropriate as an image of what human beings should spend their time doing. Nietzsche would have found Bunyan's hostility to the fair expressive of what he called the 'spirit of gravity'. The very *show* of the fair – as of the theatre – exercised a deep attraction over him. Nietzsche wanted to subvert the idea that, since the world is like a fairground, it is vain. Because he thought that there was nothing more to existence than the world around us – unlike Bunyan he had no belief in a world after or beyond this – he concluded that if one was not going to despise the world one had to embrace it in all its showy nature. And in looking at things this way Nietzsche was struck by the extraordinary *lightness* of even our deepest moral responses, including our sense of evil, of the way in which the dreadful events of the past are part of the very *spectacle* of life.

One of the best direct expressions of this lightness of moral notions I know of is to be found in a letter of Heinrich von Kleist to Wilhelmine von Zenge of 15 August 1801.

> Yes indeed, when one reflects that we need a life to learn how we ought to live, that even in death we do not grasp what heaven wants from us; when no one knows the point of his existence and his destiny; when human reason is insufficient to understand itself and the soul and life and things around it; can God demand *responsibility* from such creatures? . . . What does it mean to do something evil . . . ? What is *evil?* Absolutely *evil?* The

things of this world are connected and entwined in a thousand ways, every action is the mother of millions of others, and often the worst produce the best – Tell me, who in this world has really done something *evil*? Something which would be evil *for all eternity* – ? And whatever we hear of the story of Nero, and Attila, and Cartouche, of the Huns and the crusades and the Spanish Inquisition this planet nonetheless rolls peacefully through space, spring follows spring and human beings live, enjoy themselves and die as before . . .[6]

Kleist's point is not, I think, that, if one approves of something, one must approve of whatever led to that thing. He is saying something much subtler than that, and correspondingly more difficult to articulate. We are dealing here with a particular spiritual condition. As a way of getting at what is at issue consider the following example. Suppose that in his past someone has been the victim of certain evil deeds of others but that he has been lucky enough to learn from those experiences in such a way as to become a deeper or wiser person. Then, even though this person will have resisted the pain and suffering of those experiences at the time they happened, and even though he will not wish that anything like that should happen again, he will be able, perhaps, to look at the evil perpetrated on him in the past as being just part of the story of his life, just another of those things that have happened to him or he has done.

As I understand Kleist, he is saying that if someone looks at his life in the kind of way described then he could also come to look at the world in the same way. The point is not that one would think that the evil perpetrated on any other given individual was unimportant. Nor is this that one would think this of another even if the other's attitude towards the evil perpetrated on him was that of its having become just another part of the story of his life. The point is rather that one could look at the evils suffered by mankind as one looks at one's own life: they have just become part of the history of humanity, part of that story which is the story of all of us together. This attitude would not exclude the possibility of opposing or lamenting evil where it occurs. For, just as one would never have wished evil on oneself even if one has learnt from it, and just as one would not wish it to return and would oppose it if it did, one will also not wish evil on others and may even oppose this when it happens. But if one does share the attitude in question then, if one hears of some evil deeds perpetrated yesterday or today, and even if one tries to oppose them, one will be inclined to think that these deeds, like others that have taken place in the past, will become just another part of the story of mankind and will one day be talked of and thought about in a way devoid of emotion and concern.

It might be said that someone who looks at things this way is in some way corrupt because one *ought not* to regard the evil human beings have inflicted, and do inflict, on each other in this way. It certainly seems true that someone who comes to have the sense of things Kleist expresses might fall into despair – as Kleist did – because the very thing that is precious to him, namely, his understanding of good and evil, has come to seem in many ways to lack a certain substantiality or robustness. Good and evil have come to seem, as I put it earlier, extraordinarily *light*. This was, indeed, Kleist's position. However, it would be far too flat-footed to say that Kleist lost his sense of good and evil. It was rather that his sense of things led him to a kind of quietism. His letter continues:

> To live out one's natural term; to enjoy what blooms around us; now and again to do something good; . . . to work effectively and with pleasure; to give others life that they might carry on in this way and preserve the species; – and then to die –. To him who does this and nothing more a secret of heaven has been revealed.[7]

Nevertheless, although Kleist did not lose his sense of good and evil, it can certainly happen that someone could start from the same sense of things as Kleist did and be led, by the very idea that evil deeds form just another twist in the story of mankind, into doing evil himself. This is the spiritual condition in which Dostoyevsky's Raskolnikov finds himself in *Crime and Punishment*. For when he starts to look at things in the way in question, and when he compares himself to Napoleon whose life was seen by many as a glorification of both himself and mankind even though he sacrificed thousands of lives for his own ends, he begins to wonder why he, too, should not murder. He begins to wonder, that is, whether to kill the old moneylender really would be evil. After all, she is mean and mean-spirited, whilst he is intelligent and wishes to achieve much that is good and noble in life. He could use her money much better than she does. What does it matter if one route to this end is the murder of 'an old louse', as he thinks of her, a murder which will become just one of the many millions that are written into the story of mankind? What his remorse reveals to him when the deed is done, however, is that he has, after all, perpetrated evil. But even here things are not as simple as they might appear at first. For what he does *not* conclude is that Napoleon was evil to do what he did. He discovers, rather, that he himself, Raskolnikov, was foolish to have modelled himself on Napoleon, since he did not have the strength to carry through and bear his actions, whereas Napoleon had the strength of *his* deeds. What became clear to Raskolnikov was that he was a certain kind of person, and Napoleon was another.

At this point one might begin to feel that the concepts of good and evil have collapsed to be replaced by those of strength and weakness. Nietzsche was both appalled and fascinated by such a possibility. And part of that experience was that he shared Raskolnikov's sense that one just is a certain kind of person and there is nothing much one can do about that.

> At the base of us, right 'down there', there is indeed something un-teachable, a granite rock of spiritual fate, of predetermined decision and answer to predetermined specific questions. For every cardinal problem there speaks an unchangeable: 'This is I'.[8]

Emerson expresses a similar idea: '[N]o man can violate his nature. All the sallies of his will are rounded in by the law of his being . . . Nor does it matter how you gauge and try him.'[9] I suspect that some people will find such ideas absurd, and others will think them obviously true. But, if one agrees with the sentiments expressed by Emerson and Nietzsche, then one will see sense in speaking of one's destiny or fate. Of course, sometimes we use the notion of fate simply to express the way in which we are all of us not in complete control of our lives, for we are all to a greater or lesser extent prey to circum-stance. And if we speak in such a context of not wishing to tempt fate then, at its best, we are expressing a sense of humility with respect to what comes our way despite our desires and our best efforts. But the Emersonian-Nietzschean notion of fate goes beyond this. It suggests that one's fate will be whatever it is that the gradual unfolding of one's character is and leads one to. And the very idea that one has such a fate or destiny can itself be such as to make one feel that all is vain. For, as Kleist points out, it can take more than a lifetime to find out what kind of person one is and it can engender a sense of the pointlessness of things to realise that, however much time one has, it will never be enough to find out who one really is. In this sense, the idea that one has a fate or destiny can be felt to be oppressive.

It can also be experienced as oppressive in another way. One may, for example, discover that it is one's fate to be something one does not want to be. The case of Nietzsche is particularly interesting in this regard. Since he was, as I have already noted, very excited by the spectacle of world history – his sense of its dreadfulness was part of that excitement – he longed to be the kind of person who could stomach that spectacle in its entirety without turning away in horror. But, since someone who is able without self-deception to do that is likely to be the kind of person who could *do* the kind of appalling things of which much of history consists, he expended a great deal of philosophical energy in trying to see what the world would look like if he were that kind of person. It was his destiny to be a meek, sensitive man, but from his work one would – usually – imagine him to be utterly hard, with the spirit of a Napoleon. Nietzsche was, in fact, a sheep in wolf's clothing. For most of us, the problem is that our decency is superficial. Nietzsche was afflicted by the opposite problem and was therefore in a very unusual spiritual predicament: it would have done him a lot of good to become less decent, to live a life where he could inflict more pain on others and bear it. Morality thus seemed to him to destroy many of the better possibilities of life, but he could not see – could not think – his way around this. For him, morality was either the judge and arbiter of everything – in which case everything in life was surveyed by an eye so monstrously critical that nothing was or even could be adequate – or it was nothing. Since he could, in the end, bear neither thought, the vanity of human life haunted his every step, though – it is part of what makes him so fascinating – he spent a lot of time trying to convince himself that he was not haunted in this way, indeed, that only fools are haunted by anything at all.

What Nietzsche could not bear was the way in which, as Philip Larkin put it, 'very little that catches the imagination can get clearance from either the intelligence or the moral sense'.[10] If Nietzsche's imagination was caught by scenes from history that depict those who 'emerge from a horrific procession of murder, arson, rape, and torture with an exhilaration and peace of soul, as if it were nothing more than a students' prank, convinced they have provided the poets with a lot more material for song and praise',[11] then he thought he ought to want such people to exist. He clearly thought of this as a matter of integrity: since he was excited by the image of a certain way of life he thought there was a kind of hypocrisy in refusing to countenance its actual existence. The fear here is one of sentimentality or something similar: if one's imagination is captured by a way of life but the real existence of that way of life would appal one (as is, for example, an experience many have with respect to the Middle Ages) then one's imagination is arguably feeding from a certain sentimentality or some kind of self-deception. One then has to try to live in that condition or seek to be rid of it, either by crushing the imagination or by seeking to convince oneself that one would not be appalled by the way of life in question after all.

Larkin sought to live in that condition.

> Sometimes you hear, fifth-hand,
> As epitaph:
> *He chucked up everything*
> *And just cleared off,*
> And always the voice will sound
> Certain you approve
> This audacious, purifying,
> Elemental move.
>
> And they are right, I think.
> We all hate home
> And having to be there:
> I detest my room,
> Its specially chosen junk,
> The good books, the good bed,
> And my life, in perfect order:
> So to hear it said
>
> *He walked out on the whole crowd*
> Leaves me flushed and stirred,
> Like *Then she undid her dress*
> Or *Take that you bastard;*
> Surely I can, if he did?
> And that helps me stay
> Sober and industrious.
> But I'd go today,
>
> Yes, swagger the nut-strewn roads,
> Crouch in the fo'c'sle
> Stubbly with goodness, if
> It weren't so artificial,
> Such a deliberate step backwards
> To create an object:
> Books; china; a life
> Reprehensibly perfect.[12]

Larkin could draw nourishment for the meekness of his life from reflection on those whose lives were anything but meek but, unlike Nietzsche, he tried not to be hard on himself for being able to do so. Yet, although his thought is not uncommon, it remains mysterious how it is that the destructiveness of others can help one remain sober and industrious. Perhaps it has to do with the idea that there is some value in the sheer existence of all the different exemplars of humanity. Or maybe, and relatedly, the experience is rather like that we have when attending a tragedy: we are given energy by witnessing the pain, suffering and destruction of the tragic hero. No one knows how this happens, but, as F. R. Leavis suggested, it has perhaps to do with our capacity to take delight in the sheer fact of experiences being had, regardless of whether they are good or bad experiences and regardless of who is having them.[13] Perhaps in any case this is one reason why Nietzsche suggested that it is only as an aesthetic phenomenon that existence and the world are justified: the only way to bear the sight of the world is to think of it as one great theatre.

The sense that one has a certain destiny, given by the gradual unfolding of one's own nature, need not be experienced as wholly oppressive. It may offer some temporary shelter from the chaos of existence. *Temporary* shelter: even if a human life is perfect it can only be 'reprehensibly perfect'. It will always be the product of competing and conflicting forces of imagination, emotion, intellect, need, sense of waste and fulfilment, and so on.

But what is the connection between fate and fatalism? Does not the latter idea suggest that one is powerless?

Many would reject the idea that the notion of fatalism makes sense since it has in the past been closely connected with the existence of God, or the gods, watching over and controlling our life. Either that, or they might say that fatalism means nothing more than causal determinism, that is, the idea that everything – including human behaviour – happens on account of its being caused to take place by preceding events, just as one billiard ball *must* move in a certain way and in no other way when it is struck by another ball.

There is, however, a deep conceptual, moral and spiritual gulf between fatalism and determinism. Determinism is the sort of hypothesis which makes no distinction in kind between the events of the inanimate, the animate and the human world. If determinism is true then human behaviour is caused in just the kind of way that the growth of a plant, the fall of water over the rocks or the movements of an animal are caused. Furthermore, within the field of human behaviour determinism makes no distinction between actions which, from a human point of view, are distinguished by their being either significant in a life or utterly trivial. A man's falling in love with the woman who becomes his wife – an event which, we assume, has great meaning to him – is, from the point of view of determinism, no more and no less significant than his action of scratching his forehead to assuage an itch: both were equally caused by preceding events and both were just as unavoidable. The only difference is one of complexity.

Fatalism does not have these features at all. It directs our attention to the events in life which are most significant. It would be absurd to say that the man was fated to scratch his forehead (even if he was causally determined to do so), whereas he might well say that he was fated to fall in love with this particular woman. Saying that would be a way of recording his sense of the significance of that event – say because of the way in which it has altered, and continues to alter, his self-understanding in various ways, or on account of what it revealed to him about his nature, his needs, his temperament and the like. Or consider Werner Herzog's film *Wings of Hope* about Juliane Koepcke who, as the sole survivor of an aeroplane crash in Peru, walked for ten days through the jungle to reach safety. During the film, Herzog takes Juliane back to the sight of the crash twenty years after it occurred, and, at one point, when she is examining the wreckage on the floor of the jungle, Herzog says that Juliane has come face to face with her fate. Clearly he means to be recording the way in which the event of the crash became absolutely crucial for Juliane's self-understanding, for the meaning of her life. It would be ridiculous to suppose that anything one might say about causal determinism had anything to do with that. The notion of fate applies primarily to the world of significance which human beings inhabit and only by extension, if at all, to the rest of life.

But if invoking the notion of fate is a way of recording the meaning things have in a life, still it might be unclear why one should speak in this way rather than just saying that those events were, indeed, meaningful in various ways. Certainly it goes without saying that no one can be required to use the notion of fate in talking of his life and its meaning. Moreover, like all moral concepts, it is open to abuse, to a sentimental distortion through which one seeks to make some event in one's life look profoundly important when it is not. Nonetheless, what might make someone speak of fate in the way suggested would be that he cannot imagine his life without that particular event in it, so crucial has it become for his self-understanding. When someone speaks in a serious way about the operations of fate in his life he is articulating his sense that he sees his life under the aspect of necessity and it is the fact that he does so which makes of his life something deeper – though not necessarily happier – than it otherwise would have been. Thus if Juliane Koepcke says that it was her fate to be involved in the aeroplane crash over the Peruvian jungle and walk all that way to safety, she means by this that that event has set for her a task in her life to the demands of which she has to respond: to try to understand more deeply the nature of life and death through exploring what it means to have been the sole survivor, of chance and its relation to courage and the instinct to survive, of the brevity of life and so on. To think of one's life in terms of such a task is to express a sense of the limits of what one can imagine for one's life to be meaningful, in the absence of which one might see oneself as doing little more than filling up time between birth and death.

The conception of necessity which is at work here need not, accordingly, be felt as an infringement of one's freedom. On the contrary, it is perfectly possible that it is only in virtue of the necessity operating on one's life that one feels free: without it, one just feels that everything is aimless and thus the freedom there attainable empty.

It is nonetheless the case that the notion of fatalism can operate in a much more destructive way in one's life. In Chekov's short story 'Ward Number Six', Dr Ragin, a man who is interesting because his speech is a curious mixture of wisdom and foolishness, comments at one point: 'Life is a deplorable trap. When a thinking man attains adulthood and mature awareness he can't help feeling hopelessly ensnared.'[14] There is no reason to suppose that Ragin is propounding a belief in causal determinism. Once again, the better concept to understand what he is saying is that of fate, for he means to be referring to the way in which his life has been undermined for him by his failure to understand clearly the *meaning* of what he has been doing with his time. It would be absurd to think that he felt trapped because, say, he had been causally determined to eat a particular dish for supper.

This sense of entrapment is exemplified by the friend of mine who, to make up for early failure in life, longed for wealth and status. When, after a great deal of hard work, he got them, he came quickly to despise those who respected and deferred to him for possessing things which he now, in possessing them, believed to be unimportant. He had struggled for wealth without understanding what he was doing because he did not know what it meant to be wealthy. Yet he could not have understood that had he never become wealthy. He was trapped by fate because it is only by doing something that seemed to him meaningful that he could come to see it to be meaningless.

Are we all like this? Do we all feel this sense of entrapment which means that we are plagued by a sense that we have little grasp on the meaning of our life? Conrad was not so sure. In barely controlled disgust he spoke of those who 'walk the road of life, the road fenced in by their tastes, prejudices, disdains or enthusiasms, generally honest, invariably stupid, and are proud of never having lost their way'.[15] He thought of such persons as, in his words, 'disdained by destiny' precisely because they were satisfied that they knew what they were doing with their lives and the meaning of it all. We fool ourselves if we deny that we ever share Conrad's view of the human beings around us. G. K. Chesterton voiced something of this in a discussion of Nietzsche.

> When he makes us feel that he cannot endure the innumerable faces, the incessant voices, the overpowering omnipresence which belongs to the mob, he will have the sympathy of anybody who has ever been sick on a steamer or tired in a crowded omnibus. Every man has hated mankind . . . Every man has had humanity in his nostrils like a suffocating smell.[16]

But if we all sometimes – perhaps often – fail to see the individuality of our fellow human beings, seeing instead an undifferentiated mass, we all also feel that there is no one who does not, at times, and in private, sit and wonder what he has been doing with his life, troubled by the meaning of this strange journey to we know not where. And it is, perhaps, when we see other human beings in this way that we can most readily sense an unbreakable bond of shared destiny with them.

Perhaps it is this sense that led Larkin to write in one of his poems: 'Something is pushing them / To the side of their own lives.'[17] We are always being pushed to the side of our life because, as Kierkegaard pointed out, there is no stopping point at which we could, so to speak, put our life on hold to get its meaning in our grasp. Fate pushes us on from behind – or from the side – to we know not where. And this is not just so when we do not get what we want and need, but even when we do.

Part of what is at issue here is what Montaigne calls 'an aberration of my soul'. 'I am aware', writes Montaigne,

> that I am troubled by an aberration of my soul which displeases me as iniquitous . . . [A]s for eradicating it, I cannot: it consists in diminishing the real value of the things which I possess, simply because it is I who possess them, and in overvaluing whatever things are foreign to me,

lacking in me or are not mine . . . [O]ut of two equal achievements I always come down against my own. It is not so much that a jealous concern to do better or to amend my ways disturbs my judgement and stops me from being satisfied with myself as that our mastery over anything engenders a contempt for what we hold under our sway.[18]

Montaigne is here articulating in an especially eloquent way the perennial incapacity of human beings to be satisfied when their desires are satisfied. But he means more than this. He means that our very sense of reality is undermined by the aberration of the soul of which he speaks. For this aberration unseats our sense that we have either any kind of just understanding of the relation between our own achievements and those of others or, correlatively, and more radically, any real grasp on what it is that is valuable in life. This is perhaps why Robert Louis Stevenson said: 'There is indeed one element in human destiny that not blindness itself can controvert. Whatever else we are intended to do, we are not intended to succeed; failure is the fate allotted.'[19]

The sense of fate or destiny I have been discussing hitherto is that of a gradual growth in understanding what one is and of one's condition in life. Sometimes, however, that understanding can come to us all of a sudden through moments of especial intensity. In *Die Verwirrungen des Zöglings Törleß* (*Young Törleß*) Robert Musil describes a scene in which one of Törleß's comrades at the boarding school relates how he has come to have power over another pupil. Musil describes Törleß's condition after he had finished listening.

> From time to time a chill had run down into his finger-tips, and his thoughts rose up wildly and without order like bubbles in boiling water. It is said that this is how it is for the man who sees for the first the woman that is fated to embroil him in a destructive passion . . . There is no way of saying what is going on in such a moment. It is, as it were, a shadow the passion throws out ahead of itself; a loosening up of all earlier tensions and at the same time a condition of being newly and suddenly bound up, a condition in which the whole of the future is contained . . .[20]

Törleß is aware that through his comrade's story something is going on in him which is, as he puts it, 'irrevocable'. He has become a changed person through it. Or we could say: he now sees more clearly what kind of person he is. And because this experience is so pivotal for his self-understanding and seems to contain the whole meaning of his future life, Törleß feels himself driven to the idea that has been running through this discussion: that we each of have a nature over which we have little, if any, control.

Is it a general law that there is something in us which is stronger, bigger, more beautiful, more passionate, darker than we? Over which we have so little power that we can only scatter seeds at random until from one of them a seedling shoots up like a dark flame, which grows up right over us? . . . And in every nerve of his body there trembled an impatient 'yes' in answer.[21]

I do not think that someone who looks at things this way can prove that there is such a law. We are not talking here about anything which could be the fit object of, say, scientific enquiry, as if the science of genetics could demonstrate the existence of such a law. For even if it is true (as is, in any case, doubtful) that we are wholly formed and determined by our individual and species genetic make-up, there is, as such, nothing in that thought which could make one believe what Törleß believed. For what Törleß is concerned with is a way in which his inner life has become through his experiences a source of bewilderment and torment to him, something rebellious, demanding and frightening.

'What is it in us that lies, steals and murders?' Georg Büchner asked in a letter of 9–12 March 1834 to Minna Jaeglé, articulating in a similar way a sense of the mystery of the inner life.[22] For Büchner, the raising of this question was in part an expression of an attitude which, as commentators on his work have often noted, he displayed to many of those who did evil and who formed the object of his concern and investigation in his work. That attitude was one of pity. This pity has clear connections with the notion of fate or destiny.

Directly after raising his question, Büchner goes on to quote some words of Christ which he evidently thinks of as having relevance to the question he has asked. 'Obstacles indeed there must be, but alas for the man who provides them' (Matt. 18: 7). We could perhaps understand Büchner's moral perspective in the following way. The world just is such that there will always be individuals of different temperaments, patterns of motivation, general outlooks on life and so on. In particular, there always will be some individuals who are corrupt or evil in various ways, just as there always will be some who are decent, some who are nervous and shy, others imperious and confident, and so on. There will always be some through whom obstacles come. Suppose, now, we are faced by a given person before us whom we judge to be evil. Then we could reflect that it is only by chance or good fortune that we too are not evil. That is, if we know there will always be some who are evil, then we, too, might have been evil. This does not in any sense make it 'all right' that someone is evil, yet it opens up the possibility of that perspective on the evil-doer which is present in Büchner's work: that, as I have said, of pity. For the evil-doer simply has had the bad luck to be this particular kind of person. That was his fate. Perhaps this is what some have in mind when they say: 'There but for the grace of God go I.' Another way of expressing the same sense of things comes out in Dostoyevsky's *The House of the Dead* where he notes that some of those outside the prison thought of crime as a *misfortune* and the criminal as an 'unfortunate'.[23] And if one thinks of criminals as unfortunates then one appropriate expression of this will be that it is fate which decides whether a person's life comes to nought or issues in something valuable. Dostoyevsky is right to say that this is a profound way of looking at crime.

We should not think, however, that the moral perspective I have attributed to Büchner is something one could justify by appealing to some facts independently of that perspective. The idea that we each of us just happen to have a certain nature and in this sense to be fated in certain ways is not meant as a morally neutral hypothesis: it already *is* an expression of Büchner's pity. In that sense, there is no external justification for Büchner's view. If one comes to agree with it, or sympathise with it, this will be the result of one's experience of life and reflection on this. We are not dealing with a theoretical position which could, so to speak, become one's possession overnight as a result of arguments appealing to the intellect alone.

This sense that those who do evil are unfortunate and the victim of fate can easily be extended to those whom we would not judge to be evil but who nonetheless have committed evil. This is because we all of us, to a greater or lesser extent, share the experience that the circumstances of our life operate in ways we cannot fully fathom and which leave us with only partial control of what we are doing and where we are going. This is beautifully brought out by Sebald in *The Rings of Saturn*. Visiting his friend, the translator, critic and poet Michael Hamburger, one of whose specialisms is the poetry of Hölderlin, Sebald writes, in reflecting on Hamburger's life:

> [W]e know that we shall never be able to fathom the imponderables that govern our course through life. Does one follow in Hölderlin's footsteps, simply because one's birthday happened to fall two days after his? . . . Is it possible that one would later settle in this house in Suffolk because a water pump in the garden bears the date 1770, the year of Hölderlin's birth? . . . And did Hölderlin not dedicate his Patmos hymn to the Landgrave of Homburg, and was not Homburg also the maiden name

of Mother? Across what distances in time do the elective affinities and correspondences connect? How is it that one perceives oneself in another human being, or, if not oneself, then one's precursor?[24]

And Sebald describes how he later became the colleague of a man who, twenty-two years earlier, had invited Hamburger to spend Easter Monday at his home.

> No matter how often I tell myself that chance happenings of this kind occur far more often than we suspect, since we all move, one after the other, along the same roads mapped out for us by our origins and our hopes, my rational mind is nonetheless unable to lay the ghosts of repetition that haunt me with ever greater frequency.[25]

It would be easy, in a sceptical frame of mind, to dismiss what Sebald says as nothing other than poetic fancy, as he himself grants. Such occurrences as he speaks of are, one might say, the products of chance and carry no further significance. And sometimes, perhaps usually, we try to see a significance in things that is not there, like Zeno in Svevo's *Confessions of Zeno* who tries to find significance in dates such as 9.9.1899. But the trouble with a wholesale dismissal of the kind of thing Sebald is discussing is that the type of events in question carry a great deal of the burden of that which gives meaning to our life. It is around such happenings that we struggle to piece together, as we look back across the confusions of the years, some sense in all that we have done and been and in what has happened to us. As Mary Warnock has argued, the imagination is as much involved in our sense of the narrative of our life as is memory. This is because the faculties of memory and imagination are impossible to separate in a clear-cut way.

> [W]hether we are imagining or recalling, we are thinking of something which is not before our eyes and ears, and of something that has meaning for us, and may be imbued with strong emotions. We could say that, in recalling something, we are employing imagination; and that, in imagining something, exploring it imaginatively, we use memory.[26]

Hence: 'Telling our story, to ourselves or others, is . . . the outcome of a collaboration between memory and imagination . . . For the creative construction of a story involves seeking out what is significant, what is to feature as part of the plot.'[27]

Of course, this connection between memory and imagination as it works in the telling of the story of our life in no way requires anyone to speak of certain events in life in terms of the fate or destiny of circumstance. Someone who thought that that way of understanding things was so much rubbish cannot be proven incorrect. But by the same token, no one can be obliged not to express a sense of the mystery of human life in such terms. And there are, as Warnock's comments indicate, powers of the human mind which naturally conspire to make such a way of talking, if not amenable to reason, then not unreasonable insofar as they flow from a common experience of life. Further, as Sebald testifies, it can become hard not to speak in such terms: they can impress themselves on the mind as being the best terms in which to speak of this aspect of a human life.

In Ecclesiastes the sense of the vanity of life goes together with reflections on the nature of time. Ecclesiastes tells us that there is a time for all human activities: for giving birth, for dying, for planting, for uprooting what has been planted, for killing, for healing and so on. Where has the sense of the destructiveness of time gone in this? Does not Ecclesiastes contradict himself in saying that all is vanity and yet that there is 'a season for everything, a time for every occupation under heaven'?

To answer this last question in the affirmative would be, I think, depressingly literal-minded. And there is, in any case, no need to answer it in this way. In order to see this, consider the notion of patience as this is discussed by Kierkegaard. We might think that patience is the disposition to wait without complaining for a considerable time for the result that one desires, but that it cannot involve the idea of waiting without complaint for something that one knows cannot occur. Kierkegaard disagrees. He suggests that true patience – the kind of patience, that is, which shows up the shallowness of other forms of patience – is the capacity to wait without complaint even where there can be no justified expectation of results. This may seem absurd, but if one thinks of specific contexts in which this patience might be exercised we shall see that it is not. One of these is that of teaching. For even where there is no hope that the pupil will be able to learn, one may feel as a teacher called upon to exercise the kind of patience of which Kierkegaard speaks. Some teachers in fact do this. I once witnessed the teaching of French to some pupils so severely mentally impaired that they were barely conscious of their surroundings. The teachers in question were under no illusions whatsoever about the capacities of their pupils. They had no expectation that they would ever learn to speak and understand French. The patience these teachers displayed was one which had at its root, I think, the recognition that the only way in which, from the point of view of their capacities, their pupils could have been justifiably treated would have been to allow them to die. Yet they treated them in a way which saw their capacities as inessential to what they were. Their treatment of them expressed a determination to see them as having dignity. It expressed a sense of fellowship with them which was not dependent upon a thought about how they measured up in terms of their capacities relative to a human norm. Yet the teachers would have agreed that in one sense what they were doing was pointless. That was the sense, as I have said, in which one might think about, might hope for, results.

The sense of the vanity of life expressed by Ecclesiastes can be understood in a similar way. It does not contradict his sense of the emptiness of things that he thinks there is a time for everything. Rather, his very sense of vanity, of the destructiveness of time, enables him to accept the requirements and demands of life with grace, just as the teachers were able to accept the profound limitations of their pupils because they were not looking at things from the point of view of results. From this perspective, a life of quiet acceptance of the tasks of life is the only reasonable response to the vanity of things. Here we see the idea, picked up by many since, that quiet devotion to one's work is the only true purpose of life, an idea which reaches its apotheosis in Marx's view that it is only in the life of work that the true dignity of man and woman is to be found.

What this enables us to see is the way in which a sense of the vanity of human life can be at once a destructive and yet weirdly liberating experience. Terrifying in its undermining of that which we value, it can nonetheless help one affirm life in all its uncanny beauty. The central reason why we miss this is that we have a strong tendency to assimilate a sense of the vanity of life to cynicism. The latter really does void, or seek to void, life of any positive value. For the cynic is a consumer of persons: he cannot bear it that others should be able to draw strength and energy for life from the things around them. He seeks to undermine others by feeding on the strength they have, and this is one reason why the cynic often spends a great deal of time in manipulating others. Yet he is also a consumer of himself. He cannot bear it when he notices in himself the possibility of finding positive sources of spiritual energy. He does the alchemist's trick in reverse: he takes what would naturally offer itself to him as such a source and works on it until it becomes an empty husk.

But if a sense of the vanity of life is inconsistent with cynicism it is not inconsistent with pessimism. This is because pessimism no more excludes an affirmation of life than does a sense of life's vanity. Indeed, there is something to be said for the idea that the realistic spirit of pessimism can be crucial for some people to such an affirmation. Few have been more pessimistic than Hazlitt.

> As to my old opinions, I am heartily sick of them. I have reason, for they have deceived me sadly. I was taught to think, and I was willing to believe, that genius was not a bawd – that virtue was not a mask – that liberty was not a name – that love had its seat in the human heart. Now I would care little if these words were struck out of my dictionary, or if I had never heard them. They are become to my ears a mockery and a dream . . . I see folly join with knavery, and together make up public spirit and public opinions . . . [N]o one can live by his talents and knowledge who is not ready to prostitute those talents and that knowledge to betray his species and prey upon his fellow-man . . . In private life do we not see hypocrisy, servility, selfishness, folly and impudence succeed, whilst modesty shrinks from the encounter, and merit is trodden underfoot? . . . [T]he web of human life . . . [consists in nothing more than] various threads of meanness, spite, cowardice, want of understanding, of indifference towards others and ignorance of ourselves . . .[28]

Yet the energy of his prose belies his claim to hate the world and indicates rather an affirmation of life. For someone like Hazlitt the very act of writing about the vanity of life helped to feed such an affirmation. Yet this, too, can come to seem empty. W. B. Yeats made this point in a late poem by conceiving of the very act of writing to be like putting on display a band of circus animals. But the prancing of such animals must eventually come to an end, for they grow from, and cannot forever conceal, 'the foul rag and bone shop of the heart'.

Notes

1. John Bunyan, *The Pilgrim's Progress*, Roger Sharrock (ed.) (Harmondsworth: Penguin, 1987 [Pt. I: 1678; Pt. II: 1684]), I, p. 79.
2. Franz Kafka, 'The Next Village', in Kafka, *Stories 1904–1924*, tr. J. A. Underwood (London: Futura, 1983), p. 203.
3. W. G. Sebald, *The Rings of Saturn*, tr. Michael Hulse (London: Harvil, 1999), p. 31.
4. Arthur Schopenhauer, *The World as Will and Representation*, tr. E. F. J. Payne (New York: Dover, 1966 [1819 and 1844]), vol. I, §56–9 and vol. II, ch. XLVI.
5. Arthur Schopenhauer, *The World as Will and Representation*, Vol. II, p. 575.
6. Heinrich von Kleist, *Sämtliche Werke und Briefe in zwei Bänden*, Helmut

Sembdner (ed.) (Munich: Deutscher Taschenbuch Verlag, 1994), vol. 2, p. 683, my translation.

7. Kleist, *Sämtliche Werke und Briefe in zwei Bänden*, vol. 2, p. 683, my translation.

8. Nietzsche, *Jenseits von Gut und Böse* in Nietzsche, *Sämtliche Werke: Kritische Studienausgabe in 15 Einzelbänden*, Giorgio Colli and Mazzino Montinari (eds) (Berlin: Walter de Gruyter, 1980), vol. 5, §231, my translation.

9. Ralph Waldo Emerson, 'Self-Reliance', in Emerson, *Selected Essays*, Larzer Ziff (ed.) (Harmondsworth: Penguin, 1985 [1841]), p. 183.

10. Quoted in Andrew Motion, *Philip Larkin* (London and New York: Methuen, 1982), p. 72.

11. Nietzsche, *Zur Genealogie der Moral* in Nietzsche, *Sämtliche Werke: Kritische Studienausgabe in 15 Einzelbänden*, vol. 5, essay 1, §11, my translation.

12. Philip Larkin, 'Poetry of Departures', in Larkin, *Collected Poems*, Anthony Thwaite (ed.) (London: Marvel and Faber & Faber, 1988), pp. 25–6.

13. F. R. Leavis, 'Tragedy and the "Medium"', in Leavis, *The Common Pursuit* (Harmondsworth: Penguin, 1962), pp. 121–35.

14. Anton Chekov, 'Ward Number Six', in Chekov, *Ward Number Six and Other Stories*, tr. and ed. Ronald Hingley (Oxford: Oxford University Press, 1992 [1892]), p. 38.

15. Quoted in Tony Tanner, *Conrad: 'Lord Jim'* (London: Arnold, 1969), p. 57.

16. G. K. Chesterton 'On the Institution of the Family', in Chesterton, *Heretics* (London: Bodley Head, 1905), p. 185.

17. Philip Larkin, 'Afternoons', in Larkin, *Collected Poems*, Anthony Thwaite (ed.) (London: Marvel and Faber & Faber, 1988), p. 121.

18. Montaigne, 'On Presumption', in Montaigne, *The Complete Essays*, tr. M. A. Screech (Harmondsworth: Penguin, 1991), p. 720.

19. Quoted in William James, *The Varieties of Religious Experience* (Glasgow: Collins, 1971 [1902]), p. 147.

20. Robert Musil, *Die Verwirrungen des Zöglings Törleß* (Hamburg: Rowohlt, 1991 [1906]) pp. 45–6, my translation.

21. Musil, *Die Verwirrungen des Zöglings Törleß*, p. 92, my translation.

22. Georg Büchner, *Werke und Briefe*, K. Pörnbecher, G. Schaub, H.-J. Simm and E. Ziegler (eds) (Munich: Deutscher Taschenbuch Verlag, 1988), p. 228, my translation.

23. Dostoyevsky, *The House of the Dead*, tr. D. McDuff (Harmondsworth: Penguin, 1985 [1860]), p. 80.

24. Sebald, *The Rings of Saturn*, p. 182.

25. Ibid., p. 187.

26. Mary Warnock, *Memory* (London: Faber & Faber, 1987), pp. 75–6.

27. Warnock, *Memory*, p. 132.

28. William Hazlitt, 'On the Pleasure of Hating', in Hazlitt, *Selected Writings*, Ronald Blythe (ed.) (Harmondsworth: Penguin, 1970), pp. 409–10.

8

Morality and Life

O NE OF THE GREATEST and deepest hopes of human beings is that morality and justice might prevail all the time. The world around us is, in Samuel Johnson's words, 'bursting with sin and sorrow', and we suppose that what is needed to correct this – natural disasters excluded – is that we all be educated to be generous, kind and considerate in our relations with one another. In this, we are the inheritors of Christianity, which sees the world on a path towards greater goodness and perfection. In fact, Nietzsche suggested that we moderns even seek to 'outchristianise Christianity'. For Christianity told a story according to which the sufferings of our earthly existence would find compensation in a life to come. The modern world does not accept this story but still has to face the suffering and pain of existence. For this reason, we have set about trying to create heaven on earth, according everyone equal rights, rooting out prejudice wherever it exists, seeking to make up for the wrongs of the past. As the German philosopher Karl Löwith says in a discussion of Nietzsche:

> It is true that we no longer expect Christian redemption at the hands of a just God who judges, yet we try to offer in the same spirit a worldly political solution in the form of social justice. We no longer believe in a coming Kingdom of God, yet hold onto this in the shape of a secular utopia.[1]

The egalitarian hedonism of the modern age is, indeed, in many ways a form of secularised Christianity where the only god worshipped is human welfare and comfort. Many from both the right

112

and the left of the political spectrum have been, and are, opposed to this, on the grounds that it leads to our becoming soft and pampered. Nietzsche's own response is particularly interesting because he suggested that this softness involved our being cut off from *life* itself. Many commentators on Nietzsche have remarked that he made use of this notion in what seem to be conflicting ways. On the one hand, he believed in an affirmation of life in all its totality, including the pain and suffering it inevitably involves. On the other hand, when he remembered that the totality of life involved the small-souled, the mean-spirited and the shallow he suggested that life itself did not include such things for they were themselves already a denial of life, and thus that no affirmation of life need involve an affirmation of *these*.[2] Some people have been inclined to suppose that such tensions show that the concept of life is useless as a moral idea. For, so the thought goes, the most plausible view is that life just is everything that exists and happens, in which case it is useless for making any serious moral discriminations. If, however, someone tries, as Nietzsche did, to press the notion into serious use in a moral sense, then this will only be by excluding part of life from the notion of life. But how can one exclude any particular part of life from the concept of life itself? And even if one could do so, on what grounds would one proceed? The notion thus turns out to be vacuous or question-begging. This line of reasoning obviously applies beyond Nietzsche to anyone who seeks to use the notion of life in a moral sense.

This criticism, however, seems to me mistaken. For, although it is perfectly true that there is no univocal notion of life as a moral concept, this is also the case with all moral notions: no two people use the notion of integrity in quite the same way, for example, and no one uses it in the same way at all times of his life, yet this does not mean that it is a useless moral concept. It is part of what makes a moral concept alive that it is open to differing interpretations and uses by different people and by the same person at different times of his life. Moreover, we understand the meaning of any given moral notion from the overall context in which it is being used on a specific occasion, and we relate this to other, associated contexts and meanings. We do not require it to be defined in advance for all possible uses. If we did, that would be its death.

In any case, we nearly all of us sometimes invoke the notion of life as a moral notion, and even if we do not we can see what other people are getting at when they do. Thus, we can say that someone is full of life, glowing with life, or dead within; that someone is not completely alive or that he just floats on life; that a certain profession or occupation sucks all the life out of one; that someone loves life or bears a grudge against life; that someone's thinking is lifeless; and so on. The art critic Peter Fuller said of the work of Francis Bacon that it did the dirt on life. Orwell said that Shakespeare 'loved the surface of the earth and the process of life'.[3] And so on.

For most of us, the concept of life in a moral sense used in the kind of ways indicated is just one of many moral concepts that are important to us. But for some, it has been the central moral notion. It was so for Nietzsche, as we have seen. D. H. Lawrence is another example:

> [L]ife is not mere length of days. Many people hang on, and hang on, into corrupt old age, just because they have *not* lived, and therefore cannot go . . .
>
> And again 'living' doesn't mean just doing certain things: running after women, or digging a garden, or working an engine, or becoming a member of Parliament. Just because, for Lord Byron, to sleep with a 'crowned head' was life itself, it doesn't follow that it will be life for *me* to sleep with a crowned head . . . And living won't even consist in jazzing or motoring or going to Wembley, just because most folks do it. Living consists in doing what you really, vitally want to do: what the *life* in you wants to do . . . And to find out *how* the life in you wants to be lived, and to live it, is terribly difficult.[4]

Or again:

> Augustine said that God created the universe new every day: and to the living, emotional soul, this is true. Every dawn dawns upon an entirely new universe, every Easter lights up an entirely new glory of a new world in utterly new flower.[5]

Someone who said, 'Yes, but does Lawrence mean that God *literally* creates the world new every day?' has obviously missed the point. There is an emotional fullness – a love of life – in what Lawrence says which, if we can make it part of ourselves, will mean that the world is a place in which we can be at home. And given that hardly any of us ever wholly escapes the temptation to view life with suspicion – with a 'squinting soul', as Nietzsche put it – the struggle to make what Lawrence says part of our own life can seem to be all the more important.

A similar sense of the love of life is to be found in the life and work of Albert Schweitzer. He writes:

Ethics . . . consists in this, that I experience the necessity of practising the same reverence for life toward all will-to-live, as toward my own. Therein I have already the needed fundamental principle of morality. It is *good* to maintain and cherish life; it is *evil* to destroy and to check life . . . A man is really ethical only when he obeys the constraint laid on him to help all life . . . To him life as such is sacred. He shatters no ice crystal that sparkles in the sun, tears no leaf from its tree, breaks off no flower, and is careful not to crush any insect as he walks . . .[6]

Peter Singer, from whom I have quoted this passage from Schweitzer, finds two reasons to object to what is said here. 'The reference to the ice crystal is especially puzzling', he writes, 'for an ice crystal is not alive at all.'[7] It is certainly true that there is much in Schweitzer's position with which one might disagree, but this comment of Singer's is, I think, entirely beside the point. His remark does not constitute an *objection* to Schweitzer's position, as he thinks it does. It simply expresses a different sensibility, a refusal or inability to take a certain ethical position seriously. For if you have ever looked at an ice crystal sparkling in the sun and marvelled at its very existence, then you will know what Schweitzer is talking about. Pablo Casals expresses such a view beautifully.

> I do not think a day passes in my life in which I fail to look with fresh amazement at the miracle of nature. It is there on every side. It can be simply a shadow on a mountainside, or a spider's web gleaming with dew, or sunlight on the leaves of a tree. I have always especially loved the sea . . . How mysterious and beautiful is the sea! how infinitely variable! It is never the same, never, not from one moment to the next, always in the process of change, always becoming something different and new.[8]

Singer's second response to Schweitzer is that the latter's ethic of reverence for life is absurd since even Schweitzer had to take life in the course of his work as a doctor, that is, the life of germs and parasites. In fact, he clearly thinks that the notion that life is sacred is ridiculous, for he says:

> People often say that life is sacred. They almost never mean what they say. They do not mean, as their words seem to imply, that life itself is sacred. If they did, killing a pig or pulling up a cabbage would be as abhorrent to them as the murder of a human being. When people say that life is sacred, it is human life they have in mind.[9]

But, Singer goes on to say, hardly anyone who says he believes in the sanctity of human life really means this, since this would commit him to pacifism and most of those who think human life sacred would also be prepared to kill in self-defence and the like. He thus interprets the idea that human life is sacred as the notion that human life has a special value, an idea which he disputes.[10] He is not alone in looking at things in this way: Jonathan Glover says that the belief that human life is sacred just means believing that 'taking human life is intrinsically wrong', a principle he goes on to reject.[11] And in fact Singer articulates a widespread understanding of the sanctity of life – widespread, that is, both within and without philosophy – which is why it is worth while exploring what he says.

We might suspect that there is something wrong in Singer's argument when we recall that some cultures have believed on religious grounds that certain animals, for example, were sacred and thought, not that this forbade killing them, but that it in fact provided a special reason to do so. For example, amongst the ancient Egyptians certain animals, in particular the cat and the ibis, were associated with gods and goddesses: cats with the goddess Bastet, and ibises with the god Thota. They were considered sacred and were often mummified after their death. Yet the mummies of cats show that in some cases their necks were broken to kill them in order to mummify them. In other words, the fact that they were sacred did not mean they could not be killed. On the contrary, their being sacred meant that they were honoured by being killed and mummified.

We should also bear in mind that Christ preached an ethic of life. He insisted that those who followed him would have eternal life, and even if he meant that they would live on forever after death, he also meant that they would possess in the here and now a wonder and love of the world in all its forms. Yet Christ certainly did not think that such a sense of life committed him to a belief that it was always wrong to inflict pain, suffering or even death. He cursed the fig tree which then withered (Matt. 21: 19–21); threw the money changers and traders out of the Temple in an access of rage using a 'scourge of small cords' (John 2: 14–16); said that he had come as the bringer of dissension, setting the members of families against one another (Luke 12: 51–3); insisted that 'whosoever shall offend one of *these* little ones that believe in me, it is better for him that a millstone were hanged about his neck, and he were cast into the sea' (Mark 9: 42); cursed the cities of Chorazin, Bethsaida and Capernaum which had not repented of their ways, saying they would be brought down to hell (Matt. 11: 21–4); and spoke of a Last Judgement when those who had lived as he wanted would have eternal life and those who had rejected him would 'go away into everlasting punishment' (Matt. 25: 31–46). One could give other examples.

It is not clear to me what someone like Singer, who has no religious belief at all and no interest in the religious sensibility, would say about such examples. I suspect that he would say that the Egyptians were just involved in superstitious absurdities, but about Christ I am not so sure. Perhaps he would believe that Christ had simply got it wrong and had not thought through the implications of his ethic of life. Or maybe he would say that Christ was just talking out-moded nonsense. Or it may be that he would balk at making such a judgement. Be that as it may, given the importance of Christ and his example in Western moral thought and the way in which reflection on his life has decisively shaped our moral sensibility, it surely behoves a philosopher to pause and consider whether belief in an ethic of life really does commit one to pacifism as Singer and others suppose it does.

As I have already noted, Singer fails entirely to respond to the sense of wonder which individuals like Schweitzer express in their thinking and which is part of what leads them to place the notion of life in the centre of their moral outlook. This leads him to mistake completely the sense of the term 'life' as those such as Schweitzer intend it. For Singer understands the notion of life in a fundamentally *biological* or *classificatory* sense. But that is not what Schweitzer is talking about at all. His sense of life and the wonder it evokes in him is a distinctively *ethical* or *moral* notion and expresses a sense of the fragility of human life and of our dependence upon a natural world which is not of our creation and is not ours to re-create simply to satisfy our desires. There is here an awareness of the mystery of the coming to be and passing away of creatures and other living things, and of wonder that anything exists at all. The concept of life as used in this kind of moral sense overlaps in its reference at best only partly with the reference of the term 'life' as this is used in the biological sciences. Schweitzer's use of the term does not, for example, wait upon the deliverances of these sciences to decide whether some object is alive or not in the moral sense. This is why he can speak of the ice crystal as he does. Arne Naess, whose outlook is close to that of Schweitzer, has said of a certain mountain that it is alive and has a life of its own. You may not agree with either Schweitzer or Naess, but it is a confusion to think that you could show them wrong by drawing up a list of indicators of life that would be useful in the biological sciences for determining whether something is alive, checking a mountain or an ice crystal against the list, and ascertaining that neither is alive. Schweitzer and Naess do not speak about life in ignorance of biology – Schweitzer was a medical man! – they are speaking from a quite different perspective.

117

Consider that area of morality which philosophers call 'practical ethics', the area of morality, that is, which concerns itself with discussion of moral problems such as abortion, euthanasia, capital punishment and so on. Take the last mentioned, for example. It is usually assumed, as Singer believes, that anyone who believes in the sanctity of life must be opposed to such punishment. Indeed, it is usually assumed that this is obviously so. However, it seems to me far from clear that this is right. In fact, it appears to me possible to believe that human life is sacred and still believe in capital punishment. I do not deny that usually these will not be compatible in a given person's thought and feeling: their true compatibility would betoken a rare spiritual achievement. And the spirit in question that would need to inform one's relations to others would be given, I think, by the sense that one is jointly responsible with others for humanity. Such was the kind of thing manifested by Primo Levi in his response to those who were deeply embroiled in the evil of the Third Reich. This emerges, for example, in his discussion of Chaim Rumkowski, the Jew who contrived to get himself set up by the Nazis as the president of the Lodz ghetto and managed to exercise a dictatorship which was, as Levi says, 'an astonishing tangle of megalomaniac dream, barbaric vitality, and real diplomatic and organisational skill'.[12] For Levi says of him: 'We are all mirrored in Rumkowski, his ambiguity is ours, it is our second nature, we hybrids moulded from clay and spirit.'[13] Levi speaks in a similar way about the Nazis.

> [T]he just among us [victims of Auschwitz], neither more nor less numerous than in any other human group, felt remorse, shame and pain for the misdeeds that others and not they had committed, and in which they felt involved, because they sensed that what had happened around them in their presence, and in them, was irrevocable. It would never again be able to be cleansed; it would prove that man, the human species – we, in short – were potentially able to construct an infinite enormity of pain; and that pain is the only force that is created from nothing, without cost and without effort.[14]

Paul Bailey has written: 'What is abundantly clear is that Primo Levi . . . was on the side of life',[15] and Raimond Gaita has spoken of Levi's 'reverence for each individual life'.[16] And indeed, Levi's sense articulated in the passage quoted of sharing a common responsibility for humanity with the Nazis was itself an expression of his affirmation of life. Moreover, his freedom from hatred for the Nazis was part of this. Yet none of this means that Levi did not want the Nazis to be punished for their deeds, though he never dwelt on this in his work. It is expressed by his sense that those responsible for the atrocities of Fascism remained his enemies so long as they did not repent of their deeds and that justice should be done.

I do not know whether Levi was in favour of capital punishment, but it seems to me clear that it would be possible to be so and yet still possess a reverence for life providing one's sense of humanity and of what it is to punish someone evinced the kind of spiritual demeanour to which Levi attested. We can perhaps gain a helpful perspective on this by reflecting for a moment on Martin Buber's reaction to the hanging in Israel in 1962 of Adolf Eichmann who had been kidnapped in Buenos Aires by the Israeli secret service for his part in the Final Solution and put on trial in Jerusalem. Buber objected to the death sentence on a number of grounds, but in particular because he felt that he could not understand Eichmann's actions. Buber articulated this by saying that he had 'only in a formal sense a common humanity with those who took part' in the deeds perpetrated by the Third Reich.[17] His point was that to hang Eichmann was to allow room for the sense that he, Eichmann, was 'one of us', not simply in a formal sense – as it may be, as members of the species *homo sapiens* – but precisely as someone with whom we share a responsibility for humanity. For Buber, Eichmann's deeds meant that the latter was no longer someone whom it made sense to punish by hanging precisely because they excluded him from sharing such a responsibility. Whether or not he was right in that judgement is of no importance for this discussion. What is important is that Buber's comments respond to the sense not only that belief in capital punishment can be consistent with possessing a reverence for life but also that the carrying out of the former can be a proper – perhaps even in some cases the best – expression of the latter.

I believe, then, that we have good reason for thinking that, when Singer claims that someone who says that life is the centre of his moral experience must be committed to pacifism on pain of meaning anything serious at all by that idea, he evinces a peculiarly flattened and literal-minded perspective. However, my argument does not, of course, deny that one could reasonably be opposed to capital punishment if one believed in the sanctity of life. The point is rather that, even if a person held such a belief and took it to imply pacifism, we cannot understand his moral position with any degree of sensitivity using only the resources for this purpose which someone like Singer employs. He, like many other philosophers, misses the point that what can be most significant in what a person believes and does is the *spirit* in which he believes and does it.

Why is this so often missed? There may be many reasons. One is, no doubt, the assumption that the notion of the spirit immediately invokes implausible religious ideas. This is surely mistaken. We can often invoke the notion of the spirit in a way that does not do this at all. For example, we can say that someone suffered but his spirit was not broken; or that we did not like the spirit in which someone did something; or that we find the spirit of the landscape pleasing. George Orwell tells of an encounter with an Italian during the Spanish Civil War.

> As we went out he stepped across the room and gripped my hand very hard. Queer, the affection you can feel for a stranger! It was as though his spirit and mine had momentarily succeeded in bridging the gulf of language and tradition and meeting in utter intimacy.[18]

The other central reason why the notion of the spirit in which something is believed or done is often missed by philosophers is that such a notion is more or less useless if we are thinking about framing moral rules or laws which should govern behaviour, especially if we would like those moral laws to become laws of the land. However, just about all our moral notions are useless in this way and cannot be pressed into the service of framing rules or laws for regulating human behaviour, and they are no worse off for that. The problem, I think, is that many philosophers – and others – have a strong tendency to suppose that the primary purpose of thought about moral issues, particularly issues in practical ethics, just *is* to arrive at some set of principles or rules concerning the matter in question. Of course, one cannot deny that with respect to some ethical issues to arrive at such is something which eventually has to be done, though there are real questions why philosophers should suppose they are in a position to do so in any particularly helpful or insightful way. But even when principles and laws have to be framed, this is merely one part of what reflection on issues in ethics, including practical ethics, might offer. Moreover, we can be quite certain that such principles or laws will probably always represent a simplification of any insightful person's thought on such matters, this being the result of the kind of compromise between different people's thinking which the framing of moral rules involves. As Lawrence says: '[L]aw is a very, very clumsy and mechanical instrument, and we people are very, very delicate and subtle beings.'[19] In truth, nearly all important moral thought goes on before, after or in independence of thought about what principles or rules to follow.

Despite these points about the relation of morality to rules or principles, it might be said that what makes it possible to think in such a case as that of Levi that an ethic of life could be reconciled with the taking of life is that the punishment in question is bounded by the rule of law. It might be suggested that where the law is not operative in this way we can make less sense of such a possibility.

However, we have at least one case of someone who is on the side of life and kills, and who, in doing so, falls foul of the law and is punished for his deed. This is Melville's Billy Budd. Billy, conscripted into the navy, is young, vigorous, full of energy and life, but he is envied by the master-at-arms, Claggart, who represents the spirit of evil and wishes to destroy that which is good simply because it is good. In an interview with Captain Vere Claggart accuses Billy of hatching a plot to mutiny and then repeats the charge to Billy's face in Vere's presence. Billy is utterly astonished at the accusation and, unable to speak to defend himself, strikes Claggart who drops dead under the force of the blow and his fall to the floor. Vere convenes a drumhead court which sentences Billy to be hanged. The court sees itself as having no choice but to pass this sentence since Billy has struck a superior officer and this is the sentence for such an act. However, none of those who convict Billy believes that he is culpable from the point of view of natural justice, even though it is beyond any possible dispute that Billy has killed Claggart.

Billy has sometimes been seen as a Christ-like figure, and the comparison is certainly not wholly misleading.[20] However, Billy possesses little if anything of Christ's understanding of the ways of the world: Christ is innocent, whereas Billy is both innocent and ignorant. This suggests that a better comparison is between Billy and Adam before the Fall. Like Adam, Billy is not best understood as being goodness itself, for the distinction between good and evil is not one which operates within Billy's world, any more than it was operative in Adam's world. Rather, Billy is an embodiment of life itself, just as Adam before the Fall was immortal. This is why Billy is a 'barbarian', a foundling, without culture and civilisation, whereas Christ was steeped in the learning and teaching of Judaism.

Yet, of course, Billy kills: he kills that evil which denies life, and no one within or without the story could reasonably think that the fact that Billy has killed another human being means that he should not be seen as on the side of life after all, though of course one can reasonably regard the killing with regret or anguish. The case of Billy Budd shows that that which is on the side of life can consistently kill in the name of life. And it shows that this is so even when he who is on the side of life must be punished for his deeds.

I have already mentioned D. H. Lawrence as being someone for whom life was a central moral notion. And he, like Melville, thought that the idea of killing in the name of life was far from absurd. This comes out in his short story 'The Fox'. March and Banford live on a farmstead which they endeavour to make viable, but with little success. One day, a man, Henry, comes to the two women. Through his presence, the relationship between March and Banford is shown to be sterile: it is a living death. Henry wishes to marry March, and Banford seeks to prevent this by appealing to March's pity and loyalty, a form of manipulation which aims to prevent March's living richly and with emotional and spiritual vitality. One day, Henry is felling a tree for the women and ensures that the tree falls on, and kills, Banford so that March might be free to marry him. There is no doubt that Henry has murdered Banford. He has murdered her in the name of life, for she was herself life-denying. The point is well expressed by David Ellis in his introduction to the novella: 'The startling challenge [of the novella] . . . is whether it is not more "immoral" for Banford to live on, binding March to her with emotional blackmail, than that Henry should kill her.'[21]

The thing that most is fundamentally worrying Lawrence in this story comes out in an essay of his to which his editor has appended the title 'The Good Man'. The essay is a profound attack on what Lawrence sees as the central features of the morality of modernity. Tracing that morality to French eighteenth-century literature and its understanding of the 'good man', Lawrence writes:

> The new little monster, the new 'good man,' was perfectly reasonable and perfectly irreligious. Religion knows the great passions. The *homme de bien*, the good man, performs the robot trick of isolating himself from the great passions. For the passion of life he substitutes the reasonable social virtues. You must be honest in your material dealings, you must be kind to the poor, and you must have 'feelings' for your fellow man . . . There is nothing to *worship*. Such a thing as worship is nonsense. But you may get a 'feeling' out of anything . . . The last phase of the bluff is to pretend that we do all have nice feelings about everything, if we are nice people.[22]

He goes on:

> Now the 'good man' is all right as far as he goes. One must be honest in one's dealings, and one does feel kindly towards the poor . . . [But] the trouble about the 'good man' is that he's only one-hundredth part of a man.[23]

What has been left out? Not surprisingly, Lawrence says that life itself is missing. 'When is a man a man? When he is alight with life . . . If it is missing, there is no man, only a creature, a clod, undistinguished.'[24] We are evidently back here with the problem with which I began, that is, with the tension between a morality whose central aim is the creation of as *safe* a life for as many as possible and a morality whose centre is rather to be found in the concept of life itself. But we have now, perhaps, a better perspective on that problem. For we often suppose that in seeking to reduce suffering as much as possible we are in the most authentic manner on the side of life itself. But we might now, having discussed such cases as that of Christ, of Primo Levi, of 'Billy Budd, Sailor' and of 'The Fox', begin to suspect that what being on the side of life is customarily understood to involve could actually be a corruption of a proper understanding of life. If this is right we can see why Nietzsche thought that the fundamental problem of modern existence was: morality *versus* life.[25]

Notes

In writing this chapter I have especially benefited from discussion with and advice from Michael Newton.

1. Karl Löwith, 'Nietzsches Vollendung des Atheismus', in Hans Steffen (ed.) *Nietzsche: Werk und Wirkungen* (Göttingen: Vandenhoeck & Ruprecht, 1974), pp. 7–18, at p. 8, my translation.
2. This aspect of Nietzsche's thinking is explored at length and with great insight by Henry Staten, *Nietzsche's Voice* (Ithaca: Cornell University Press, 1990).
3. George Orwell, 'Lear, Tolstoy and the Fool', in Orwell, *Inside the Whale and Other Essays* (Harmondsworth: Penguin, 1962 [1947]), pp. 116–17.
4. D. H. Lawrence, 'Blessed Are the Powerful', in Lawrence, *Phœnix II*, Warren Roberts and Harry T. Moore (eds) (New York: Viking Press, 1970), pp. 437–8.
5. D. H. Lawrence, 'A Propos of "Lady Chatterley's Lover" ', in Lawrence, *Phœnix II*, Roberts and Moore (eds), p. 504.
6. Quoted by Peter Singer, *Practical Ethics* (Cambridge: Cambridge University Press, 1979), p. 91.
7. Singer, *Practical Ethics* , p. 91.
8. Pablo Casals, *Joys and Sorrows: Reflections by Pablo Casals, as Told to Albert E. Kahn* (New York: Simon & Schuster, 1970), p. 17.
9. Singer, *Practical Ethics*, p. 72.
10. Ibid., p. 73.

11. Jonathan Glover, *Causing Death and Saving Lives* (Harmondsworth: Penguin, 1982), ch. 3.
12. Primo Levi, *The Drowned and the Saved*, tr. R. Rosenthal (London: Abacus, 1988), p. 45.
13. Levi, *The Drowned and the Saved*, p. 50.
14. Ibid., p. 66.
15. Paul Bailey, 'Introduction' to Levi, *The Drowned and the Saved*, p. xiv.
16. Raimond Gaita, *A Common Humanity* (London: Routledge, 2000), p. 152.
17. Quoted in Hannah Arendt, *Eichmann in Jerusalem: A Report on the Banality of Evil* (Harmondsworth: Penguin, 1994 [1963]), p. 251.
18. George Orwell, *Homage to Catalonia* (Harmondsworth: Penguin, 1989 [1938]), pp. 1–2.
19. D. H. Lawrence, 'Study of Thomas Hardy', in Lawrence, *Phœnix I*, Edward D. McDonald (ed.) (London: Heinemann, 1961), p. 405.
20. The comparison was suggested by Hannah Arendt, *On Revolution* (Harmondsworth: Penguin, 1990 [1963]), pp. 80ff. and is questioned by Harold Beaver in his introduction to Melville's *'Billy Budd, Sailor' and Other Stories* (Harmondsworth: Penguin, 1985), pp. 41ff., where a comparison with Adam is alluded to.
21. David Ellis in D. H. Lawrence, 'The Fox', in Lawrence, *The Fox. The Captain's Doll. The Ladybird*, David Ellis (ed.) (Harmondsworth: Penguin, 1994), pp. xvi–xvii.
22. Lawrence, 'The Good Man', in Lawrence, *Phœnix I*, D. McDonald (ed.), p. 751.
23. Ibid., p. 752.
24. Lawrence, 'Study of Thomas Hardy', p. 421.

9

Sex

E VER SINCE SOCRATES, PHILOSOPHY has been interested in asking
such questions as: What is art? What is morality? What is love?,
and the hope has been to find a definition of such areas of human
concern, delineating each such form of attention to the world from
other forms. Philosophers have often been attracted to such a
procedure because it seems to hold out the prospect of genuine
understanding and insight, and to promise to provide a method for
settling disputes. Thus, if we take ourselves to be in possession of a
definition of what, say, art is, then we shall be able to take any object
and decide whether it does or does not have the properties which
make it a work of art. This will allow us to sort out the real from the
bogus, something which seems these days an especially great problem
in the art world when a common reaction to many objects on display
in public galleries is that they are not works of art at all and should not
be there.

Some philosophers and others have adopted such an approach
with respect to sexual desire. They have wanted to provide a definition of such desire, and one of the things that has motivated them to
do so is the hope that, armed with a definition of what sexual desire is,
they will be able to indicate which kinds of sexual activity, if any,
express perversions of sexual desire or otherwise unacceptable forms
of it. For example, Roman Catholicism bases its teaching concerning
the morality of sex on a notion of what Nature, as an expression of
God's design, intends. But what Nature intends, so it is said, is that sex
shall be between a man and a woman, and that it shall issue in the
birth of children. The raising of children is, however, a long and

arduous process, and what the person engaging in sex commits himself to is seeing this through to completion. This requires the stable institution of monogamous marriage. Further, such a marriage flourishes if it is an expression of love between two people on the model of God's love for human beings. Hence, Roman Catholic teaching confines morally decent sex to that which takes place between a man and woman in marriage for the purposes of procreation and the expression of the love that exists between them.

As I have noted, such a view of sex purports to tell us *what sex is* and hence which kinds of sexual activity are morally permitted: those that do not accord with such a definition will be in various ways unacceptable, and some will be perverted. Few people these days accept the Catholic view, and even many who call themselves Catholic would reject it, for it is extremely restrictive in its sense of what counts as acceptable sexual activity. But there are other views which have similar ambitions to provide a definition of what sexual desire is. Thus Roger Scruton, in what is certainly by a long way the most interesting and insightful philosophical account of sexual desire produced by modern analytic philosophy, has argued that any instance of sexual desire possesses an individualising intentionality. By this he means that sexual desire is founded upon the thought of the other as the specific individual he or she is.[1] Hence, according to this account, if a man desires two women at the same time, he will be experiencing two different desires, each of which will be a desire for one of the two women. From this account it also follows that there cannot be any such sexual desire as an unfocused desire for no particular man or woman. Scruton considers the case of the sailor storming ashore with the thought 'woman' in his mind: he might be thought to desire a woman, but no particular woman. Scruton claims that this is not so: until the sailor actually meets a specific woman he desires, he desired no woman; he was rather in the condition of desiring to desire.[2]

Such a view of sexual desire has to find an adequate response to such phenomena as that of Casanova, described by Stefan Zweig:

> His passion, flowing away at the purely erotic level, knows nothing of the ecstasy of uniqueness. We need have no anxiety, therefore, when he seems reduced to despair because Henriette or the beautiful Portuguese lady has left him. We know that he will not blow out his brains; nor are we surprised to find him, a day or two later, amusing himself in the first convenient brothel. If the nun C.C. is unable to come over from Murano, and the lay-sister M.M. arrives in her place, Casanova is speedily consoled. After all, one woman is as good as another![3]

Scruton writes: 'If John is frustrated in his pursuit of Mary, there is something inapposite in the advice "Take Elizabeth, she will do just as well." '[4] Not, apparently, if one is Casanova! It seems, then, that Scruton has two options. Either he could insist that he has provided a true account of sexual desire, in which case Zweig has totally misunderstood and misdescribed the case of someone like Casanova, and, indeed, that a lot of what looks like sexual desire where what is desired is *someone or other* is not really sexual desire after all since it does not display an individualising intentionality; or he could say that such cases display sexual desire all right, but a perverted or otherwise morally unacceptable form. In fact, Scruton seems to waver between the two, for, although, as we have seen, he claims that in cases such as that of the sailor the man in question experiences no sexual desire until he comes into contact with the woman he desires, he also grants, at the end of his book, and looking over his argument as a whole, that 'my analysis has included a large prescriptive component'.[5] In other words, he seems to concede that his analysis is not an analysis of sexual desire as such but a moral view about the best form that sexual desire can take.

Actually, it seems to me that, whatever the weaknesses of his account, what Scruton is offering is a picture of sexual desire which helps to make sense of the fact that there can be deeper and shallower ways of understanding and experiencing our sexuality. I am sure that the Catholic view attempts the same. Some accounts, it seems, do not. Thus Igor Primoratz has argued that sexual desire 'is sufficiently defined as the desire for certain bodily pleasures, period'.[6] It is hard to see how such a view can make sense of the fact that sexual desire is capable of finding deeper forms of expression in human life, let alone the fact that it often seeks to do so. For it seems to assimilate sexual desire to something like the desire to scratch an itch, and the possibilities of a deepened understanding of itch-scratching are severely limited, to say the least. This is not to say that only deepened forms of expression of sexual desire are morally legitimate, or anything like that: it is merely to say that any account of sexual desire must be able to make sense of the possibility of those deeper forms of expression.

In any case, Primoratz' account of sexual desire has some odd consequences. It leads, he argues, to the conclusion that any putative sexual act which is devoid of pleasure for the person engaged in that act is not, after all, a sexual act at all. Thus he claims that a prostitute who gains no pleasure from intercourse with a customer is not engaged in a sexual act (whereas the customer is). Further:

> As for the couple who have lost sexual interest in each other but still engage in routine coitus, the less pleasurable it gets, the less valuable it is as sex. If, at some point, it becomes utterly bereft of sexual pleasure, would it be so odd to say that they were performing acts that for most people ordinarily involve at least a modicum of sexual pleasure, but that *they* were merely going through the motions, that *for them* there was no sex in it any longer?[7]

One might suspect that Primoratz is not, after all, just trying to tell us what sex is, but prescribing a particular form of it, that is, one through which one experiences as much pleasure as possible. For he clearly believes that the less pleasurable sex is, the less valuable it is. Still, leaving that aside, it does, surely, seem odd to suppose that the bored couple in Primoratz' example are not actually engaged in a sexual act. One might as well say that what it is to feel hunger is to have a desire for certain bodily pleasures so that if one eats something utterly bland which fails to fill the stomach (modern mass-produced strawberries, for example) one is not really eating at all.

In fact, I do not think that Primoratz need deny on his account that the prostitute or the bored couple are engaged in sex even if they get no pleasure from such acts. His view expresses a confusion between sexual desire and sexual acts. One is, after all, still eating if there is no pleasure in doing so. The prostitute might not, indeed, possess any sexual desire for her clients, but it does not follow from that that she is not engaged in sexual acts with them. The same may be the case for the bored couple. In the same way, I might for some reason have no hunger, no desire for food, yet still be eating. It is possible to defend the 'pleasure view' of sex and grant that sexual acts which involve no pleasure are still genuinely sexual acts.

Still, even if Primoratz' account can be repaired in the way suggested, it is still exposed to the earlier criticism that it cannot make sense of the possibility of a deepened understanding of sex. Scruton's view, as we have seen, also has weaknesses. They are both questionable because, however much they differ from each other, they share the same fundamental aspiration which I mentioned at the outset, namely, the desire to provide a definition of sexual desire, to find some feature which any and every experience of sexual desire possesses. And it seems to me that what is mistaken about this is that it is far too restrictive. Sexual desire is a huge, sprawling phenomenon, which casts its shadow over almost every aspect of our inner life and can find expression in a fantastic variety of acts. It seems unlikely that we shall ever be able to define it. Wittgenstein suggested that if we consider the concept of a game we should not assume that there must be some feature or features which they all – football, patience, ring-a-ring-a-roses, chess, noughts and crosses, and so on – have in common. He suggested, rather, that as we compare one game with another, and then with another, and so on, we shall see that there is 'a complicated network of similarities overlapping and criss-crossing: sometimes overall similarities, sometimes similarities of detail'.[8] And he goes on:

> I can think of no better expression to characterize these similarities than 'family resemblances'; for the various resemblances between members of a family: build, features, colour of eyes, gait, temperament, etc. etc. overlap and criss-cross in the same way. – And I shall say: 'games' form a family.[9]

I would say the same about sexual desire. We are not going to get far, I think, if we try to provide a definition of sexual desire or of what constitutes a sexual act, for we shall in such a case always end up ruling out some desire or act which, in the absence of the definition, we should have no difficulty in regarding as sexual. The different acts and kinds of desire which one can think of as sexual resemble one another in the way members of a family resemble one another, with overlapping and criss-crossing characteristics, as Wittgenstein puts it. The desire some adult men have to dress up in nappies and be mothered by a woman is a sexual desire, but whatever it is that makes this a sexual desire has little to do with the sexual desire which finds expression in the wish to make love to one's partner whom one cherishes. They are connected as being both sexual by bearing family resemblances to each other and to other forms of sexual desire. Or again, consider the following passage from Heinrich Böll's story 'Im Tal der donnernden Hufe' ('In the Valley of the Thundering Hooves'). Paul is waiting in church to go to confession. A woman tells him that it is his turn. He shakes his head and indicates that his turn is after hers. Böll writes:

> [T]he intensity with which he desired her tormented him; he had not even seen her face; the gentle smell of lavender, a young voice, the soft and yet hard noise of her high heels as she walked the four paces to the confessional: this rhythm of the high heels, hard and yet so soft, was only a fragment of the unending melody which raged in his ears all day and night. In the evenings, he would lie awake, the window open, and would hear them walking along the asphalt of the pavement: shoes, heels, hard,

soft, unsuspecting; he heard voices, whispering, laughter under the chestnut trees. There were too many of them, and they were too lovely: some opened their handbag, in the tram, at the box-office in the cinema, on the counter in the shop; they left their handbags lying around in cars and he could look inside: lipstick, handkerchiefs, loose change, crumpled-up tickets, packets of cigarettes, powder compacts.[10]

This wonderful evocation of adolescent sexuality, of the time when the entire world seems to take on a sexual hue and everything seems to have some sexual aspect; of a time when, for a boy at least, more or less any object associated with the opposite sex can take his breath away and make him yearn – this nameless, glorious, tormenting, fear-filled, anxious longing has little in common with, say, the cynical, brutal de-humanised forms of the sexual desire of the pimps, prostitutes, murderers and queens which Jean Genêt describes in his *Our Lady of the Flowers*. What links them is, once again, a series of family resemblances. And such resemblances are not just interpersonal ones, but intrapersonal: they have to do with the way in which, later in life and reflecting on the changes to which our own sexual desires have been subject, we see that what makes all of them sexual desires is that they bear family resemblances to one another. For what one finds sexually appealing or exciting at the age of, say, forty, may be utterly unlike that which one found sexually appealing at the age of fifteen; and the fifteen-year-old would have been, perhaps, uncomprehending about the forty-year-old's pattern of desires. Yet, at the same time, one can see how the one type of desires developed into the other; and one might think that it is only through telling the story of the changes in one's desires that one could come to see how it is that *these* things later in life could be sexually exciting at all.

None of this is to say, however, that the accounts of sexual desire offered by Roman Catholic teaching or by Scruton or Primoratz have nothing to be said for them. On the contrary, the very amorphousness of sexual desire is such that these accounts certainly do latch onto part of that to which any sensitive understanding of sexual desire should draw our attention.

Consider again the Catholic emphasis on the relation between sexual desire and procreation. To many people, such an emphasis seems absurd, and it is easy to find arguments to criticise the idea that every sexual act not 'by nature' aimed at procreation is morally suspect.[11] But it by no means follows from this that an adequate understanding of sexual desire may leave out the notion of procreation as, for example, the accounts of both Scruton and Primoratz do.

We can see this by the simple reflection that a species of creature which had all our experiences of sexual desires but in whom sexual desire had no connection with procreation would have a profoundly different understanding of sexual desire from the one we have. As so often in philosophy, the real problem is to find a way of expressing this point which does not fall foul of some unhelpful generalisation, such as that which the Catholic view involves.

At one point D. H. Lawrence writes:

> Sex is the balance of male and female in the universe, the attraction, the repulsion, the transit of neutrality, the new attraction, the new repulsion, always different, always new. The long neuter spell of Lent, when the blood is low, and the delight of the Easter kiss, the sexual revel of the spring, the passion of mid-summer, the slow recoil, revolt, and grief of autumn, greyness again, then the sharp stimulus of long winter nights. Sex goes through the rhythm of the year, in man and woman, ceaselessly changing: the rhythm of the sun in his relation to the earth.[12]

It goes without saying that many, if not most, do not share this view of sex, wonderful though it is. And there are lots of ways in which one might pursue or develop or respond to the thoughts Lawrence articulates. For our purposes what is important is that Lawrence connects sex to the natural cycle of life, and does so in such a way as to express a sense of the wonder and mystery of sex. But if we ask ourselves how it is possible to see sex in this way, then I think that we shall not be able long to resist the thought that it is the fact that sex is related to conception and procreation that allows us to do this. For it is *this* fact about it which most immediately and forcefully connects it to the notions of corruption and regeneration and hence allows it to be brought into contact with our sense of the natural cycle of the seasons. And if, as we do, we can wonder at that cycle, at its utter familiarity together with the strangeness that each spring green shoots sprout from what looks like dead wood, we can also see why it is that we can wonder at sex, at the strangeness of a force at once so familiar and yet *unheimlich* – this incomparable German word, which means 'uncanny' or 'spooky' or 'frightening', captures the sense of something's not being like that which one meets with at home (*Heim*), that which is unfamiliar or upsets one's ingrained and habitual ways of dealing with things.

We could perhaps get at the significance of procreation for an understanding of sexual desire in another way. Many people experience a sense of wonder and mystery at the birth of a child. And this very sense can cast in a certain light the sexual act which directly led to this birth, can remind us of the strangeness and mystery of sex. But to speak here of a reminder is not to suggest that anyone might actually have forgotten anything, for we are all familiar with the fact that sexual desire has its own demands and needs which well up and grip us in ways we cannot fully fathom, and that it attaches us to people in ways we cannot properly comprehend. We all know that sex, where what is craved is so clear and yet weirdly elusive, seems at once completely natural and an intrusion from another world into our daily activities. The issue is rather that of such knowledge becoming deeper and more alive as an object of wonder in a person, much as, say, suffering but surviving a dreadful accident might be said to remind one of one's mortality. Thus the connection with sex of reproduction and all it involves casts its shadow over sex in the kind of way that mortality casts its shadow over human life. And this is so even if a given person never thinks of procreation (except, perhaps, to prevent his or her sexual acts leading to conception), just as it is so even if a person never thinks of his own mortality (except to suppress or ridicule the thought). For the kinds of thought I have said people have about the birth of a child and those that people have who have survived death form part of the collective experience of mankind, of the wisdom concerning what it is to be a human being and thus of our sense of who and what we are.

I am not claiming, of course, that reflection on the connection of sex with reproduction is the only way in which it is possible for one to come to a deepened understanding of human sexuality. I am just saying that it is a central or permanent way in which this can happen for creatures such as we are, and thus that any account of sexual desire which leaves it out must be inadequate.

I earlier suggested that the view that sexual desire is a desire for pleasure and nothing else is misleading because it seeks to reduce the variety of desires which are correctly understood to be sexual desires to one type. But some have suggested that the idea is absurd for other reasons. Thus, in a brilliant discussion of the nature of sexual desire, Jean-Paul Sartre argued that sexual desire cannot be understood to be a desire merely for pleasure, for this view would not allow us to make sense of how it is that such desire could come to 'attach' itself to an object: why would masturbation not be enough?[13] Roger Scruton and Thomas Nagel have echoed Sartre's claim.[14] Is this view correct? The basic problem with it seems to me this: even if it is true that not all sexual desire can be understood to be a desire for pleasure, it does not follow from this that sexual desire is never simply desire for pleasure. And if a particular person understands his own sexual desire to be nothing more than a desire for pleasure we can, *pace* Sartre, account for the way in which his desire attaches itself to an object, for the pleasure which comes from having sex with a person might seem to him greater or to offer more variety or the like than does masturbation.[15] I do not think, therefore, that Sartre is right to say that sexual desire *cannot* be a desire simply for pleasure or orgasm. No purely philosophical thesis can legislate out of existence a particular experience of, and attitude towards, sex, however much one might judge it to be inhuman or thoughtless or shallow or degrading (if one does).

Still, the fact remains that for most people sexual desire is much more than a desire for pleasure, though it is also at least that. As Stuart Hampshire has put it:

> It is unhistorical, and contrary to experience, a Manichean error, to think of erotic feeling as comparable with hunger and thirst, as a primitive need . . . [O]ur sexual desires and practices vividly express individual natures as well as something of the customs of a particular culture. They are penetrated by thought, by symbolism and by imagery, and therefore by that kind of thought which is called imagination.[16]

This very complexity of sexual desire, and the way in which it expresses something of one's very nature as a person – as Freud put it with exaggeration but point, 'The sexual behaviour of a human being often *lays down the pattern* for all his other modes of reacting to life'[17] – this very complexity gives a reason for thinking that the pleasure which sex affords must itself be complex. And, indeed, as others have pointed out, the pleasure that sex brings is peculiar amongst our many pleasures in often being experienced as strangely hollow. Of course, all of our pleasures can fail to bring satisfaction: nothing is more common than to satisfy a desire and remain unsatisfied oneself. But the point about sexual desire goes deeper than this: it is that it seems in some way doomed to frustration, as Sartre in his account proposes. Why should this be so? Here is a suggestion: sexual desire seems to be a deeply unstable desire. On the one hand, it is roving, largely undiscriminating about the individuals to whom it attaches itself, restless: one wants 'woman' or 'man'. On the other, it can be especially excited by, and become fixated upon, a specific individual. This lends sexual desire a strange fragility: for, in desiring a given individual, one also desires him or her as man or woman, as a representative of the male or the female sex. There accordingly seems to me to be a way in which what one wants in the sexual act is two things that one cannot have: one wants this individual man or woman and one wants *all* men or *all* women. That is, one wants all men or all women in and through this one individual. But this is impossible. Yet this is why it is that one of the most recurrent sexual fantasies is that of not knowing who one's sexual partner is.

Roger Scruton holds a similar view, and he traces sexual jealousy to the very fact that if one is desired, one is desired as an example of one's sex, for this means that one is always in principle replaceable by another as an object of desire.[18] This understanding of jealousy comes out well in Büchner's great play *Woyzeck* – from which Berg made an opera and Herzog a film – his study, based on real sources, of the sexual jealousy of the eponymous down-trodden soldier who murders his common-law wife when he discovers she has been sleeping with the Drum-Major. The scene in which Woyzeck confronts her with this is extraordinary:

> *Woyzeck* (staring at her, shaking his head). Hm! I don't see anything, I don't see anything. Oh, you think you'd see it – you'd think you could catch hold of it.
> *Marie* (frightened). What's up, Franz? You're raving, Franz.
> *Woyzeck* A sin so big and so fat. It stinks so you'd think it'd smoke the angels out of Heaven. You've got a red mouth, Marie. No blisters on it? Goodbye, Marie, you're as beautiful as sin. Can mortal sin be so beautiful?
> *Marie* Franz, you're talking like you were mad.
> *Woyzeck* To hell with it! – Did he stand like that or like this?
> *Marie* As the day is long and the world old lots of people can stand in the same place, one after the other.
> *Woyzeck* I saw him.
> *Marie* You can see a lot if you've got two eyes and aren't blind and the sun's shining.[19]

The whole scene expresses in a wonderfully economical fashion – and, it must be said, in language which cannot be adequately captured in translation – horror at the thought that in sexual desire one person can be replaced by another. When in Herzog's film of the play Woyzeck, played by Klaus Kinski, asks 'Did he stand like that or like this?', Kinski places himself right in front of Marie and thrusts his pelvis now this way, now that, into her groin, and this gesture perfectly captures the horror at the replaceability of individuals in sexual desire.

Yet it captures more than horror, for there is disgust in Woyzeck's reaction. This is why he immediately associates Marie's infidelity with disease. And the disgust is also captured in Kinski's portrayal of the soldier: during the scene, he bends down and buries his nose in the turned-back sheets and blankets of the bed, smelling for the animal-like scent of the sex act. (Büchner was very influenced by Shakespeare, and one cannot help thinking in this connection of Hamlet's 'Nay, but to live / In the rank sweat of an enseamed bed, / Stew'd in corruption, honeying and making love / Over the nasty sty!',[20] and Kinski – or Herzog – may have had this in mind.) There is an important connection between disgust and sexual jealousy.

In a valuable essay, David Pole has analysed the concept of disgust.[21] He argues that disgust always carries a charge of attraction, and I think that this attraction is evident in Woyzeck's reaction to Marie: witness the association of her beauty with sin and the emphasis on the diseased redness of her mouth, dreadful yet enticing. Pole also suggests that we get our central notion of disgust from organic matter that is decomposing in some way, which would help explain why such things as slugs – to take one of Pole's examples – are experienced as disgusting: for the slug's slimy body, which it appears to be losing as it crawls along, seems to be caught in a process of decay and corruption. One of the most disgusting things I have ever seen was the neck of an otherwise healthy horse, gashed wide open by barbed wire, into which had buried themselves thousands of maggots which were feeding on the blood oozing in clots from the wound. A friend told me of his disgust on seeing a frog which has a loose back like a string vest into which the young flee to seek shelter and be carried for safety. Organic decay, then, or what looks like it, or smells of it, is perhaps the core of disgust.

Consider now the sexual act. In this act the bodies of those involved undergo profound changes: the flushing of the face, the erection of the penis, the tumescence of the nipples, the secretions of the vagina. One is overwhelmed in desire by one's body, as Sartre puts it: one's will is here in abeyance. All of these things can, of course, be received as an expression of excitement. But there is no doubt that they can be seen as disgusting, and often have been so seen. For, by their very nature, and in their triumph over the will, they are redolent of a body in decay. This is why desire for the other in his or her flesh can so easily, in certain persons, tip over into disgust with his or her flesh. And in sexual jealousy such disgust is to the fore: for the sexually exciting transformations of the beloved's body resemble nothing so much as the disgusting decay of that body when they are provoked by, and express desire for, a rival. Yet the transformations of one's beloved's body, even when they are connected with one's rival, remain exciting, and they do so even partly because they disgust, for that which is disgusting is appealing, as we have already noted. Disgust, one might say, adapting a Sartrean idiom from another context, lies coiled like a worm at the heart of desire, and it is brought to the light of day by betrayal. Sexual jealousy may begin in the recognition of one's dispensability as a sexual partner, but once it has been evoked it feeds upon the primordial disgust which lies hidden in all sexual acts. It is *this* recognition which animates the brilliance of Büchner's treatment of Woyzeck's jealousy and Kinski's portrayal of it.

It might be said that the idea that disgust lies at the heart of sexual desire is absurd. And it is, of course, true that not everyone will be susceptible to the sense that the transformations of the body in sexual excitement are redolent of a body in decay, however latent this might be. But there are other reasons for supposing that disgust is inherent in sexual desire. For example, it just seems to be the case that sexual desire (especially male desire?) is often ignited and intensified by a sense of doing something which involves disgust. This is connected with the fact that in sex we suspend or overcome our normal sense of disgust. As William Ian Miller says:

> [S]exual desire depends on the idea of a prohibited domain of the disgusting. A person's tongue in your mouth could be experienced as a pleasure or as a most repulsive and nauseating intrusion depending on the state of relations that exist or are being negotiated between you and the person. But someone else's tongue in your mouth can be a sign of intimacy *because* it can also be a disgusting assault.[22]

But can it be right to say that modern sexual desire, whose expression is so free in comparison with that of previous ages, carries a sense of disgust at its core? Perhaps the idea is not as absurd as it might seem, for A. Béjin has argued that

> present day [sexual] norms tend to provoke a conflict between immediate surrender to the demands of the senses, and an increased conscious mastery of the organic processes . . . One must . . . abandon oneself to sensation, without ceasing to submit one's actions to a rational calculation of 'sexual expedience'.[23]

The claim is that we have done a great deal to subsume our sexual practices under the same kind of cost-benefit calculus that applies in so many other areas of our life. If this is right, then modern sexual desire, for all its seeming liberation from older forms of control, may be thought to express a powerful asceticism which itself testifies to a sense of disgust with sex.

I mentioned earlier Sartre's thought that in desire one is overwhelmed by the body. He makes this point in the context of his discussion of the caress which expresses sexual desire. Such a caress – it may be a caress of the hand or the eye – constitutes an attempt to *incarnate* the other. The other, he says, is born as flesh under my caress, whence the idea that I want him or her to be overwhelmed by his or her body: 'Desire is the attempt to strip the body of its movements as of its clothing and to make it exist as pure flesh.'[24] If the other responds to my caress then this person will experience his or her arousal as 'troubling', as 'clogging' consciousness. Yet, at the same time, my experiencing my own desire is felt by me in the same way, and I, too, in responding to the caress of the other, am born as flesh for him or her.

This process of mutual incarnation leads Sartre to speak of a 'world of desire'.

> If my body . . . is lived as flesh, then it is as a reference to my flesh that I apprehend the objects in the world. This means that I make myself passive in relation to them and that they are revealed to me from the point of view of this passivity . . . Objects then become the transcendent ensemble which reveals my incarnation to me. A contact with them is a *caress*; that is, my perception is not the *utilization* of the object, but to perceive an object when I am in the desiring attitude is to caress myself with it. Thus I am sensitive not so much to the form of the object and to its instrumentality, as to its matter (gritty, smooth, tepid, greasy, rough etc.). In my desiring perception I discover something like a *flesh* of objects . . .[25]

This passage, typical in both its insight and incantatory quality of the whole of Sartre's discussion, could be read as a philosophical explication of Heinrich Böll's description of the adolescent boy's sexual excitement at the objects he associates with women. But it is more than that. For it helps provide an explanation of why it is that in desire the lovers can want the entire world to become sexualised, made over in the image of their desire: there is in desire a hostility to that which does not support and feed the desire itself. The lovers attempt to discover, so to speak, the sexual qualities of the objects around them. This is why there is an ancient connection between sex and food. For it is not just that we like eating and associate its pleasures with those of sex, as if we were dealing here with two intense forms of pleasure and wanted to have them both simultaneously. Rather, because we like eating anyway, and because when we eat we are profoundly aware of the *matter* of what we eat (its smoothness, greasiness and so on), we seek in sex to co-opt the experience of food to that of sex, to sexualise our food, discover its flesh, which is why a shared meal is so often a desired prelude to the sex act. Or again, fashion itself, which helps construct our sense of gender as men and women, is, amongst other things, the construction of a style through which, in the world of desire, one can be aware of the fleshliness of the material of one's clothes not simply as clothes but as representations of one's existence as man or woman. One's clothes, after all, are things constantly in contact with one's flesh, and they are therefore the first objects to whose fleshliness one responds in the world of desire: it is thus gratifying that they should be invested in such a moment with the imagery and symbolism of gender. Even the act of love itself does not rest content until it discovers to itself the flesh of objects. This is why especially manufactured sex toys are readily incorporated into the sex act itself. Such toys discover to the lovers the fleshliness of the world around them, and help preserve the fantasy that the world itself can be made over in the image of their desire, that the world is compliant to their will. Similar things may be said about the kind of fantasy clothing that typically serves to raise sexual excitement and about the materials from which it is made: leather, plastic, rubber, fur. The lovers want to discover the fleshliness of such materials which is one reason why the clothing made from such fabric is often conceptualised as a 'second skin': for in this way it can subserve the desire to be both the skin of the lover and partake of the nature of the inanimate world, thus discovering to the lovers both their own nature as flesh and the flesh of the world around them.

I referred just now to the lovers' imposition of their will on the world in the wish in sexual desire that the world itself co-operate in supporting and feeding that desire. There is something apposite about this way of speaking. For, as we have seen, in desire one is overwhelmed by one's body: the will is cancelled, especially in one's properly sexual parts. Thus we might speculate that the attempt to make the world over in the image of one's desire can be interpreted as an attempt to impose one's will at one site (the world) which has been put in abeyance at another site (the body). And this itself, if correct, deepens our understanding of the seemingly inevitable frustration of sexual desire, discussed earlier: for such an attempt is, of course, futile.

I have suggested, following Sartre, that such stratagems of desire involve an attempt to sexualise material objects. But this very attempt contains within itself its own mirror image: the desire to turn the object of sexual interest into a material object. This is clear from a great deal of pornography, for example, where the individuals presented often appear 'dollified'. Hence it is that the deeper meaning ('project', as Sartre would say) of pornography is not that of its being a substitute for a sexual partner, though, it may, of course, serve this purpose, but of its being the object of a distinctive kind of sexual desire: that, once again, of sexualising the entire world. This reaches its apotheosis, perhaps, in such wonderfully bizarre phenomena of the modern world as telephone sex, where the very emptiness of the sexual encounter – merely auditory, and devoid of tactile, olfactory, visual and gustatory qualities – together with the insistence of topic awakens the fantasy that the world of objects is a world of sexual objects, for there is no object in the world which does not subserve a sexual purpose, all other objects having been destroyed. That is, there is in this fantasy only one object – and it is a sexual object – the voice of the other person on the end of the line, and this object is omnipresent, emanating from every person because it emanates from no particular person one knows. Perhaps we should see in this some version of the Christian conception of God: for the caller speaks to the voice at the end of the line as the person in prayer speaks to God, that is, by speaking into the aether. And it is, as I have said, an omnipresent voice. Moreover, it is an omniscient voice, for it knows one's desire through and through; and omnipotent, since it can give one what one wants. There is even a kind of supplication in both the masturbator on the telephone and the believer. But, in the end, the voice is an inversion of God: for he required that one bend one's desires to his will; the voice exists merely to satisfy one's desire.

I spoke earlier of the possibility of a deepened understanding of sex. I have also spoken of the disgust which is implicit in sex. These two ways of thinking can certainly pull us in different directions, making us think of sex as now something full of grace and light, now as something mean and shabby. But they can pull in the same direction. For the experience of sex can be deeply consoling. If we ask why this is so, then a key part of the answer is surely that, given the wretchedness of the human heart and its potential to fill one with disgust, it can seem little short of a miracle that one person should consent to the intimacy with another that making love involves. In other words, in some moods it can seem that when two people make love this act will depend upon, and involve, mutual forgiveness. Responding to such a thought, some have seen in sex the possibility of a quasi-religious act. Such an idea is certainly blasphemous, but it helps us see that, in an age of decay of religious belief, there may lie secretly in the modern obsession with sex a kind of longing for a redemption no longer available in traditional terms.

There is, for some people, something melancholy in the fact that sex can be both a source of the kind of consolation I have mentioned, as well as being rampant and imperious in the way I have also discussed. We often long for it to express only the most tender of feelings. Yet one can also be glad of this discrepancy in our experience of what sex is, since it makes of sex one of those mysteries of the human condition which help us hold onto the sense that life is worth living because what it offers us is inexhaustibly rich and varied.

Notes

1. Roger Scruton, *Sexual Desire* (London: Weidenfeld & Nicolson, 1986), ch. 4.
2. Scruton, *Sexual Desire*, pp. 89–90.
3. Stefan Zweig, *Casanova: A Study in Self-Portraiture*, tr. Eden and Cedar Paul (London: Pushkin Press, 1998 [1928]), pp. 88–9.
4. Scruton, *Sexual Desire*, p. 76.
5. Ibid., pp. 362–3. Cf. also Igor Primoratz' discussion of Scruton's views in *Ethics and Sex* (London: Routledge, 1999), ch. 3.
6. Primoratz, *Ethics and Sex*, p. 46.
7. Ibid., p. 49.
8. Ludwig Wittgenstein, *Philosophical Investigations I*, tr. E. Anscombe (Oxford: Blackwell, 1983 [1953]), §66.
9. Wittgenstein, *Philosophical Investigations I*, §67.
10. Heinrich Böll, 'Im Tal der donnernden Hufe', in Böll, *Als der Krieg ausbrach: Erzählungen* (Cologne: Deutscher Taschenbuch Verlag, 1971), pp. 140–1, my translation.
11. Many of them are offered by Primoratz in *Ethics and Sex*, ch. 2.
12. D. H. Lawrence, 'A Propos of "Lady Chatterley's Lover" ', in Lawrence, *Phœnix II*, Warren Roberts and Harry T. Moore (eds) (New York: Viking Press, 1970), p. 504.
13. Jean-Paul Sartre, *Being and Nothingness*, tr. Hazel Barnes (London: Methuen, 1984 [1943]), II, iii, 2.
14. Scruton, *Sexual Desire*, p. 74; Thomas Nagel, 'Sexual Perversion', in

Nagel, *Mortal Questions* (Cambridge: Cambridge University Press, 1979), pp. 39–52.

15. This point is made by Primoratz, *Ethics and Sex*, p. 47.

16. Stuart Hampshire, *Innocence and Experience* (Harmondsworth: Penguin, 1989), pp. 125–6.

17. Sigmund Freud, '"Civilized" Sexual Morality and Modern Nervous Illness', in Freud, *Civilization, Society and Religion,* tr. Angela Richards (Harmondsworth: Penguin, 1991 [1908]), p. 50.

18. Scruton, *Sexual Desire,* p. 163.

19. Georg Büchner, *Woyzeck,* in Büchner, *Werke und Briefe,* K. Pörnbecher, G. Schaub, H.-J. Simm and E. Ziegler (eds) (Munich: Deutscher Taschenbuch Verlag, 1988), scene 7, my translation. (Büchner left behind four unfinished versions of the play when he died, and since no one knows what final order of the scenes he intended, this scene appears in a different place in the play in some published editions.)

20. William Shakespeare, *Hamlet,* Harold Jenkins (ed.) (London: Arden, 1997 [1603]), III, iv, 91–4.

21. David Pole, 'Disgust and Other Forms of Aversion', in Pole, *Aesthetics, Form and Emotion,* George Roberts (ed.) (London: Duckworth, 1983), pp. 219–31.

22. William Ian Miller, *An Anatomy of Disgust* (Cambridge, MA: Harvard University Press, 1997), p. 137.

23. A. Béjin, 'The Influence of the Sexologists', in P. Ariès and A. Béjin (eds), *Western Sexuality: Practice and Precepts in Past and Present Times* (Oxford: Basil Blackwell, 1985), p. 211.

24. Sartre, *Being and Nothingness,* p. 389.

25. Ibid., p. 392.

10

The Need to Sleep

I N THE FIRST FEW moments after he has murdered Duncan,
Macbeth wails his despair at what he has done:

> *Macbeth*
> Methought, I heard a voice cry, 'Sleep no more!
> Macbeth does murther Sleep,' – the innocent Sleep;
> Sleep, that knits up the ravell'd sleeve of care,
> The death of each day's life, sore labour's bath,
> Balm of hurt minds, great Nature's second course,
> Chief nourisher of life's feast; –
> *Lady Macbeth*
>   What do you mean?
> *Macbeth*
> Still it cried, 'Sleep no more!' to all the house:
> 'Glamis hath murther'd Sleep, and therefore Cawdor
> Shall sleep no more, Macbeth shall sleep no more!'[1]

It is incredible that these meditations on sleep are just about the *first*
thing that Macbeth says after the murder, following directly on his
complaint that 'Amen' stuck in his throat. Why is he thinking about
sleep at such a time? There are obvious dramatic reasons: Duncan has
been murdered in his sleep, his two sons are themselves asleep in the
next chamber. But there are deeper reasons which lead us into a
philosophical perspective on sleep – a topic on which there exists, to
my knowledge, no serious philosophical work at all. Of course, there
are in philosophy numerous discussions of the fact that we dream, but
this is evidently not the same as discussing the fact that we sleep.
Scientists have been more interested than philosophers in sleep, and

a lot of scientific research on sleep has been carried out, but this will not enlighten us – at least not directly – about the meaning of sleep, which is what a philosophical approach to the matter is after.

'The innocent sleep', says Macbeth. The idea, obviously enough, is that those who have a clear conscience sleep. In his book on Kafka, Pietro Citati writes:

> Sleep is the purest and most innocent of divinities: a mild blessing, which descends only on the eyelids of pure beings. Sleepless men are guilty, because they do not know the quiet of the soul and are tortured by obsession.[2]

But it is not just the innocent who have a clear conscience and thus sleep well. Akira Kurosawa made a film called *The Bad Sleep Well*. And they do sleep well just so long as they have the strength of their own evil.

An instructive case is presented by Napoleon. About one episode during his Egyptian campaign Evangeline Bruce writes:

> When the fortress of Jaffa in Palestine (now a suburb of Tel Aviv) surrendered after a short siege, it was sacked and looted and its garrison, including women and children, massacred. The army would never forget the shame of what came afterwards – the murder of three thousand Turks who had capitulated after a promise that their lives would be spared – nor the full horror of the circumstances. Three days after they had surrendered, General Bonaparte [as he then was] ordered them to be drowned or bayoneted in order to save gunpowder. He could not, he said, feed both them and his army. French troops were forced to wade in after those who attempted to swim out to sea, sometimes with their children still clinging to them.[3]

Napoleon, however, was not in the slightest bit worried by what he had done: his conscience was quite clear. He had no problem sleeping at all. In fact, Vincent Cronin writes, 'he was able to sleep at will even when guns were thundering a few yards away'. He goes on: 'This ability to sleep at will is one of the most revealing things about Napoleon. It presupposes great calm. Though his senses were sharp, and he felt things keenly, Napoleon seldom worried, and was hardly ever seriously ruffled.'[4] Unlike Macbeth, Napoleon had the strength of his evil. We can say: it is not the evil who do not sleep but the good who do bad or evil deeds and are consequently kept awake by the sting of their conscience.

Citati refers to sleep as a divinity. He is not alone. Throughout classical literature sleep appears in this guise. Those who do not sleep have not been touched by God's hand. If human beings are prepared to think of sleep as a god this suggests that sleep is one of their most fundamental needs. Why does it matter to us so much that we sleep? Why is it such a terrible thing to be unable to sleep?

Some people try to understand the fundamental needs and features of human life in the terms offered by evolutionary adaptive biology. But in the case of sleep such an explanation seems inadequate. Elias Canetti makes the point well.

> Anyone who lies down disarms himself so completely that it is impossible to understand how men have managed to survive sleep. It is true that in their primitive state they lived, when they could, in caves, but even there they were not secure; and the miserable shelter of leaves and twigs with which many had to content themselves gave no protection at all. The marvel is that there are still men in existence. One would expect them to have been exterminated long ago, when they were many fewer . . . This one fact of sleep – defenceless, recurrent, and prolonged – shows the inadequacy of all the theories of adaptation to environment which are put forward as explanations of so much that is inexplicable.[5]

It is of course true that what we seek in sleep is refreshment for the body and mind. But what kind of refreshment? Once in the newspaper there was a report of a man who had suffered an accident, some kind of a blow to the head, which left him completely unable to sleep but otherwise healthy. At night he would lie down and rest, and, in the morning, he felt as refreshed as if he had slept. Yet he craved sleep. Whether the story is true or not, it alerts us to the possibility that what we need in sleep is a very complicated and subtle form of refreshment.

Citati does not say: 'the guilty are sleepless'. He says instead: 'the sleepless are guilty'. It is true, as we have noted, that the good who do something evil cannot sleep on account of their guilty conscience. But Citati is suggesting that, regardless of whether one has done anything evil, the fact of not being able to sleep makes one guilty. The notion of what one has done and whether it is good or evil is less fundamental for a philosophical understanding of sleep than is the fact that being unable to sleep itself makes one guilty. Or, at least, many feel this way about their inability to sleep. Citati says that Kafka understood his insomnia to be his sin itself – not the *result* of his sin.

What we need in sleep is *to be rid of ourselves*. Macbeth rages about sleep because he knows that he will never be free of himself, that he must drag the ball and chain of himself – of his self – around with him until the end. The man who had the accident, despite his ability to rest and feel refreshed, was unable to be rid of himself. Life is short and we can be afflicted by the sense that there is not enough time to do everything we want to do. But even as we think this we can be oppressed by time on our hands, by the sense that there is nothing to do. We can, in short, be bored. In boredom, says Hazlitt, we want to compress all of time and arrive at a point where we are no longer bored: 'We would willingly, and without remorse, sacrifice not only the present moment, but all the interval (no matter how long) that separates us from any favourite object.'[6] And, according to Baudelaire, boredom is the worst state one can be in; we would do anything to relieve ourselves of it. Hence he says, in the preface to his *Les Fleurs du mal* (*The Flowers of Evil*), that more evil than anything else which crawls around in the human soul is that which 'would lay waste the earth quite willingly, / And in a yawn engulf creation. Boredom! Its eyes with tears unwilling shine, / It dreams of scaffolds, smoking its cheroot'. If we cannot sleep to rid ourselves of boredom then our boredom may well incite us to fantasise the rage and destruction of which Baudelaire speaks. Sleep is a central refuge to which we can repair to preserve us from this guilt.

To be unable to be rid of oneself in sleep is to be cursed, to be guilty. It is to be *alone*, excluded from the community of sleepers, from those who let the world turn peacefully on its axis and speed through the heavens. It is to feel excluded from the common lot of human beings of which sleep reminds us. For the famous and the obscure, the rich and the poor, the gifted and the dull-witted are all united in their need to sleep, in their need, once a day, to sink into oblivion. And the *attitudes* we adopt whilst asleep form a graphic reminder of this – of, one might say, the way in which we are all equally ridiculous and of the emptiness of our worldly differences from each other. The idea is wittily expressed by Leigh Hunt in a short essay on sleep.

> [S]leep plays the petrifying magician. He arrests the proudest lord as well as the humblest clown in the most ridiculous postures; so that if you could draw a grandee from his bed without waking him, no limb-twisting fool in a pantomime should create wilder laughter . . . Imagine a despot lifted up to the gaze of his valets, with his eyes shut, his mouth open, his left hand under his right ear, his other twisted and hanging helplessly before him like an idiot's; one knee lifted up, and the other leg stretched out, or both knees huddled up together. What a scarecrow to lodge majestic power in![7]

Sleeplessness means feeling that there is no one to help one, that the common bond of humanity is broken. The only others who are not sleeping either need as much help as one does oneself, or they have forced themselves to stay awake to help – to sit, perhaps, at the end of a telephone line and take one's call. There is no one who can help simply because he *happens* to be there. He is there to help, if he is, by design: he has *planned* to stay awake. There is no one at night, as there is during the day, who will help simply through a spontaneous gesture of warmth of heart. Such are the thoughts of the man or woman who cannot sleep as he or she lies in agony: they are the thoughts of one who feels himself excluded from all community, from all fellowship. To be unable to sleep is to be like a leper, an untouchable.

It is because sleep reminds us that as human beings we share in a common lot that Macbeth wails that he has murdered sleep itself. For, in doing what he has done, he has excluded himself from the community of men and women. And we each of us, to a greater or lesser extent according to temperament, need the community of others to preserve us. This is why Lady Macbeth says to her husband: 'You lack the season of all natures, sleep.' What she has in mind is the kind of seasoning that salt is, that is, a seasoning which preserves. Macbeth lacks the community that can preserve him.

The failure of sleep is one of the themes played on in the figure of Dracula in order to make clear this character's expulsion from the community. In a sense, his condition is worse than that of Macbeth since he sleeps, but does so during the day. He is the unhuman, whereas Macbeth, in his ambition and crime, is human, all too human. Yet Dracula's sleep during the day is not all it seems, for it is not the extinction of consciousness that sleep is for mortal men and women, where it intimates death and, in a sense, helps prepare us for it. The Count's sleep is more a kind of biding time, a waiting for the moment at which he can disturb the sleep of others and bring them into his realm of darkness. For he is deathless, at least so long as he is not caught by the rays of the sun. Hence the irony of the fact that he sleeps in a coffin: this is a coffin which brings none of the rest to be found in death. Werner Herzog's Dracula, in his film *Nosferatu*, articulates his expulsion from the human community by saying that his life is completely devoid of love, and by this he clearly means the kind of sexual love that can exist between a man and a woman. And the reference to sexual love is linked to the motif of sleep in the film. For, at least until fairly recently, sexual joy has usually been confined in both literature and film to a world of darkness that exists off the page or off-screen, mirroring a pervasive feature of quotidian existence. The darkness in which Nosferatu lives is one which cannot know this joy. His craving for love is of a piece with his craving for sleep, the longing to use darkness as ordinary mortals do to hide two of their most catastrophic experiences: the eclipse of the mind in sleep and sex. We sleep at night, in the dark, not simply because we are less able to negotiate the world at this time than during the day. After all, modern technology can erase for us the darkness of night, if we wish this. We sleep at night because we need to hide from each other the total vanquishing of the soul by the body in sleep, this shameful reminder of our inability ever to escape our corporeal nature. A. Alvarez says in *Night* that, when he went to a hospital in South London to visit a sleep investigation unit and watched one patient sleep, he felt that he should not be there, that he was invading the patient's privacy. The nurse in charge of the unit felt the same way about her observation of her patients.[8]

It is not just the evil-doer, like Macbeth, or the figure of horror, like Dracula, whose exclusion from the community is symbolised by lack of sleep. In the Garden of Gethsemane Christ prayed that his cup might pass from him, but three times he found Peter, James and John asleep even as he had asked them to keep awake and pray. They slept, comfortable in their humanity, in their ordinary human condition, whilst Christ, whose passion was shortly to begin, was utterly alone. The truly good man, like Christ, can be, perhaps always is, as excluded from the community of human beings as is the evil man. Why should this be? Hannah Arendt has suggested a line of response. Discussing the nature of goodness and good acts, she writes:

> [G]oodness . . . harbors a tendency to hide from being seen or heard . . . For it is manifest that the moment a good work becomes known and public, it loses its specific character of goodness, of being done for nothing but goodness' sake. When goodness appears openly, it is no longer goodness, though it may still be useful as organized charity or an act of solidarity. Therefore: 'Take heed that ye do not your alms before men, to be seen of them.' Goodness can exist only when it is not perceived, not even by its author; whoever sees himself performing a good work is no longer good, but at best a useful member of society or a dutiful member of a church. Therefore: 'Let not thy left hand know what thy right hand doeth.'[9]

She draws from this line of reflection the following conclusion: 'The man who is in love with goodness . . . must remain essentially without testimony and lacks first of all the company of himself . . . [W]hen living with others he must hide from them . . .'.[10] Christ, then, can never actually be part of any human community in the fullness of what he is, and neither can any other truly good man or woman. If Christ must keep awake whilst his disciples sleep, this is a literal expression of the fact that he must keep awake so that he not be tempted to relax his vigilance and become a merely useful man. Which is not to say that he guards his goodness – for, as Arendt says, were he to have knowledge of his goodness, his goodness would vanish. It is rather that he must keep watch over what he must do. The focus of his thoughts is not what he is but what his task is. Hence the appropriateness of the reference to Christ's sleeplessness in the Garden of Gethsemane just before his Passion.

Nevertheless, however important sleep is to us as a symbol of our community with others, we can come to fear sleep. For in sleep we lose ourselves. When we worry or feel guilty or are anxious we can be glad because at least in these feelings we are brought up against ourselves in a peculiarly acute and stark way. This is why we can reap such happiness from worrying and the like. We are, in such a state, at least aware of our own existence. Further, sleeplessness can, we like to think, testify to our sensitive apprehension of the world: we are not dull like those who can so easily sink into oblivion. And whilst asleep we are subject to an immense lassitude of will which runs counter to our usual desire to be aware of what is going on, plan for possibilities, be on our guard, keep a watch over – and keep up – the compulsive round of our thoughts. And that can be so frightening that we can come to want the curse of insomnia. We can come to be afraid of something – sleep – which we crave.

In fearing the loss of ourselves in sleep, however, what we fear at the most fundamental level is the passage of time, the flow of time over us that leaves no mark on our existence. In refusing to let ourselves sleep even as we crave it, we are seeking *to arrest the flow of time*. Citati says of Kafka's solitary nights alone, writing: 'He would have liked to cancel day and summer, dawn and sunset, prolong the night beyond its brief confines, transforming it into an interminable winter.'[11] Kafka wanted time to come to a halt. Western culture since Christianity has been marked by the same fantasy. Insofar as we are able to understand it, and insofar as the faith of Christians allows them to try and imagine it, existence with God is supposed to be like a healthy sleeplessness, a condition in which there is no flow of time but in which all our faculties are at their sharpest and the mind does not prey upon itself in worry and anxiety.

Animals, in one perfectly good sense, never sleep. What we call sleep in an animal actually marks nothing more than a change in *degree* in the animal's consciousness, whereas in a human being sleep marks a change in *kind* from wakening consciousness. For animals never feel the need to be rid of themselves as a person does; they are never burdened by themselves. This is because animals live only in the present. And hence we can so easily envy them. In an early essay, Nietzsche makes the point with style:

> Behold the cattle grazing near you: they know nothing of yesterday or today, jump around, eat, rest, digest, jump again, and so on from morning until night and from day to day, accepting both their pleasures and displeasures, that is, bound to the moment and therefore neither melancholy nor bored. This is a hard sight for man, for he tells himself that in his humanity he is superior to the animals, but he looks with envy at their happiness – for he wants nothing but to live like an animal, neither bored nor in pain, and yet this is a futile desire because he refuses to have such things in the way an animal has them.[12]

We sleep, of course, in a special piece of furniture, a bed, and in a special room, a bedroom. Yet human beings have, of course, not always separated off a special place for sleeping, and in medieval society it was normal to receive visitors in rooms that contained beds. Moreover, it was normal for many people even in the upper classes to sleep together in the one room – the master with his servants, the mistress with her maid or maids. We often wear special clothing, a nightshirt or pyjamas, when we sleep. About the clothing that we wear at night Norbert Elias has written:

> A special nightdress only came into use roughly at the same time as the fork and handkerchief. Like the other 'implements of civilization,' it made its way through Europe quite gradually. And like them it is a symbol of the decisive change taking place at this time in human beings. Sensitivity toward everything that came into contact with the body increased. Shame became attached to behavior that had previously been free of such feelings.[13]

Part of what Elias is getting at is that the increased use of such pieces of equipment as the nightdress and all that goes with it has helped us to constitute an area of life which we call 'private life' and which we separate from the rest of our activities that we think of as our public or social life. Correlatively, such implements have helped us develop rituals which prepare us for sleep – washing or bathing, cleaning the teeth and so on. As such, they serve symbolically and practically in helping us complete that task by which we are faced once every twenty-four hours, namely, bringing the day to an end. This need to bring the day to an end in a private sphere has become in the modern world increasingly central to our understanding of adult life and the responsibilities it brings with it, for in our bureaucratised and managed world we live our days under the critical glare of our fellows and the private sphere and its rituals constitute a retreat from this where we may put that exposure to the scrutiny of others behind us. Some such point about the relation between sleep and adult life is made by Robert Musil in *Die Verwirrungen des Zöglings Törleß* (*Young Törleß*), his masterly study of adolescence. At one point the narrator says this of the central figure:

> The patient plans which, without his noticing it, bind together for the adult the days, months, and years, were unknown to him. And so, equally, was that dullness of sensibility which is never even puzzled when yet another day comes to an end. His life was focused on each day. Each night was for him a nothing, a grave, it meant being extinguished. The ability to lie down every day and die without reflecting on what it all meant was something he had not yet learnt.[14]

The child or adolescent who does not yet know that negotiation of the adult with himself and the world which involves the permanent necessity and strain of matching means to ends and vice versa sleeps from biological necessity, and he resents and is puzzled by the requirement to sleep when the body does not require it. For adults, things are different. We need to mark out our lives into stages or fragments. For most of what we have to do in life is unmanageable taken as a whole. We have to break up our time into manageable units or segments, to have an overview of the tasks by which we are faced, to relax the appalling self-surveillance which modern existence demands of us. Sleeping and carrying out the rituals connected with it in privacy enable us to do this better.

Sleeplessness, especially over a long period of time, returns us to the condition of a child: we are irritated by the smallest things; we wish to bicker and squabble; we want the world to be warm and snug, and we see it as hostile and dangerous. The fatigue of long-term sleeplessness makes us want to hurt others: in such a condition we lose, if only temporarily, our conscience and we become like the child, a creature of monstrous egoism and self-concern. Sleeplessness is, after all, like a disease and, as Johnson remarked, 'Disease produces much selfishness. A man in pain is *looking after ease*.'[15] In all the work on the philosophy of crime, no thought has been given, so far as I know, to the part that fatigue plays in sin. How many would have lived out their days in peace if only they could have slept, but instead have ended up punished and ruined, we do not know. The idea may seem bizarre, but Chekov at least would not have thought so. He wrote a short story, 'Sleep . . . Sleep . . .', in which a nursemaid loses herself through lack of sleep and strangles the crying baby in the cot that she might have silence and sleep.

Lady Macbeth does not suffer from the disease of sleeplessness. Her disease is that of a sleep which is itself disturbed, for she walks in her sleep. This is part of her having bad dreams or nightmares. It is not just the ability to sleep that symbolises for us our position as part of the community of human beings but also the *quality* of our sleep. Discussing Kafka's sleep, Citati says:

> In the evening he fell asleep, but after an hour he woke up as though he had placed his head in the wrong hole. He was perfectly awake, had the impression of not having slept at all or having slept covered by a very thin skin, and he still had ahead of him the effort of falling asleep. Then he fell asleep again; his body slept alongside itself, while his self thrashed about and struggled with dreams.[16]

The only sleep of which Kafka was capable was thus a sleep which made him in even greater need than he would otherwise have been of escaping himself.

Kafka's dreams were like wild animals which crawled up out of him when he went to sleep. He felt that there were *animals living in him* over which he had no control and which would come out whilst he slept. Why was this? The animal, I have said, does not sleep in the way human beings do: it does not feel the need to be rid of itself. The animals that inhabited Kafka's body and came out at night in his fitful sleep (when he slept) were thus received by him as a *rebuke to his condition as a man*, a rebuke to the fact that he needed, as we all do, to rid himself of himself in sleep, but could not do so. But Kafka did not just dream that he was inhabited by animals. He dreamt also that he was animal. Citati entitles the chapter in his book on which I have been drawing here 'The Writer as Animal'. But the kind of animal that Kafka could actually envisage himself as being was one that could only be an even greater burden to itself than a man or woman is to him- or herself. He dreamt of himself as being a huge insect which yet had a man's mind, a man's hopes, fears and wishes. Not for him some of the metamorphoses that Ovid discusses in which human beings find peace in being transformed into animals.

In his sleep, then, as much as in his sleeplessness, there was for Kafka no escape from himself. To a greater or lesser extent we all of us share in Kafka's situation, for we are all of us sometimes disturbed by dreams which means that we are not even free from ourselves in sleep. And if our dreams wake us then, whilst we may be relieved that, if they are bad dreams, they are now over, we are nevertheless left with the darkness and silence of the night which can make us feel lonelier than ever.

Notes

1. William Shakespeare, *Macbeth*, Kenneth Muir (ed.) (London: Arden, 1997 [1623]), II, ii, 34–42.
2. Pietro Citati, *Kafka*, tr. Raymond Rosenthal (London: Secker & Warburg, 1990), pp. 53–4.
3. Evangeline Bruce, *Napoleon and Josephine: An Improbable Marriage* (London: Orion, 1996), p. 248.
4. Vincent Cronin, *Napoleon* (Harmondsworth: Penguin, 1976), pp. 227–8.
5. Elias Canetti, *Crowds and Power*, tr. Carol Stewart (Harmondsworth: Penguin, 1973), pp. 453–4.
6. William Hazlitt, 'On the Love of Life', in Hazlitt, *The Round Table (Essays on Literature, Men and Manners)* (New York: Chelsea House, 1983 [1817]), p. 2.
7. Leigh Hunt, 'A Few Thoughts on Sleep', in Hunt, *Selected Essays* (London: Dent, 1929), pp. 261–2.
8. A. Alvarez, *Night* (London: Jonathan Cape, 1994), p. 72.
9. Hannah Arendt, *The Human Condition* (Chicago: University of Chicago Press, 1958), p. 74.
10. Arendt, *The Human Condition*, p. 76.
11. Citati, *Kafka*, pp. 54–5.
12. Nietzsche, 'Vom Nutzen und Nachtheil der Historie für das Leben', *Unzeitgemäße Betrachtungen II*, §1, in Giorgio Colli and Mazzino Montinari (eds), *Sämtliche Werke: Kritische Studienausgabe in 15 Einzelbänden* (Berlin: Walter de Gruyter, 1980), vol. 1, my translation.
13. Norbert Elias, *The Civilizing Process*, tr. Edmund Jephcott (Oxford: Basil Blackwell, 1995 [1939]), p. 135.
14. Robert Musil, *Die Verwirrungen des Zöglings Törleß* (Hamburg: Rowohlt, 1991 [1906]), p. 34, my translation.
15. Quoted in Walter Jackson Bate, *Samuel Johnson* (London: Hogarth Press, 1978), p. 9.
16. Citati, *Kafka*, p. 54.

11

The Fear of Death

O UR GREATEST FEAR IS that of death. This being so, many
philosophers have sought perspectives on death which help
to alleviate our fear of it. Of course, those with a traditional Christian
belief can be presumed to have such help through their faith. But
supposing one does not have this faith, what kind of consolation can
philosophical reflection provide?

The most well-known argument offered in philosophy to console us
in our fear of death – indeed, to rid us of it – is that of Lucretius.[1]
According to him, our fear of death is based on a confusion, namely,
that of supposing we shall have some experiences when dead. We
suppose, that is, that, once we are dead, we will in some sense still be
around to lament our own sufferings, such as the cremation of our
body, and, indeed, the very fact of our no longer existing. But we
shall, of course, no longer be around at all once we are dead, and are
thus beyond being harmed. Lucretius says that the situation after
death is symmetrical with that which obtained before our birth: just as
all the ages which passed before our birth were then, as now, nought
to us, since we did not then suffer good or ill, being non-existent, so,
after we are dead, all the ages that are yet to come will be nothing to
us, for we shall once again be non-existent.

Very few philosophers have agreed with Lucretius in seeing a
symmetry between the time before we were born and the time after
our death. In disagreeing, they have sought to indicate just what kind
of harm death is for us. Thomas Nagel has suggested that, although
we will no longer be once we are dead, death is still a loss and harm to
us, just as someone's betrayal of us is a loss and a harm, even when we

do not know we have been betrayed.[2] And Martha Nussbaum has suggested that the harm of death depends upon the fact that all our projects and patterns of life – work, love, marriage, citizenship and so on – demand a temporally extended structure for their pursuit, and that such a structure is cut off when we die.[3]

These arguments are certainly not irrelevant to understanding the harm that death is, but, I think, they fail properly to understand the nature of death in relation to human existence. This is because they understand it to be simply an event at the end of life, something towards which one moves through life. But, as Heidegger pointed out,[4] death does not enter into a human life in this way: it is not – or not simply – some event at the end, marking the outer limit of a life. It has a more intimate relation with life as it is lived.

There is a sense in which we die throughout a life. I do not mean that the body is always slowly decaying towards death, or something of that order – though this is of course true. I mean, rather, that in many of our activities as human beings we have a sense of the presence of death. Thus there are many ways in which unanticipated forms of weakness, cowardice, compromise, loss, self-betrayal and so on are knit up into the fabric of our interactions with ourselves and each other. It may seem an exaggeration to call these an experience of death, but it is not. For they are precisely the kinds of experiences which can lead us to describe our life as a living death. Our compromises and ways of betraying ourselves can gradually corrode us until we are dead within: it is as if death were within our life, eating away at it, never to be escaped just because it is already inside. Hence we readily identify a life without such compromises as one in which there is no death: Adam and Eve, lodged in the wholeness and completeness of life which was paradise, knew no death before they ate from the tree of knowledge of good and evil. Christ promised eternal life as a form of existence which knew no compromise or human frailty.

It was, perhaps, such reflections on the presence of death in life which led Heidegger to argue that most of us are embroiled in what he called an inauthentic relationship to death. His thinking on this point is very complicated and, in part, very dark, but he seems to have had something like the following in mind. He brings the notion of death into connection with that of authenticity. For Heidegger, we all have a tendency to follow what he calls *das Man*, which is a sub-stantivised form of the impersonal pronoun *man*, in English: 'one' (compare the French '*on*'). *Das Man* is, roughly, public opinion, and in following what *das Man* does the individual is (thoughtlessly) following what *they* do, the *others*, simply in order to fit in. In doing this, one stands in an inauthentic relationship to what one is, for one is behaving as if one had no individuality, no independent centre of action and thought. Heidegger suggests that this inauthenticity comes out also in one's relationship to one's own death. We suppress all thoughts of our death, terrified of it as we are, and in this way fail to own up to what we are, namely, individuals, with our own life to lead. And, indeed, there is a way, for Heidegger, in which to follow *das Man*, to be inauthentic, just is to have an inauthentic relation to death.[5] For his idea is that at least many of the compromises we make in our life are, as I suggested, forms of death in life and that we commit them often simply because we are following *das Man*. Heidegger concluded from this that our mortality gives our life meaning, or can do so, since its presence challenges us to find our own authentic individuality.

Whether one finds any consolation in one's fear of death from such a way of looking at things is probably going to be a matter of temperament. After all, if death is a presence in life in the way discussed this is more likely, perhaps, to fill one with despair at the whole thing. Heidegger probably did not mean that one should spend a great deal of time mulling over death, but if one starts to look at things in his way one may find that such thoughts come to one whether one will or no. I suspect that there is more likely to be consolation in the recognition that death is present in life in certain situations where we suffer a welcome extinction of consciousness. One of these, obviously enough, is sleep, and the image of sleep's being the brother of death is common. Or again, our mind and spirit suffer temporary obliteration in sexual ecstasy. And these experiences are ones we welcome into our lives, indeed, often crave. But our need for sleep and sex rises and falls, waxes and wanes. Hence, our experience of them – two of the standing conditions of human existence, to which any philosophy must pay attention if it is to understand the nature of human existence – can give us a sense that the life of each of us is cyclical. Yet if, from the inside view on our life, we welcome certain forms of extinction of the mind as part of a cycle, this might help us gain a sense that our life viewed from the outside is also part of a cycle, that is, part of the cycle of nature wherein we must yield our place to others. That is, the temporary but repeated and welcome obliteration of the mind in life can in some way seem to find or seek its fitting completion in the total closing of the mind in death as part of a bigger cycle of growth and decay. A certain understanding of sleep and sex can thus, perhaps, provide some consolation for our mortality.

For some, as for Philip Larkin, all that will seem inadequate.

> The mind blanks at the glare. Not in remorse
> – The good not done, the love not given, time
> Torn off unused – nor wretchedly because
> An only life can take so long to climb
> Clear of its wrong beginnings, and may never;
> But at the total emptiness for ever,
> The sure extinction that we travel to
> And shall be lost in always. Not to be here,
> Not to be anywhere,
> And soon; nothing more terrible, nothing more true.[6]

Yet *is* there no way of ameliorating the terror we feel in the face of death, a terror so palpably present in Larkin's poem? Maupassant once commented: 'I am always thinking of my poor Flaubert and I would like to be dead if I knew for sure that someone would think of me as I think of him.'[7] It is a fine sentiment. Assuming that Maupassant was sincere and not being frivolous in what he said, it seems clear that he found some consolation for his own mortality in the thought that he might be the object of another's love and reverence as Flaubert was for him. Flaubert lived on, one might say, as the object of obligations on Maupassant's part, for if Maupassant had come to forget his love for Flaubert then he would have judged that a moral failure, a kind of betrayal. Of course, in one sense this kind of thing is not at all unfamiliar. The dead often figure in our thoughts as the object of certain obligations, as when we erect gravestones and other votary objects or hold ceremonies of remembrance. But the case with Maupassant is somewhat different because there is here a *personal* obligation, not an obligation like that which one might take oneself to have, for example, to those who died for one's (and their) country long before one was born. Maupassant could feel as he did about Flaubert after the latter's death because he, Maupassant, was grateful for the personal generosity Flaubert had shown him.

It is possible, however, that Maupassant's way of looking at things can deepen one's terror of death because one might live on, not as the object of others' love, but of their scorn or contempt. The point is finely expressed by D. H. Lawrence.

Old men, old obstinate men and women
dare not die, because in death
their hardened souls are washed with fire, and washed and seared
till they are softened back to life-stuff again, against which they
   hardened themselves.[8]

In another poem Lawrence writes:

Oh build your ship of death, oh build it in time
and build it lovingly, and put it between the hands of your soul.

Once outside the gate of this walled silvery life of days,
once outside, upon the grey marshes, where lost souls moan
in millions, unable to depart,
having no boat to launch upon the shaken, soundless,
deepest and longest of seas,
once outside the gate,
what will you do, if you have no ship of the soul?[9]

Lawrence speaks here of the soul, and of the fate of the soul, after
death. The philosopher will, if he is moved by such speech, be
burdened by the worry about how to understand it – assuming, that
is, that one cannot take such talk at face value as indicating the soul's
literal survival of the death of the body. For if he cannot take it
literally, but cannot find a way to understand what Lawrence says such
that the intellect is satisfied, he will suspect that what Lawrence says
may well be emotionally or spiritually appealing but strictly speaking
false. And should one not seek to divest oneself of such empty
emotions, however appealing or spiritually sustaining?[10] Whence
the idea that philosophy works to disenchant the world. 'Do not
all charms fly / At the mere touch of cold philosophy?', as Keats has
it.[11]

   If there is any consolation for our mortality in these lines – as there
seems to be – then we shall have to look in a different direction. It
seems to me, as it seems to many, that such lines of Lawrence's will
always be able to move men and women if they are worthy of their
humanity. What this means is that they challenge us to come to a finer
and more sensitive response to life around us. They hold out the
possibility of a fuller, richer existence and in doing so they open up
for us the possibility of a relationship to life in all its forms which helps
us to see life itself as a gift. In one sense, of course, much art aims at
the same thing, which is why some have seen art as the highest of
activities and, on occasion, as some kind of substitute for religious
belief. But Lawrence's poem explicitly turns our thoughts towards

death, and, in so doing, helps us bring the thought of death into connection with those better possibilities of living I mentioned. But this means that it challenges us to seek to view our own death not as a moment at which we shall lament the failures and wasted chances of our life but as a moment in which we can rejoice in what has been. In other words, it challenges us to live from now on in such a way that we shall, at the moment of our death, be able to look at our own life in the way described. Our ship of death is nothing we shall have after death, Lawrence is saying, but something we can build now, in life and for life. But that ship, if we have built it, will, he suggests further, carry us over into death without our succumbing to despair. Lawrence's poem, therefore, renews the ancient wisdom that it is by truly living for life that we can prepare ourselves for death and be consoled for the fact that one day we must die.

At one point in Proust's *A la recherche du temps perdu* the narrator says the following:

> I feel that there is much to be said for the Celtic belief that the souls of those whom we have lost are held captive in some inferior being, in an animal, in a plant, in some inanimate object, and thus effectively lost to us until the day (which to many never comes) when we happen to pass by the tree or to obtain possession of the object which forms their prison. Then they start to tremble, they call us by our name, and as soon as we have recognised their voice the spell is broken. Delivered by us, they have overcome death and return to share our life.[12]

The narrator is led to find that there is a lot to say for the Celtic belief on account of an experience of his to which it is similar. In a famous passage, Proust's narrator describes his experience on mixing some pieces of madeleine – a kind of cake – in some tea and drinking the mixture.

> No sooner had the warm liquid mixed with the crumbs touched my palate then a shudder ran through me and I stopped, intent upon the extraordinary thing that was happening to me. An exquisite pleasure had invaded my senses, something isolated, detached, with no suggestion of origin. And at once the vicissitudes of life had become indifferent to me, its disasters innocuous, its brevity illusory . . . I had ceased now to feel mediocre, contingent, mortal.[13]

What the narrator realises, as he struggles to understand the nature and meaning of this experience, is that the taste of the madeleine mixed with the tea reawakens in him the memory, long thought dead, of an earlier period of his life when he had drunk tea in which pieces of madeleine had been soaked. His own past had lain trapped in the taste of the tea and cake and was waiting there to be released. And this release could only happen by chance – the chance of drinking, once again, morsels of madeleine soaked in tea. In coming into contact once again with his past, the narrator feels that his own former soul is given back to him, reawakened from the dead and joined with his present soul so that the waste and pointlessness of the intervening years – in short, his mortality – is overcome.

There is little doubt that the narrator's experience is a mystical experience. It has all the features of such, helpfully listed by William James in *The Varieties of Religious Experience*: ineffability, the inability properly to be described in words; noetic quality, the sense of opening up depths of experience not normally encountered in everyday life; transience; and passivity, the sense of the will's being in abeyance. Moreover, the narrator's experience corresponds to many of the mystical experiences James reports and discusses.[14] And some at least of these involve a sense of overcoming death. Thus Tennyson, who himself had mystical experiences, said that in such an occurrence it seemed that 'death was an almost laughable impossibility'.[15]

It goes without saying that most of us have not had a mystical experience, and probably not many more have had the memory experience – involuntary memory, as Proust's narrator calls it – which we find in *A la recherche*. But that some have had such an experience is beyond doubt. Similarly, I doubt that many of us have had the 'Celtic experience'. Yet there seems no good reason to deny that it can happen and that it might happen to us. The philosophical issue is what to make of it. For just as Proust's narrator does not pretend that the experience with the madeleine shows that he is *literally* immortal or that his soul was *literally* trapped in some material object, neither does he believe – and nor should we – that the souls of those we love are *literally* trapped in some material object. Yet these disclaimers do nothing to impugn the value and human significance of the experience.

Places and objects matter to us in strange, even mysterious ways. They often become heavily invested with an emotional charge for us as a result of experiences we have with them or on account of our relations with people with whom we associate them and so on. Artists and others often make use of this, as, for example, Ingmar Bergman did in his masterpiece of a film *Wild Strawberries*, in which the aged professor returns to the house where he had spent summers as a boy and finds that he is thrown by the memories the house carries for him into profound reflections on his time then and his life since. A further example, beautiful and moving, is provided by Raimond Gaita in some reflections on his childhood in Australia.

> [T]he glorious, tall, burnt-yellow grasses (as a boy they came to my chest and sometimes over my head) moving irregularly against a deep blue sky, dominated the images of my childhood and gave colour to my freedom and also to my understanding of suffering. In the morning they inspired cheerful energy of the kind that made you whistle; at midday, in partnership with an unforgiving sun and alive with insects and other creatures, they intimidated; but in the late afternoon, towards dusk, everything was softened by a light that graced the area in a melancholy beauty that could pierce one's soul . . .
>
> Religion, metaphysics or the notions of fate and character as they inform tragedy are suited to that light and landscape . . .[16]

The Celtic experience draws on such possibilities of human life. Perhaps what happens is that our friend loved or found solace in some place or object, or in some peculiar combination of colour and light. Then, when we find ourselves in this place, come across this object or are confronted by these sensations, we suddenly respond to what we see, or feel, or taste as we know our friend responded. It is, perhaps, a response on our part which is new to us, or which we had shared with our friend when he was alive, but which had seemed lost to us. And thus his sense of the world comes flooding in on us, and we feel that we are on the inside of his view on life, not standing outside, observing. We are, we feel, looking at the world through his eyes. This may seem odd or obscure, but actually it is familiar from an analogous case: art. According to Proust, the artist embodies and expresses in his work his own utterly unique view on existence, his sense of what the world looks like through his eyes. And it is the value of art that we come to know this point of view by attending to the artist's work. But most of us are, of course, not artists, and we have to content ourselves with something less than the creation of works. For many, the artistic work of others can make good our own inability to create, and the objects a given artist produces can become central to our own view on life. A painting or a poem or a piece of music can come to express our sense of existence, not just that of the artist. And if a particular work of art means a lot to our friend then one central way in which we can reach an understanding of his sense of life is through that work of art. We might say: if we respond to the work of art as our friend does, then we are suddenly no longer in that condition of spiritual loneliness which characterises the normal run of life, but are, for a moment, at one with another. I take it that something like this is what F. R. Leavis meant when he remarked that a work of art is a place where one mind can communicate fully with another. That this communication may not often take place does not mean it cannot happen. And in the Celtic experience, I suggest, the same kind of communication takes place. We might express this by saying that the soul of our dead friend was trapped in whatever natural object it was to which we responded as our friend had responded.

If one ever has such an experience it will be something to which one will feel the need to bear witness. How might this be manifested? Here is a suggestion. A sense that the soul of someone we have loved has lain trapped in some object or animal will encourage us to cultivate a loving attention to the material conditions of existence and to have at the same time a sense that part of what it is that we value in those objects is human mortality, that we can only truly find delight in the material world because one day we shall 'have shuffled off this mortal coil'. This idea seems to find expression in Wim Wenders' extraordinary film *Der Himmel über Berlin*, known in English as *Wings of Desire*. In this film, one of the angels chooses to become mortal because he has become tired of a purely spiritual existence. He longs to eat a meal, to feel his bones as he walks, to feed the cat, to blacken his fingers from reading the newspaper, to get fever, to stretch out his legs after a long day . . . He wants all these things even though it will mean that he will one day die. Perhaps one could say: because it means he will die. The suggestion is clearly that we could not marvel at the corporeality of existence unless we paid for it with our mortality. The two are part of the one experience, and the idea that the dead souls of those we have loved are trapped in some material object or animal helps to remind us of this feature of our existence. It is possible, if we are lucky, that in this we might find some consolation for our mortality.

Hazlitt writes:

> The effeminate clinging to life as such, as a general or abstract idea, is the effect of a highly civilised and artificial state of society. Men formerly plunged into the vicissitudes and dangers of war, or staked their all upon a single die, or some one passion, which if they could not have gratified, life became a burthen to them – now our strongest passion is to think, our chief amusement is to read new plays, new poems, new novels, and this we may do at our leisure, in perfect security, *ad infinitum*.[17]

Certainly Hazlitt has a point. His complaint is part of a concern which many thinkers have been raising for at least two hundred years. That is the complaint of the 'atrophy of the heart and the dulling of the senses in a world where conformism and commerce, the civil service and bourgeois taboos, have taken the place of heroism and adventure'.[18] Hazlitt goes on: 'A life of action and danger moderates the dread of death. It not only gives us fortitude to bear pain, but teaches us at every step the precarious tenure on which we hold our present being.'[19]

Nothing could be more alien to the spirit of his – and our – age than that of Hazlitt's comments. And he is, in fact, offering us an ancient understanding of death. It is one which we find in the pre-Christian, pagan world. For the Greeks and the Romans, a life without honour was of no real value: better to die with honour than to live on without it. Christian thought, on the other hand, is in many ways hostile to the notion of honour since honour has to do with worldly success and standing, something which Christianity scorns. Of course, Christian thought never completely eradicated the pagan view of the relation between honour and life, and often it existed in an uneasy truce with pagan thinking. But that our post-Christian moral thinking, which has been deeply and decisively influenced by that religion, in many ways carries a scepticism about the pagan view is beyond doubt. The ancients would have been aghast at our belief in the value of life even in a state of mental or physical eclipse and would have mocked our strenuous attempts to preserve ourselves even when in such a condition.

A tremendous example of the ancient conception of the relation between death and honour is to be found in Herodotus.[20] Solon tells Croesus the story of a lady who was in danger of arriving late for the festival of Hera: the two oxen required for taking her to the temple were not available. Her two sons, Cleobis and Biton, harnessed themselves to the cart and dragged their mother some six miles to her destination. Joyous at her sons' devotion and strength, the lady prayed that they might have the greatest blessing that could befall them. After the festivities, everyone slept, including the two boys. But the boys never woke, for the gods had granted them what their mother had wished for them: the greatest blessing of a mortal man. 'A heaven-sent proof of how much better it is to be dead than alive', comments Solon. Statues of the two were made and sent to Delphi to celebrate their glory. It would be hard to find a better example to illustrate Hazlitt's comments.

There are two aspects to the perspective on death which such an example provides. The first is that of a 'timely' death. This is the idea of the glory of a death suffered at the height of one's powers and achievements. And, as the example from Herodotus shows, if one values such a death one will be able to find consolation even in a demise seemingly absurd. This classical idea – or ideal – has sometimes been alive in much later thinkers. For example, Goethe, who had in many ways a deeply pagan sensibility, wrote an essay on Winckelmann, the great eighteenth-century scholar of Greek art. At the end of the essay he speaks of Winckelmann's murder in Trieste.

> [I]n possession of the greatest happiness he could have wished for, Winckelmann departed from this world. His fatherland awaited him, his friends reached out to welcome him, and all the expressions of love he so much craved for, all the testimonies of public esteem he valued so highly were about to be lavished on him as soon as he arrived. And in this respect we may well call him fortunate, for he ascended to the realm of the blessed from the summit of human existence . . . He did not experience the infirmities of age or the waning of his mental powers . . . He lived as a man, and as a complete man he went from hence. He now enjoys in the remembrance of posterity the distinction of appearing eternally able and eternally strong.[21]

The second aspect of the kind of heroic death which the example from Herodotus provides is that in the ancient world the celebration of the death of heroes was central in giving to a group of people a sense of itself as a community. And those who were thus celebrated possessed a kind of immortality. We have not, of course, completely lost this sense of immortality, but the experience of community is now so weak in the highly fragmented societies of the West (and elsewhere) that that sense is but a pale shadow of what it once was. We are left to face our own death more or less as individuals, devoid of the idea that, once we are dead, we could live on as part of the ranks of those to whom the community is permanently and irrevocably indebted. This is, according to Hannah Arendt, but one aspect of the destruction of our political life which is at present proceeding apace.[22]

Yet if the kind of honour ethic which enabled the ancients and others to find a certain kind of consolation for death is largely lost to the modern world there is perhaps an analogy to this which is available to modern people. For I suspect that many find some consolation for their mortality in the thought that when they die they will go through what others have gone through. I do not mean the suffering that is often the prelude to death. I mean the very fact of being dead. Thus, a friend of mine once said to me that he drew a certain consolation from the thought that, as many of those he admired are dead, when he died he would be in the same condition as they are, joining them in their condition of death. But is this anything more than the illusion that after one's death one will in some sense still be around to meet those one admires? Does this consolation express anything more than the inability which we all share to imagine our own extinction?

There is, perhaps, a more generous way of understanding the thought in question. We could perhaps see it as an invocation of an imaginative vision of man according to which all human beings share the same fate, the same doom, which is death. It invokes a sense of solidarity with one's fellow man, indeed, provides a way in which it makes sense to think of another human being as a fellow man. Were we immortal, one could say, we would not be able to look upon one another as fellow human beings as we are now able to, for we would be devoid of the sense that each of us is on a journey between birth and death, a journey so strange and perilous that much will go wrong in it and there will be no time to make good the loss.

Perhaps, then, my friend was expressing such a sense of fellowship when he spoke of drawing consolation from the fact that many of those he admired are dead. And perhaps he was right to draw consolation from such a thought. But the highways and byways of human self-deception are legion, and it may be that one can find no true consolation in this, just as one may, in the end, see no real consolation in any of the other perspectives on death I have discussed. Perhaps, as Conrad suggests, only those who have confronted death know its full horror.

> I have wrestled with death. It is the most unexciting contest you can imagine. It takes place in an impalpable greyness, with nothing underfoot, with nothing around, without spectators, without clamour, without glory, without the great desire for victory, without the great fear of defeat, in a sickly atmosphere of tepid scepticism, without belief in your own right, and still less in that of your adversary. If such is the form of ultimate wisdom, then life is a greater riddle than some of us think it to be.[23]

Notes

1. Lucretius, *On the Nature of the Universe,* tr. R. E. Latham, rev. John Godwin (Harmondsworth: Penguin, 1994), bk. III, 830ff.
2. Thomas Nagel, 'Death', in Nagel, *Mortal Questions* (Cambridge: Cambridge University Press, 1979), pp. 1–10.
3. Martha Nussbaum, 'Mortal Immortals: Lucretius on Death and the Voice of Nature', in Nussbaum, *The Therapy of Desire* (Princeton: Princeton University Press, 1996), pp. 192–238.
4. Martin Heidegger, *Sein und Zeit* (Tübingen: Max Niemeyer Verlag, 1967 [1927]), §47ff.
5. Cf. Julian Young, 'Death and Authenticity', in Jeff Malpas and Robert C. Solomon (eds), *Death and Philosophy* (London: Routledge, 1998), pp. 112–19.
6. Philip Larkin, 'Aubade', in Larkin, *Collected Poems,* Anthony Thwaite (ed.) (London: Marvel and Faber & Faber, 1988), p. 208.
7. Maupassant, quoted by W. M. Landers in his introduction to Guy de Maupassant, *Boule de suif et autres contes de la guerre* (Walton-on-Thames: Nelson, 1984), p. 12, my translation.
8. D. H. Lawrence, 'Death', in Lawrence, *Complete Poems,* Vivian de Sola Pinto and F. Warren Roberts (eds) (Harmondsworth: Penguin, 1993), p. 663. I am grateful to Michael Newton for drawing my attention to the significance, for my thinking, of Lawrence's poems on death.
9. Lawrence, 'Ship of Death', in Lawrence, *Complete Poems,* p. 962.
10. This is one way of putting the central issue of Erich Heller's explorations of German philosophy and literature in *The Disinherited Mind* (London: Bowes & Bowes, 1975), and elsewhere.
11. John Keats, 'Lamia', in H. W. Garrod (ed.), *Keats: Poetical Works* (Oxford: Oxford University Press, 1987), p. 176.
12. Marcel Proust, *Remembrance of Things Past: 1,* tr. C. K. Scott Moncrieff and Terence Kilmartin (Harmondsworth: Penguin, 1983), p. 47.
13. Proust, *Remembrance of Things Past: 1,* p. 48.
14. William James, *The Varieties of Religious Experience* (Glasgow: Collins, 1971 [1902]), lecture III.
15. James, *The Varieties of Religious Experience,* p. 370.
16. Raimond Gaita, *Romulus, My Father* (London: Review, 1999), p. 128.
17. William Hazlitt, 'On the Fear of Death', in Hazlitt, *Selected Writings,* Ronald Blythe (ed.) (Harmondsworth: Penguin, 1970), pp. 479–80.
18. J. P. Stern, *Idylls and Realities* (London: Methuen, 1971), p. 37.
19. Hazlitt, 'On the Fear of Death', p. 481.
20. Herodotus, *The Histories,* tr. Aubrey de Sélincourt, rev. John Marincola (Harmondsworth: Penguin, 1996), bk.I, 31.
21. Goethe, 'Winckelmann', in H. B. Nisbet (ed. and tr.), *German Aesthetic and Literary Criticism: Winckelmann, Lessing, Hamann, Herder, Schiller and*

Goethe (Cambridge: Cambridge University Press, 1985 [1805]), pp. 235–58, at p. 258.

22. Hannah Arendt, *The Human Condition* (Chicago: University of Chicago Press, 1958), §27.

23. Joseph Conrad, *Heart of Darkness* (Harmondsworth: Penguin, 1989 [1902]), p. 112.

Bibliography

Alvarez, A., *Night* (London: Jonathan Cape, 1994).

Anscombe, Elizabeth 'Modern Moral Philosophy', *Philosophy*, 33, 1958, pp. 1–19.

Arendt, Hannah, *The Human Condition* (Chicago: University of Chicago Press, 1958).

Arendt, Hannah, *On Revolution* (Harmondsworth: Penguin, 1990 [1963]).

Arendt, Hannah, *Eichmann in Jerusalem: A Report on the Banality of Evil* (Harmondsworth: Penguin, 1994 [1963]).

Aristotle, *Nicomachean Ethics*, tr. T. Irwin (Indianapolis: Hackett, 1985).

Auerbach, Erich, *Mimesis: The Representation of Reality in Western Literature*, tr. Willard R. Trask (Princeton: Princeton University Press, 1953).

Bate, Walter Jackson, *The Achievement of Samuel Johnson* (Oxford: Oxford University Press, 1955).

Bate, Walter Jackson, *Samuel Johnson* (London: Hogarth Press, 1978).

Béjin, A., 'The Influence of the Sexologists', in P. Ariès and A. Béjin (eds), *Western Sexuality: Practice and Precepts in Past and Present Times* (Oxford: Basil Blackwell, 1985).

Berlin, Isaiah, 'Two Concepts of Liberty', in Berlin, *Four Essays on Liberty* (Oxford: Oxford University Press, 1989).

Böll, Heinrich, 'Im Tal der donnernden Hufe', in Böll, *Als der Krieg ausbrach: Erzählungen* (Cologne: Deutscher Taschenbuch Verlag, 1971).

Boswell, J., *Life of Johnson* (Harmondsworth: Penguin, 1980 [1791]).

Bruce, Evangeline, *Napoleon and Josephine: An Improbable Marriage* (London: Orion, 1996).

Büchner, Georg, *Werke und Briefe*, ed. K. Pörnbecher, G. Schaub, H.-J. Simm and E. Ziegler (Munich: Deutscher Taschenbuch Verlag, 1988).

Bunyan, John, *The Pilgrim's Progress*, ed. Roger Sharrock (Harmondsworth: Penguin, 1987 [Pt. I: 1678; Pt. II: 1684]).

Camus, Albert, *La Peste*, ed. W. J. Strachan (London: Methuen, 1965 [1947]).

Canetti, Elias, *Crowds and Power*, tr. Carol Stewart (Harmondsworth: Penguin, 1973).

Čapek, Karel, *The Cheat*, tr. M. and R. Weatherall (London: George Allen & Unwin, 1941).

Casals, Pablo, *Joys and Sorrows: Reflections by Pablo Casals, as told to Albert E. Kahn* (New York: Simon & Schuster, 1970).

Casey, John, *Pagan Virtue* (Oxford: Oxford University Press, 1990).

Chekov, Anton, 'A Boring Story', in Chekov, *Lady with Lapdog and Other Stories*, tr. and intro. David Magarshack (Harmondsworth: Penguin, 1987 [1889]).

Chekov, Anton, 'Ward Number Six', in Chekov, *Ward Number Six and Other Stories*, tr. Ronald Hingley (Oxford: Oxford University Press, 1992 [1892]).

Chesterton, G. K., 'On the Institution of the Family', in Chesterton, *Heretics* (London: Bodley Head, 1905).

Citati, Pietro, *Kafka*, tr. Raymond Rosenthal (London: Secker & Warburg, 1990).

Conrad, Joseph, *Lord Jim* (Oxford: Oxford University Press, 1983 [1900]).

Conrad, Joseph, *Heart of Darkness* (Harmondsworth: Penguin, 1989 [1902]).

Cronin, Vincent, *Napoleon* (Harmondsworth: Penguin, 1976).

Diamond, Cora, 'Eating Meat and Eating People', *Philosophy*, 53, 1978, pp. 465–79.

Dostoyevsky, Fyodor, *The House of the Dead*, tr. D. McDuff (Harmondsworth: Penguin, 1985 [1860]).

Elias, Norbert, *The Civilizing Process*, tr. Edmund Jephcott (Oxford: Basil Blackwell, 1995 [1939]).

Eliot, George, *Middlemarch* (Harmondsworth: Penguin, 1994 [1872]).

Eliot, T. S., *Collected Poems 1909–1962* (London: Faber & Faber, 1986).

Emerson, Ralph Waldo, *Selected Essays*, ed. Larzer Ziff (Harmondsworth: Penguin, 1985).

Freud, Sigmund, ' "Civilized" Sexual Morality and Modern Nervous Illness', in Freud, *Civilization, Society and Religion*, tr. Angela Richards (Harmondsworth: Penguin, 1991 [1908]).

Frisch, Max, *Biedermann und die Brandstifter* (Frankfurt: Suhrkamp, 1958).

Gaita, Raimond, 'Integrity', *Proceedings of the Aristotelian Society, Supplementary Volume* 1981, pp. 161–76.

Gaita, Raimond, *Good and Evil: An Absolute Conception* (London: Macmillan, 1991).

Gaita, Raimond, *Romulus, My Father* (London: Review, 1999).

Gaita, Raimond, *A Common Humanity* (London: Routledge, 2000).

Glover, Jonathan, *Causing Death and Saving Lives* (Harmondsworth: Penguin, 1982).

Goethe, J. W. von, 'Winckelmann', in *German Aesthetic and Literary Criticism: Winckelmann, Lessing, Hamann, Herder, Schiller and Goethe*, ed. and tr. H. B. Nisbet (Cambridge: Cambridge University Press, 1985 [1805]), pp. 235–58.

Grayling, A. C., 'Editor's Introduction', in A. C. Grayling (ed.), *Philosophy: A Guide through the Subject* (Oxford: Oxford University Press, 1995).

Hampshire, Stuart, *Innocence and Experience* (Harmondsworth: Penguin, 1989).

Hazlitt, William, *The Round Table (Essays on Literature, Men and Manners)* (New York: Chelsea House, 1983 [1817]).

Hazlitt, William, *Selected Writings*, ed. Ronald Blythe (Harmondsworth: Penguin, 1970).

Heidegger, Martin, *Sein und Zeit* (Tübingen: Max Niemeyer Verlag, 1967 [1927]).

Heller, Erich, *The Disinherited Mind* (London: Bowes & Bowes, 1975).

Herodotus, *The Histories*, tr. Aubrey de Sélincourt, rev. John Marincola (Harmondsworth: Penguin, 1996).

Holland, R. F., *Against Empiricism* (Oxford: Basil Blackwell, 1980).

Humphreys, A. R., 'Johnson', in B. Ford (ed.), *The Pelican Guide to English Literature 4: From Dryden to Johnson* (Harmondsworth: Penguin, 1966).

Hunt, Leigh, 'A Few Thoughts on Sleep', in Hunt, *Selected Essays*, intro. J. B. Priestley (London: Dent, 1929).

James, William, *The Varieties of Religious Experience* (Glasgow: Collins, 1971 [1902]).

Johnston, Paul, *Wittgenstein and Moral Philosophy* (London: Routledge, 1991).

Kafka, Franz, *Stories 1904–1924*, tr. J. A. Underwood (London: Futura, 1983).

Kafka, Franz, *Das Urteil und andere Erzählungen* (Frankfurt: Fischer, 1989).

Kant, Immanuel, *The Groundwork of the Metaphysics of Morals*, tr. H. J. Paton as *The Moral Law* (London: Hutchinson, 1953 [1785]).

Kant, Immanuel, *The Metaphysics of Morals*, tr. Mary Gregor (Cambridge: Cambridge University Press, 1993 [1797]).

Keats, John, *The Letters of John Keats*, ed. R. Gittings (Oxford: Oxford University Press, 1970).

Kierkegaard, Søren, *Concluding Unscientific Postscript*, tr. David F. Swenson and Walter Lowrie (Princeton: Princeton University Press, 1974 [1846]).

Kleist, Heinrich von, *Sämtliche Werke und Briefe in zwei Bänden*, ed. Helmut Sembdner (Munich: Deutscher Taschenbuch Verlag, 1994).

Larkin, Philip, *Collected Poems*, ed. Anthony Thwaite (London: Marvel and Faber & Faber, 1988).

Lawrence, D. H., *Phœnix I*, ed. Edward D. McDonald (London: Heinemann, 1961).

Lawrence, D. H., *Phœnix II*, ed. Warren Roberts and Harry T. Moore (New York: Viking Press, 1970).

Lawrence, D. H., *Complete Poems*, ed. Vivian de Sola Pinto and F. Warren Roberts (Harmondsworth: Penguin, 1993).

Lawrence, D. H., *The Fox. The Captain's Doll. The Ladybird*, ed. David Ellis (Harmondsworth: Penguin, 1994).

Levi, Primo, *The Drowned and the Saved*, tr. R. Rosenthal (London: Abacus, 1988).

Leavis, F. R., *The Common Pursuit* (Harmondsworth: Penguin, 1962).

Leavis, F. R., 'Introduction', in Leavis (ed.), *Mill on Bentham and Coleridge* (London: Chatto & Windus, 1971).

Louden, Robert B., 'Kant's Virtue Ethics', in Daniel Statman (ed.), *Virtue Ethics: A Critical Reader* (Edinburgh: Edinburgh University Press, 1997).

Löwith, Karl, 'Nietzsches Vollendung des Atheismus', in Hans Steffen (ed.), *Nietzsche: Werk und Wirkungen* (Göttingen: Vandenhoeck & Ruprecht, 1974).

Lucretius, *On the Nature of the Universe*, tr. R. E. Latham, rev. John Godwin (Harmondsworth: Penguin, 1994).

McCarthy, Mary, *Birds of America* (Harmondsworth: Penguin, 1974).

McDowell, John, 'Values and Secondary Qualities', in T. Honderich (ed.), *Morality and Objectivity* (London: Routledge, 1985).

MacIntyre, Alasdair, *After Virtue* (London: Duckworth, 1981).

MacIntyre, Alasdair, *A Short History of Ethics* (London: Routledge, 1987).

MacIntyre, Alasdair, *Whose Justice? Which Rationality?* (London: Duckworth, 1988).

MacIntyre, Alasdair, *Three Rival Versions of Moral Enquiry* (London: Duckworth, 1990).

McNaughton, David, *Moral Vision* (Oxford: Basil Blackwell, 1996).

Magarshack, David, *Dostoyevsky* (London: Secker & Warburg, 1962).

Malcolm, Norman, *Ludwig Wittgenstein: A Memoir* (Oxford: Oxford University Press, 1989).

Maupassant, Guy de, *Boule de suif et autres contes de la guerre* (Walton-on-Thames: Nelson, 1984).

Melville, Herman, *'Billy Budd, Sailor' and Other Stories*, ed. Harold Beaver (Harmondsworth: Penguin, 1985).

Meyer, Michael, *Strindberg* (Oxford: Oxford University Press, 1988).

Miller, William Ian, *An Anatomy of Disgust* (Cambridge, MA: Harvard University Press, 1997).

Mochulsky, K., *Dostoyevsky: His Life and Work*, tr. M. A. Minihan (Princeton: Princeton University Press, 1967).

Montaigne, Michel de, *The Complete Essays*, tr. M. A. Screech (Harmondsworth: Penguin, 1991).

Motion, Andrew, *Philip Larkin* (London and New York: Methuen, 1982).

Murdoch, Iris, *The Sovereignty of Good* (London: Ark, 1970).

Musil, Robert, *Die Verwirrungen des Zöglings Törleß* (Hamburg: Rowohlt, 1991 [1906]).

Nagel, Thomas, *Mortal Questions* (Cambridge: Cambridge University Press, 1979).

Nehamas, Alexander, *Nietzsche: Life as Literature* (Cambridge, MA: Harvard University Press, 1985).

Nietzsche, Friedrich, *Sämtliche Werke: Kritische Studienausgabe in 15 Einzelbänden*, ed. Giorgio Colli and Mazzino Montinari (Berlin: Walter de Gruyter, 1980).

Nozick, Robert, *Anarchy, State, and Utopia* (Oxford: Basil Blackwell, 1984).

Nussbaum, Martha, *The Fragility of Goodness* (Cambridge: Cambridge University Press, 1986).

Nussbaum, Martha, *Love's Knowledge* (Oxford: Oxford University Press, 1992).

Nussbaum, Martha, 'Aristotle on Human Nature and the Foundations of Ethics', in J. E. J. Altham and R. Harrison (eds), *World, Mind, and Ethics: Essays on the Ethical Philosophy of Bernard Williams* (Cambridge: Cambridge University Press, 1995).

Nussbaum, Martha, *The Therapy of Desire* (Princeton: Princeton University Press, 1996).

Orwell, George, *The Road to Wigan Pier* (Harmondsworth: Penguin, 1987 [1937]).

Orwell, George, 'Lear, Tolstoy and the Fool', in Orwell, *Inside the Whale and Other Essays* (Harmondsworth: Penguin, 1962 [1947]).

Pender, Malcolm, *Frisch: Biedermann und die Brandstifter* (Glasgow: University of Glasgow, 1998).

Platts, Mark, *Ways of Meaning* (London: Routledge, 1979).

Pole, David, *Aesthetics, Form and Emotion*, ed. George Roberts (London: Duckworth, 1983).

Primoratz, Igor, *Ethics and Sex* (London: Routledge, 1999).

Proust, Marcel, *Remembrance of Things Past: 1*, tr. C. K. Scott Moncrieff and Terence Kilmartin (Harmondsworth: Penguin, 1983).

Regan, T., *The Case for Animal Rights* (Berkeley: University of California Press, 1983).

Rorty, Richard, *Contingency, Irony, Solidarity* (Cambridge: Cambridge University Press, 1992).

Russell, Bertrand, *Unpopular Essays* (London: George Allen, 1950).

Sartre, Jean-Paul, *Being and Nothingness*, tr. Hazel Barnes (London: Methuen, 1984 [1943]).

Schneebaum, Tobias, *Where the Spirits Dwell* (London: Weidenfeld & Nicolson, 1988).

Schopenhauer, Arthur, *The World as Will and Representation*, tr. E. F. J. Payne (New York: Dover, 1966 [1819 & 1844]), vols I and II.

Screech, Michael, *Montaigne and Melancholy* (Harmondsworth: Penguin, 1991).

Scruton, Roger, *Sexual Desire: A Philosophical Investigation* (London: Weidenfeld & Nicolson, 1986).

Bibliography

Sebald, W. G., *The Rings of Saturn*, tr. Michael Hulse (London: Harvil, 1999).

Shakespeare, William, *Hamlet*, ed. Harold Jenkins (London: Arden, 1997 [1603]).

Shakespeare, William, *King Lear*, ed. Kenneth Muir (London: Arden, 1991 [[1608]]).

Shakespeare, William, *Macbeth*, ed. Kenneth Muir (London: Arden, 1997 [1623]).

Singer, Peter, *Practical Ethics* (Cambridge: Cambridge University Press, 1979).

Singer, Peter, *Animal Liberation* (Wellingborough: Thornsons, 1984), 2nd edn.

Spender, Stephen, *Eliot* (Glasgow: Fontana, 1975).

Staten, Henry, *Nietzsche's Voice* (Ithaca: Cornell University Press, 1990).

Statman, Daniel, 'Introduction', in Daniel Statman (ed.), *Virtue Ethics: A Critical Reader* (Edinburgh: Edinburgh University Press, 1997).

Stern, J. P., *Idylls and Realities* (London: Methuen, 1971).

Strawson, P. F., *Freedom and Resentment and Other Essays* (London: Methuen, 1974).

Tanner, Michael, 'Sentimentality', *Proceedings of the Aristotelian Society*, LXXVII, 1977, pp. 127–47.

Tanner, Tony, *Conrad: 'Lord Jim'* (London: Arnold, 1969).

Taylor, Richard, *Reflective Wisdom*, ed. John Donnelly (New York: Prometheus Books, 1989).

Tester, Keith, *Moral Culture* (London: Sage, 1997).

Tooley, Michael, 'Abortion and Infanticide', in Peter Singer (ed.), *Applied Ethics* (Oxford: Oxford University Press, 1986).

Trilling, Lionel, *Sincerity and Authenticity* (London: Oxford University Press, 1972).

Warnock, Mary (ed.), *John Stuart Mill: Utilitarianism, On Liberty, Essay on Bentham, Together with Selected Writings of Jeremy Bentham and John Austin* (London: Fontana, 1962).

Warnock, Mary, *Memory* (London: Faber & Faber, 1987).

Watson, Gary, 'On the Primacy of Character', in Daniel Statman (ed.), *Virtue Ethics: A Critical Reader* (Edinburgh: Edinburgh University Press, 1997).

Wiggins, David, *Needs, Values, Truth* (Oxford: Basil Blackwell, 1987).

Williams, Bernard, *Ethics and the Limits of Philosophy* (London: Fontana, 1985).

Williams, Bernard, *Moral Luck* (Cambridge: Cambridge University Press, 1986).

Winch, Peter, 'Can We Understand Ourselves?', *Philosophical Investigations*, 20: 3, 1997, pp. 193–204.

Wittgenstein, Ludwig, *Philosophical Investigations*, tr. E. Anscombe (Oxford: Blackwell, 1983 [1953]).

Bibliography

Wittgenstein, Ludwig, *Culture and Value*, ed. G. H. von Wright and Heikki Nyman, tr. Peter Winch (Oxford: Basil Blackwell, 1980).

Woolf, Virginia, *A Room of One's Own/Three Guineas* (Harmondsworth: Penguin, 2000).

Yeats, W. B., *The Poems*, ed. Daniel Albright (London: Dent, 1991).

Young, Julian, 'Death and Authenticity', in Jeff Malpas and Robert C. Solomon (eds), *Death and Philosophy* (London: Routledge, 1998).

Zweig, Stefan, *Casanova: A Study in Self-Portraiture*, tr. Eden and Cedar Paul (London: Pushkin Press, 1998 [1928]).

Index